Soap Operas Worldwide

ALSO BY MARILYN J. MATELSKI

The Soap Opera Evolution:
America's Enduring Romance with Daytime Drama
(McFarland, 1988)

Broadcast Programming and Promotions Worktext

Variety Sourcebook I: Broadcast-Video
Co-edited with Dr. David Thomas

Daytime TV Programming

TV News Ethics

Variety: The Year in Review (1990)

Variety: The Year in Review (1991)

Vatican Radio: Propagation by the Airwaves

Messages from the Underground:
Transnational Radio in Resistance and in Solidarity
Co-authored with Nancy Lynch Street

Soap Operas Worldwide

Cultural and Serial Realities

by

MARILYN J. MATELSKI

McFarland & Company, Inc., Publishers
Jefferson, North Carolina, and London

PN
1992.8
S4
M273
1993

British Library Cataloguing-in-Publication data are available

Library of Congress Cataloguing-in-Publication Data

Matelski, Marilyn J., 1950–
    Soap operas worldwide : cultural and serial realities / by Marilyn
J. Matelski
       p.   cm.
    Includes bibliographical references and index.
    ISBN 0-7864-0557-0 (library binding : 50# alkaline paper) ∞
    1. Soap operas—History and criticism.   2. Soap operas—Social
aspects.   I. Title.
PN1992.8.S4M273   1999
791.45'6—dc21   98-37978
                                               CIP

Manufactured in the United States of America

McFarland & Company, Inc., Publishers
  Box 611, Jefferson, North Carolina 28640

For Nina Moon

Acknowledgments

In 1986 I decided to embark on one of the most challenging experiences of my career—writing a book. Because my interests lay in broadcast programming, cultural communication and serial drama, the idea of tracing the evolution of soap operas in America seemed to be a "natural." I had a great deal of information and felt a tremendous commitment to the project. Unfortunately, as a first-time author I had no track record. Luckily (for me), McFarland & Company, Inc., Publishers decided to give me a chance.

Today, more than ten years (and nine books) later, I can think of no one for whom I'd rather write than the people at McFarland. I'd like to take this space to thank them for their kindness and dedication to a first-time author. I will never forget them.

Because of the scope of this particular project, I am indebted to many other people as well. The Undergraduate Research Assistance Program and a Research Expense Grant from the Office of Research Administration at Boston College allowed me to defray costs and hire people to help with my research. One of my colleagues at BC, Dr. Michael Keith, also gathered data and conducted several interviews for me in Tanzania (garnering some very important comments from Franco Tramontano, at Dar es Salaam TV) while lecturing there for the U.S. State Department. Another colleague and friend, Dr. Michael Resler, chair of Germanic Studies, translated some of the public relations material I obtained from the German television networks. Victoria Barges, an administrator in the School of Nursing (and former student of mine), provided needed insight in the sections on viewer telenovela preferences. In addition three undergraduate students—Mark DiGregorio, Kristin Pugh and Ereka Vetrini—were extremely helpful, "surfing" the net for valuable Lexis-Nexis information and using their Spanish skills and Portuguese dictionaries to translate some of the telenovela titles in this book.

Special thanks to the station/network personnel and syndication services supervisors who responded to the questionnaire: Barbara A. Brady, D'Arcy Masius Benton & Bowles, Inc.; Sigurour G. Valgeirsson, Rikisutvarpid-Sjonvarp,

Iceland; Maria Waldau Ekelund, TV4 AB Stockholm; Kirsi Tormanen, YLE, Finland; Eva Bergquist, Sveriges Television, Sweden; Erik Christiansen, Danmarks Radio, Denmark; Jean Mino, La Cinquième, France; Rudolf Fehrmann, ORTF, Austria; Dr. Ronald Grabe, WDR, Germany; Silvia Maric, ARD, Germany; Cordelia Wagner, VOX, Germany; Andrea Kellermayer, DSF, Germany; Josef Burri, SF/DRS, Germany; Inga Chalizova, Tele 3, Lithuania; Michell Dieckmann, Ceska Televize, Czech Republic; Dermot Horan, RTE, Ireland; Enver Lekaj, Albanian Radio Television; Paula Sandes, CBC/SRC, Canada; Tele-Sahel, Niger; Martin Goosarran, Guyana Television Broadcasting Co.; Valerio Fuenzalida, Televisión Nacional de Chile; Stella Sim, TV 12, Singapore; Chantasanee Chuthong, Army Television, Thailand; Ray Sorimachi, NTV, Japan; Ken Mishima, Fuji Television, Japan; Emily Ng, RTHK, Hong Kong; Sarah Wiltshire, Nine Network Australia Pty.; Connie Telfer-Smith, Norfolk Island Broadcasting Service; John Taylor, EMTV, Papua New Guinea; David Compton, TAB, New Zealand; Christophe Lassagne, Canal Polynesie, Tahiti; Amalia Ahmad, Anteve, Indonesia; Urusan Seri Paduka Baginda, Malaysia; Florecita Lizardo, Télé-Haiti, Haiti; Andrea Martin, St. Thomas-St. John Cable TV; Angela Patterson, JBC, Jamaica; and Anestine Lafond, Marpin TV Company, Commonwealth of Dominica.

My new e-mail "pen pals," Betsi Curdi and Yolette Nicholson, gave me essential information and perspective on certain soaps and novelas outside the United States, and longtime friend, Mark Harbin, found books for me that were impossible to obtain locally.

My colleague and sometime coauthor, Dr. Nancy Street, helped with some of the more "challenging" novela titles and contributed intercultural perspectives and contacts, most especially in China and Hong Kong.

Last, but certainly far from least, my favorite "soap consultant" and proofreader (who also happens to be my mom), Carolyn Matelski, contributed countless hours and considerable talents to help me with yet another book. Her suggestions in research and writing were invaluable, her encouragement unflagging. Most important, she offered an enlightened view of the world that few of us can claim. She is truly a "touchstone" for me—in every way—and I continue to grow as an author, teacher and person because of her.

Contents

Introduction

> *Television can entertain and educate, but no place is safe from it.... It unites us in mediocrity. It gives us all its one-eyed vision of the world, and it tries to reduce everything to the simplest terms, so the simplest among us will hear the message.*[1]

This passage from William Martin's acclaimed novel *Nerve Endings* could also be applied more specifically to TV soap operas. Everyone loves to "hate" them, and everyone seems to have some criticism of the "substandard" production quality, script writing, direction or acting. Even the musical scores and story titles have found a place on the comedy circuit. However, despite the friendly (or not-so-friendly) sport of "soap bashing," no one can deny the apparent, decades-old appeal of serial drama replete with star-crossed lovers, unknown (and incurable) illnesses, tragic deaths, broken marriages, questionable parentage or natural disasters. According to media scholars Bradley S. Greenberg and Rick W. Busselle, soap operas have endured more than most other forms of media entertainment for several reasons:

First, the legacy of soaps goes back 60 years in radio and 40 years in daytime television. Soaps have been the most consistent content staple created in broadcast entertainment programming. Second, the viewing audience is large. In a national survey of 3,800 adults in July 1994, 17% said they were regular viewers of soaps; this extrapolates to 30,000,000 adults in the United States who admitted to regular soap viewing. If the same percentage were applied to American teenagers—and it likely is higher—another three to four million are regular viewers. Third, and more pertinent to the issue of the social importance of soaps, regular soap viewers systematically consist of higher proportions of specific population subgroups. The less educated (27% with less than a high school education compared to 9% with a four-year degree), those with lower incomes (36% with family incomes less than $10,000 vs. 9% with incomes more than $50,000), nonwhites (27% nonwhites compared to 15% of the whites), women (26% vs. 7% of the men), and particularly nonworking women (36% vs. 10% of working women) are all significantly more likely to self-identify as regular viewers.[2]

In fact, one could argue that daytime programming (and specifically soap operas) may be the best "deal" in the TV business—serving large audiences at comparatively low costs and providing an impressive yield for its investment in the United States and abroad. The "business" of soaps doesn't stop with the remote control, however. As British author Charlotte Brunsdon observes:

> The central fiction of the genre, that the communities represented exist outside the box, as well as on it … is supported and sustained across a range of media material. Newspaper articles, novels, souvenir programmes, *TV Times* promotions, even cookery books, function to support the simultaneous co-existence of them and us. It is possible to wear the same clothes, use the same decor, follow the same recipes and even pore over the same holiday snaps as the people on the Street, the Close and the Motel.[3]

Serial drama is also an effective way to teach culture—as well as language—to non-native speakers. Nowhere is this better shown than in the Phoenix ELT book series, in which two texts, *Soap Opera—The Reader* and *Soap Opera II—The Sequel*, trace "the passion, the pain, the greed, the joys and the surprises of the Collins and Rawlins families," while teaching English at the same time.[4]

The purpose of this book is to explore the unique genre of TV soap operas worldwide—their origin, their ability to adapt to outside influences, their creation of "cultural landscaping" through which audiences can learn both positive and negative sociopolitical behaviors, and their potential as a device for cultural imperialism and change via the relatively new technologies of satellite and cable transmission. Before exploring the phenomenon of soap operas, however, it is important to define more specifically the genre and the focus and scope of this study.

Definition of Terms

Author Robert C. Allen, in his introduction to *To Be Continued... Soap Operas Around the World*, spends a great deal of time defining and describing serial narrative drama.[5] Although some of his interpretations may differ slightly from my own, he draws an important distinction between soap operas and telenovelas: the former use "open" serial form; the latter are "closed." According to Allen, "open" serials (like those found in the United States, Great Britain and Australia) are not determined by any particular time frame—and no one expects them to be. They are, in short, never-ending stories. Conversely, "closed" serials (popular in Latin America, South America and parts of Asia and Africa) are designed to have specific conclusions (although the number of episodes needed to move the story line may vary).[6]

Along with this major distinction come other definitive differences (which will be addressed in the next several pages) between the two narrative forms. Both are also drawn together by similarities in melodramatic plotlines, popularity of the characters and profitability from both domestic and foreign distribution.

The Soap Opera

Many scholars have defined the soap opera genre, but none have been more articulate than Christine Geraghty, a prolific writer and professor of media studies at Goldsmiths' College, University of London. In her 1981 article, "The Continuous Serial—A Definition," (written as part of a television monograph for the British Film Institute), Geraghty gives several identifying features of soap opera form: the organization of time, the sense of a future, the interweaving of stories and the presence of an ensemble cast.[7]

Organization of Time. Serial viewers are particularly comforted to know that there are specific days and times for the soap. This creates for them a "ritual of regularity," allowing them to drop in at any time and "catch up," even if several episodes have been missed. Unlike an episodic series, serial drama has no specific story within a capsule. Characters and plotlines cross over into several (maybe many) episodes; the passage of time and personal crisis is generally more similar to real life.[8] Holidays (like Christmas or July 4 in the United States; the Silver Jubilee in England) are often celebrated at the same time as the actual event, lending a credibility to the time line of "realistic drama."

Time orientation is no minor aspect to serial drama, as Geraghty asserts:

> The strength of this convention can be illustrated by what happens when it is broken. When a lorry crashed into the Rover's Return in "Coronation Street" in 1979, the dramatic nature of the incident was underlined by the spinning out of time. Two or three hours of narrative time dealing with the clearing of rubble and the discovery of victims took days and weeks of real time: tension was emphasised in this way and the normal feeling of day-to-day life was gone.[9]

Without this sense of time passage, viewers felt cheated. It is as if an event took place without their knowing about it.

Conversely, soap operas can also create pseudoevents for fans, who also experience them in "real" time. One of the most dramatic examples of this phenomenon was the months-long rape of Laura and then her romance with Luke on *General Hospital*. It became such a national obsession that critic Ruth Rosen observed, "In September 1981, the star-crossed lovers appeared on the cover of *Newsweek*; that November, fourteen million people, a full 43 percent of the television-viewing audience, made daytime rating history as they witnessed the couple's long-awaited wedding, adorned with a guest appearance by Elizabeth Taylor."[10] Actors Anthony Geary and Genie Francis left *General Hospital* for several years to pursue other projects but returned to the show in mid–1990 with lucrative contracts. Luke and Laura came back—this time with their son, Lucky—to the delight of their many fans.

The Sense of a Future. Otherwise known as the "permanent" postponement of plot resolution, serials have no season "finale" or "cliffhanger." They seem to go on forever. Geraghty elaborates: "Even events which would offer a suitable ending in other narrative forms are never a final ending in the continuous serial: a wedding is not a happy ending but opens up the possibilities of stories about married life and divorce; a character's departure from a serial does not mean that s/he will not turn up again several years later, as Lillian Bellamy does in 'The Archers.'"[11] Only death seems to be irreversible, and even this has been changed from time to time with such story conventions as evil twins, mistaken identity or temporary amnesia. One classic character who cheated death on American soaps was Roman Brady on *Days of Our Lives.*

Roman Brady was first introduced on *Days* in the early 1980s as a police investigator and romantic interest of psychiatrist Dr. Marlena Evans Craig. Roman and partner Abe Carver soon became the leading crime fighters in Salem, cracking local cases such as the Salem Strangler, as well as international syndicates with leaders like Stefano DiMera and Kellam Chandler. Unfortunately, during one of his many attempts to capture and arrest the evil Stefano DiMera, Roman was "killed," dying in his brother Bo's arms.

Roman Brady's death sent tremors throughout Salem (and apparently throughout the viewing nation). Marlena was so grief stricken that she left their daughter with Roman's first wife, Anna, and took their twins to Denver. She later returned but to the continual harassment of psychotic patients and romantic suitors. She began to wonder about her own mental stability, when she noticed that one of her patients, John Black, bore an amazing likeness to Roman. Indeed it was Roman. He had lived through his ordeal, but he had lost his memory and become a pawn for Stefano and his cohort, Victor Kiriakis.

As this book goes to press, Roman Brady is still alive and well, and Stefano DiMera (also a victim of several mistaken deaths) continues his villainy in Salem. In fact, the story line of Roman's exaggerated demise was not so much the whim of a creative scriptwriter as the result of audience mail and contract renewals. Such is the life of a soap opera actor.

The Interweaving of Stories. The serial nature of soap operas lends itself to several stories being presented at the same time, although in different stages. These plotlines usually involve different characters, but they "cross over" to each other many times, usually in situations where large groups of people meet. For example, at a 1996 New Year's Eve party on *The Young and the Restless*, Katherine Chancellor hosted a newly married couple (who had overcome enormous difficulties before their wedding), a newly divorced man as a possible love interest for Katherine (the man's ex-wife later crashed the party), and the divorced man's son, who was courting a love interest of his own. These three (or four) separate stories merged for a brief time, as everyone took time to reflect on the previous year. Story "blending" can also be found at weddings, funerals, murders and court cases, in addition to parties. A 1997 plot in *As the World Turns* involved a murder investigation, tying together at least six different suspects for quite separate reasons.

The serial script-writing device has several hard-and-fast rules that must be followed. Despite different stages of development, the same amount of airtime is usually devoted to each narrative during the course of a week, unless one of the plots is close to resolution (or seeming resolution) or a particular story has taken hold with the viewers during a ratings sweep month. At least two stories are always in progress; frequently, it's three or more. Although the stories may be very different, they are always bound by established elements of "the signature tune, the setting, long-standing characters"[12] because, as Christine Geraghty writes, "the unfamiliar is introduced within a context of the very familiar, the audience is able to cope with enormous shifts in style and material, even within one episode, which might otherwise be expected to occur across a whole evening's viewing."[13] Through these conventions, characters can have what soap writer Marnie Winston-Macauley calls a "DPU," or "Direct Pick-Up." This means that the audience can be cued quickly to a change in scene within a show or placed quickly into the context of the next day's drama.[14]

The Presence of an Ensemble Cast. An ensemble cast is essential to serial drama for its ability to provide both continuity and transition for the audience in the midst of potentially extreme plotline diversity. Until the 1980s most American soap operas had one "core" family as a referent to the action taking place on-screen. Since then, the number of "core" families has blossomed into two, three or sometimes even four, each representing a different racial, ethnic or economic identity. In *The Bold and the Beautiful*, for example, the primary family is the Forresters, consisting of fashion design founder Eric, matriarch Stephanie, two sons and two daughters. The daughters seem to come back only occasionally; the mother, father and sons provide for more than adequate amounts of narrative. Since the show's premiere in 1987, several other "core" families have been linked to the Forrester family either biologically, maritally or professionally. They include the Spectras (headed by Sally Spectra, the lower-line clothier rival who is forever competing for recognition, fame and social status and whose daughter has married one of the Forrester sons), the Logans (a middle-class family "from the Valley," whose mother was once linked romantically to Eric Forrester and whose daughter, Brooke, has apparently followed the family tradition by falling for Forrester son Ridge), and the Cortezes (the most recent addition to the soap, a single-parent family of illegal Salvadoran aliens, one of whom, Claudia, has found both work and romance with the Forresters). The number of characters and their relationships would challenge even the most sophisticated mind, but once these families are established, the number of story possibilities in one town is endless.

Another type of "core" family is one that is not biological but occupational. Examples of such relationships are the primary characters in *General Hospital* or *Sunset Beach*. In these cases the central action takes place around a certain place of employment, such as a medical center or beach patrol, where characters discuss their love lives, family problems and the latest crisis.

An ensemble cast provides stability, which can then allow for wild plotline swings and changes. Viewers are more likely to identify with the characters in serial drama; thus, story lines are for the most part secondary and malleable.

American Soap Operas

Although Geraghty provides some excellent guidelines for general soap opera identification, serial drama in the United States can be further distinguished as "daytime" and "primetime"—with differences far greater than the scheduled telecast. These differences include viewer influence, the writing/ production schedule, program costs and character identification.

Viewer Influence. In *Writing for Daytime Drama* Jean Rouverol (a daytime-script-writing veteran) describes viewer feedback as an essential element in story-line development:

> Reading the fan mail is another of the headwriter's regular tasks.... [T]hese are always read, tabulated, and considered, along with the ratings, as an indication of how well or poorly a given story line is doing. (Oddly, there is not necessarily a correlation between the mail and the ratings.) Because daytime is a commercial genre, even a slight dip in the ratings or any indication of viewer dissatisfaction will bring worried phone calls and general pressure from the sponsors or network people to hype the story.[15]

In the 1990s "fan mail" has been enhanced to include voice mail, email and newsgroup chats, as well as Internet Web pages. In addition, a plethora of soap opera magazines has emerged with 1-900 phone numbers for viewer polls. An example of this is found in a March 1997 copy of *Soap Opera Magazine*:

> What's your opinion? We'd like to know, and we're not alone. THE NETWORKS ARE LISTENING is our way of compiling and tabulating your views on the hottest soap opera topics for all the world to see, including the people who decide what happens to your favorite daytime characters and storylines. Network executives and producers carefully listen to what the fans have to say ... SO YOUR VOTE CAN MAKE A DIFFERENCE![16]

The magazine presents two questions for deliberation, as well as the results (with statistics, no less) of the questions posed in the previous issue. Most relevant issues during the week of March 4, 1997, were 1) newly widowed Trevor (on *All My Children*) and his choices for a future wife to help him raise his two children in Pine Valley and 2) story-line suggestions for the reconstituted writing staff of

Another World. The questions from the previous week (reactions to Aaron Spelling's recently introduced soap, *Sunset Beach*, and the abrupt dismissal of *Bold and the Beautiful* actor Jeff Trachta) were analyzed statistically and given summaries. Question #1 drew a 64 percent rave review of *Sunset Beach*; 10 percent veto; and 26 percent undecided. Question #2 uncovered a 74 percent viewer support statement for Jeff Trachta on *B&B*; 26 percent felt that Trachta's replacement, Winsor Harmon, should be given a chance. One can conclude (based on Rouverol's experience) that although not associated with the networks per se, these polls filter in to the decision-making process.

Although viewer feedback is also important to primetime television, chances are it is neither as immediate nor as influential as in daytime drama. This is due in part to the overwhelming demands of writing and production in daytime television, as well as basic economics.

Writing/Production Schedule. In *Writing for Daytime Drama* Rouverol also details the hectic "assembly-line" approach to daytime soaps:

> Simply put, the writing of a daytime series can be thought of as a straight line carved into ever smaller units at each stage of planning. Methods of work differ from show to show, but the general procedure is the same: The long-range projection is broken up into (roughly) 13-week segments, which are in turn carved into 1-week segments (the weekly overview, or *thrust*); and these are carved yet again into daily segments. The daily outline is called (almost too descriptively) a *breakdown*, and is the blueprint for the final product, the script.[17]

In addition, the head writer must adjust the pace of each primary story to reach a "climax" during a sweeps week (in February, May, July or November). However, as noted earlier, soap opera plotlines are never completely resolved. Thus, Rouverol modifies the term, "climax," saying, "Usually when a major story has peaked and its crisis is at least temporarily resolved, it can be moved to a back burner and one or another of the secondary stories will then be moved to the foreground."[18]

Given the breakneck schedules and inherent pressures of the genre, as well as the sheer volume of scripting material necessary to provide 2½ to 5 hours of programming each week, it is not difficult to understand the importance of outside sources (such as viewer feedback, advertiser and network suggestions and current issues of social relevance) in creating the cultural "temperature" of the story line. There's not enough time to do all the research necessary for every plot; and even if there was, there's no guarantee the final product would be acceptable to the target demographics. In a genre not defined by overnight ratings (but still susceptible to sweeps weeks), writers and producers are more flexible and open to external suggestions, which only enhance the number of creative possibilities and help keep costs relatively low.

Cost Factors. Generally speaking, a week's worth of daytime soap opera episodes costs about half as much as a single primetime drama. The primary reasons for relatively low prices are 1) the choice of videotape over film; 2) the style of writing, favoring interior scenes over outdoor panoramas;[19] and 3) the comparatively low actor salaries. Regarding the latter point, an August 1996 issue of *Soap Opera Update* quotes a personal manager's estimates of the payscale ranges: "On the low-end, primetime actors make $5,000 per episode, but for network shows, it is closer to $10,000 per episode. For a solid soap star, working three to four years on a show, they can earn anywhere from $3,000 to $4,500 per week on average. Of course, there are those who make more and those who make less."[20] In addition, primetime actors work on a 22-week cycle, leaving them time to pursue other projects in film or theater. Soap stars may take time off, but it is far more difficult to do so. Also, many are more limited in the means available to supplement their incomes—rather than movies or stage plays, they tend to schedule personal appearances, which usually average $1,000 to $5,000 per show.[21]

This "economy of scale" helps to support other programming on network schedules. And although overall soap opera ratings have dipped slightly in recent years, they still provide a high yield for relatively low expenditures. In short, daytime drama provides an economic foundation for nighttime drama.

Character Identification. A final and important distinction should be made between characters in daytime serials and those found on primetime. Because of their salaries and promotional exposure, primetime stars are often identified by their stage names. Daytime stars, on the other hand, are associated with their character names. Thus, people find themselves describing a newcomer to a soap opera as "the old Nola on *Guiding Light*" or "the former Matt in *The Young and the Restless.*" Even magazine writers use this same identifying style. Moreover (and sometimes more dangerously), viewers may have difficulty separating the actor from his or her role. Actress Kelley Menighan Hensley recalls a brief incident in 1997, shortly after her character, Emily, was left lying motionless after having been brutally raped on *As the World Turns*:

One woman was in a wheelchair and another woman was trying to pull her into a building. I stopped to hold the door. The one in the wheelchair looked up, grabbed my arm and said, "I knew it! You're not dead!" They were blocking the entrance, but the woman kept talking. She said, "In real life, you're not like Emily. You're holding the door for me!" I said, "Get in there. People are waiting—get going."[22]

Viewers may confuse the actors with their character *personas*, but they nonetheless are a very loyal, caring and protective group. Most daytime stars recognize and appreciate this allegiance—their careers depend upon it.

The Telenovela

Media scholars who study Latin American telenovelas (or teleromanas) trace their origins to TV soap operas aired in the United States during the

1950s and 1960s.[23] Because of this factor, the first programs of this type quite obviously displayed many of the characteristics found in American serial drama; however, for the last several decades, the telenovela form has adopted its own style and identity, creating subject matter specific to a particular culture and targeted audience. For example, Brazilian teleromanas are quite unique from those found in Cuba, Mexico, Chile, Colombia or Argentina.[24] Further, as the genre has expanded and redefined itself in Asian and African countries, its common threads have become more sparse. Despite these limitations, several general comparisons between telenovelas and soap operas can be made. They include certain time constraints, scheduling priorities and cost, actor/actress identification, writing style and national identity.

Organization of Time. Unlike those who follow TV soap operas, viewers of telenovelas expect a definitive conclusion to the story. The number of episodes will vary, but a conclusion still occurs. Author Heidi Nariman explains: "A key difference between the U.S.-style soap opera and the Latin American telenovela is that the U.S. soap opera is an open-ended story that continues as long as advertisers and ratings are in sufficient abundance; each telenovela, on the other hand, consists of a finite number of episodes (three months to one year of half-hour to one-hour broadcasts Monday through Friday) in which a central story is told until its conclusion."[25]

Often these stories are variations of a more traditional play, novel or folk tale—something the audience is familiar with—adapted to a different geographic location, historical era or ethnic culture, as described by Doraluz Vargas, editor of *TV y Novela* magazine, read by over 20 million Spanish speakers in Latin America and the United States: "The themes are timeless. I think the first telenovela was the theater of ancient Greece. And Shakespeare's 'Romeo and Julietta' was a telenovela. It's about the love between a man and a woman and the problems that they have with their families. Many telenovelas are based on old stories, like 'Cinderella,' about a poor woman who's looking for a prince."[26] Viewers, familiar with the basic content of the specific play or folk tale, thus have a rudimentary idea of how the story will progress but can enjoy the "new flavor" of different settings and adaptations. According to audience polls and focus group research, they also expect a climax and resolution to the plot within a reasonable period of time. Hence, the average lifespan of a telenovela is between 90 and 100 episodes.[27]

Importance on the Programming Schedule. Whereas most American soaps find themselves scheduled in an afternoon time slot, telenovelas are considered one of the most important, profitable areas of primetime entertainment, reaching millions of viewers each evening. And the most popular stars can be found on telenovelas, as media scholar Ana M. Lopez notes:

> Many US soaps continue to be sponsored by soap companies, are generally produced as daytime entertainment aimed at a female audience, are primarily destined for the national market, and are still considered a form

of "slumming" by its workers (work on a soap being second best to film or theatrical work). On the other hand, telenovelas are prime-time entertainment for all audiences, financed directly by TV networks (or, most recently, by independent producers who subsequently sell advertising slots), widely exported, and definitive of the Latin American star system. Unlike the case in the US, where "stardom"—either of actors or writers and directors—is still defined by Hollywood, to work in a telenovela today is often to have reached the apex of one's professional career.[28]

The concentration on exotic plotlines, the targeting of large, heterogeneous audiences, and the "star billing" of telenovelas set them apart from most serial drama (aired either in daytime or primetime) on American television. Production companies and television networks also pay hefty sums (including cast/crew salaries, travel and production costs) to ensure viewer popularity and satisfaction. In short, telenovelas are considered highly competitive, costly and extremely important to a programmer's schedule, as demonstrated through a 1994 dramatization of the novel *Nano*, by Argentinean Enrique Torres. The summary (obtained via Internet) reads as follows:

> Nano (short for Manuel) runs an oceanarium, Mundo Marino, in spite of the fact that his father, Noel, wants him to join the family enterprise as is expected of an aristocrat. Nano, an idealist, prefers to work in the magical and silent world of the animals he so loves—the dolphins, Orca whales, sea lions and penguins. By day he runs the oceanarium and the foundation to protect animals, but at night he comes to the aid of people. Secretly, he is "the Cat"—a sort of Robin Hood who steals from the rich and corrupt and gives to the poor. He will even steal thousands of dollars from his father's own safe to distribute to the workers who were fired by his father. Connected to his office is his secret "cave" where together with his closest friend, Sebastian, he plans the "cat's" actions. Also connected to his office is his little apartment where he finds peace and quiet away from his nagging wife, Rosario, whom he does not love. Although he has a lover, he says that he never experienced the magical love that, by his definition, is felt from the waist up. Until he meets Camila. Camila, who became deaf and mute as a result of a childhood trauma (her parents were murdered), silently watches Nano at the oceanarium without him seeing, and photographs him without end. Her silent world joins to the silence of his world of water. They meet and fall in love. But will they be able to overcome the dark secrets of their past and the evils of the present to live and love in their magical world? What will happen when Camila remembers her past and recognizes Nano's father, Noel, as the murderer of her father? Will Nano's wife succeed in her insane schemes? And will Nano's and Camila's love for each other, that began in their long lost childhood, triumph in the end?[29]

Certainly, familiar themes of complicated love and romance are present but with a scenic backdrop unknown to most American soap opera viewers.

Actor/Actress Identification. Unlike actors on daytime soap operas in the United States, the actors/actresses on Latin American/Asian/African telenovelas easily retain their "real world" identities after taping is complete—they are not lost to the characterizations defined by the particular program. In fact, it is not unusual for famous acting duos to move from one telenovela to another after the story's end. According to Professor Ana Lopez, audiences actually enjoy the "fictional reincarnation" and seem curious to see if the actors can make the imaginary leap from one setting to another. [30]

The tendency of viewers to identify with actors rather than the characters they portray does not diminish viewer loyalty, however. In March 1995, when TV Globo fired one of Brazil's most famous stars (Vera Fischer) from the country's most popular telenovela (*Pátria Minha/My Homeland*), the move made front-page headlines. According to a report in *Television Business International*,

> TV Globo had never before fired a starring actor or actress and knew the sacking would hurt ratings. The network, nonetheless, broke with precedent after Fischer and her estranged husband Felipe Camargo (who had a bit part in the telenovela) began constantly arriving late on the set and fighting with fellow actors. Fischer's late arrivals became so predictable that her on-screen husband Tarcisio Meira refused to leave home for the set till Fischer arrived there. And those late arrivals slowed the soap's shooting schedule so that the normal time-lag of more than a week, between taping of one of Fischer's scenes and televising it, was reduced to one day. So TV Globo decided to give both Fischer and Camargo's characters the ax by killing them in a hastily-scripted hotel fire. [31]

Sometimes the most creative scripts are truly "character-driven."

Hollywood Style versus New York Style. Another important difference between telenovela and soap opera form lies in the style of writing and production. As described earlier, soap operas adopt an assembly-line approach in their scripts and production. The taping is done using two or three (sometimes maybe four) indoor sets during the course of a week. Although some exterior footage may be involved, the creative form generally reflects a Broadway stageplay, or "New York," style of writing and production.

Telenovelas, on the other hand, often adopt a more "Hollywood" approach to production, employing large amounts of exterior footage and thus taking more time to complete each episode. Most "Hollywood" style programs in the United States are filmed (costing exorbitant amounts of money); telenovelas save some of their production costs by using videotape but maintain the "feel" of Hollywood production. [32]

Despite the "Hollywood" approach in writing and production values, characters in telenovelas are anything but the buffed, hardbodied, chisel-faced stars of American daytime drama. Reporter Anne Valdespino describes some of the most popular faces on Latin American TV as "meddlesome grandmothers, snoopy maids, concerned priests, bratty children, and fat, bald uncles"— throwbacks to traditional theater rather than Hollywood tinsel. [33] They rely on raw emotions, not technology, to get their points across. Comedy also plays a central role in many telenovelas; it is not unusual to see a small bit, here and there, reminiscent of vaudeville.

National Identity. No one would deny that international program distribution is important. Rede Globo in Brazil, for example, dubs its productions into several languages for broadcast in 130 countries.[34] However, even with program exports as an acknowledged business priority, telenovelas still reflect much of the culture and "feel" of their homeland through both content and stylistic presentation. Professor Lopez elaborates:

> Mexican telenovelas are notorious for their weepiness, extraordinary Manichean vision of the world, and lack of specific historical references. At the opposite end of the spectrum, the Brazilian telenovelas are luxurious, exploit cinematic production values, and are considered more "realistic" for their depiction of ambiguous and divided characters in contemporary (or specific historical) Brazilian contexts. The Venezuelan and Colombian telenovelas lie between these two extremes assuming certain characteristics and establishing their own differences. The Venezuelan telenovelas are like the Mexican in so far as they tend to privilege primal emotions over socio-historical context, but they substitute dialog and utterly Spartan sets for signifying baroqueness of the Mexicans' *mise-en-scène.* The Colombians, on the other hand, have followed the Brazilian model, making specific and pointed reference to the history and culture of the nation, although not by recourse to "realism," but through the use of an ironic/parodic mode that combines the melodramatic with comedy.[35]

As telenovelas face a future of growing international distribution, the national identity of the genre could give way to a more cross-cultural perspective. Programming might soon be more reflective of a technological world of coaxial cables, fiber optics and satellite dishes than that of ethnic nationalism.

Soap operas, too, are no longer limited by geography, economics, political borders or socioeconomic class. They have evolved in both size and scope during the last 70 years. Today, in the United States alone, an estimated 50 million people are considered to be regular viewers of America's 10 existing daytime dramas. Even in Athens, Greece, over 50,000 crazed fans once crowded together to glance at their favorite characters from *The Bold and the Beautiful.*[36] In short, serial drama has made its way around the globe, showing little evidence of imminent extinction. And as subsequent chapters show, its influence in cultural transmission has only begun to be realized.

Scope of Project

To address the effects of televised serial drama throughout the world, it was necessary to define the area of analysis clearly. As a result, primetime soap operas in the United States—such as *Dallas, Dynasty, Melrose Place* and

Beverly Hills, 90210 are not included. Marketing and distribution figures are in constant flux for these soaps, and because some of them have already been terminated, they were not as relevant to cultural studies as were the soap operas found on American daytime television. In addition, the primetime costs of serial drama overseas more closely approximate daytime soap opera budgets in the United States. Thus, American daytime drama—its production, audience composition, story line and distribution—seemed more congruous for analysis and comparison to other countries than primetime soap opera fare.

The information for this book is based on "snapshots" of soap opera/telenovela programming shown throughout the world in the 1996-1997 season, compiled from the *1998 World Almanac* and Internet information, as well as "snail mail" and phone surveys from over 200 countries. The resulting data have been organized into eight regional chapters, each providing a thumbnail sketch of population, media accessibility and serial programming strategies, as well as a brief analysis of the impact of soaps in each region.[37] These analytical "capsules" include a brief history of serial drama, audience demographics (where available) and possible goals and objectives of the TV network or service airing these soap operas/telenovelas, as well as specific, "profile" countries where serial drama has had a particular influence on commercial, educational or governmental directives. Because the profile countries tend also to be major importers or exporters of serial drama throughout the world, they, in turn, have the power to dictate a "worldview" of different cultures through their programming.

Finally, two appendixes of selected soap operas/telenovelas are provided at the end of the book, including brief descriptions of each and the names of the countries that produce them.

Notes

1. William Martin, *Nerve Endings* (New York: Warner Books, 1994), 112.
2. Bradley S. Greenberg and Rick W. Busselle, "Soap Operas and Sexual Activity: A Decade Later," *Journal of Communication* (autumn 1996): 153.
3. Charlotte Brunsdon, *Screen Tastes: Soap Opera to Satellite Dishes* (London: Routledge, 1997), 19.
4. Charlyn Wessels, *Soap Opera II—The Sequel* (Hertfordshire, UK: Phoenix ELT, 1996), 1.
5. Robert C. Allen, ed., *To Be Continued... Soap Operas Around the World* (London and New York: Routledge, 1995).
6. *Ibid.*, 17–24.
7. Christine Geraghty, "The Continuous Serial—A Definition," in *Television Monograph 13: Coronation Street* (London: British Film Institute, 1981): 9–26.
8. This is not always true, however. Many times, depending on viewer feedback, ratings or actor changes, the time frame for a particular event is altered drastically. Most notable are the examples of painfully long pregnancies followed by children who seem to grow older by the month instead of by the year.

9. Geraghty, 11.
10. Ruth Rosen, "Search for Yesterday," in *Watching Television*, ed. Todd Gitlin (New York: Pantheon Press, 1986), 55.
11. Geraghty, 11.
12. *Ibid.*, 12.
13. *Ibid.*
14. Quoted in Seli Groves, *The Ultimate Soap Opera Guide* (Detroit: Visible Ink Press, 1995), xiii.
15. Jean Rouverol, *Writing for Daytime Drama* (Stoneham, MA: Focal Press, 1992), 44.
16. *Soap Opera Magazine* (March 4, 1997), 42.
17. Rouverol, 12.
18. *Ibid.*, 11–12.
19. Usually, this style of writing—utilizing two or three sets, with sequential taping of scenes—is referred to as the New York style (taken from the Broadway onstage prototype). Most primetime drama is "Hollywood" style—filming multiple scenes (many of which are exteriors) out of sequence.
20. "Do Soap Stars Make Big Bucks?" *Soap Opera Update* (August 6, 1996), 63.
21. *Ibid.*
22. *Soap Opera Magazine*, 35.
23. For more detailed analyses, see Ana M. Lopez, "Our Welcomed Guests: Telenovelas in Latin America," in *To Be Continued... Soap Operas Around the World*, ed. Robert C. Allen (London: Routledge, 1995), 256–275; and Heidi Noel Nariman, *Soap Operas for Social Change: Toward a Methodology for Entertainment-Education Television* (Westport, CT.: Praeger, 1993).
24. This "uniqueness" does not diminish the worldwide popularity of telenovelas, however, which is described in the chapters that follow.
25. Nariman, 13–14.
26. Anne Valdespino, "A Novela Approach: Spanish-Language Soap Operas, the Highest-Rated Programming in Latin America, Are Gaining Fans in the United States," *Orange County Register* (September 29, 1996), F12 [database on-line]; available from Lexis-Nexis.
27. *Ibid.*
28. Lopez, 258.
29. Telenovela archives received from <yoletten@x.site.net> [database on-line]. This particular summary was prepared by Beth Lerner.
30. Lopez, 259.
31. "Brazil: Fiery Star Written Out of Globo Telenovela," *Television Business International* (March 1995): 12 [database on-line]; available from Lexis-Nexis.
32. Lopez quotes the cost of an "ambitious" Brazilian telenovela as about $120,000 in 1992 (p. 259). This figure would compare to costs of about $1 million for a primetime drama each week or $60,000 for a daytime soap opera episode during the same time period.
33. Valdespino, F12.
34. Rede Globo Web site <redeglobo.com.br> [database on-line].
35. Lopez, 261–262.
36. "The Koppel Report: Technology in a Box," aired by ABC-TV (September 1989).
37. These regions are defined by the *World Radio TV Handbook, 1996 Edition*, ed. Andrew G. Sennitt (New York: Billboard Books, 1996) and the *World Radio TV Handbook, 1997 Edition*, ed. Andrew G. Sennitt (New York: Billboard Books, 1997).

The Soap Opera/Telenovela Genre —A Brief History

Decades before computer-generated "virtual reality" became part of everyday life, people could still enhance their sense of love, romance, personal success and failure through vicarious experiences. One of the most effective ways to create an "awareness" of life (without paying its full price) was through a genre first popularized on American radio known as the "soap opera."[1] This chapter traces the evolution of the American soap opera—its crossover into television, its influence overseas and its reflection of cultural values. In addition, serial drama in Great Britain and Australia are discussed, as well as the origins of the popular *telenovela** format in Latin America (which has also served as a programming model for Asia and Africa).

The Development of Soap Operas in the United States

Initially, the notion of serial drama on American radio was considered risky and programmatically unwise. Most network executives thought that the listening audience would accept only those story lines that were resolved within a series episode. However, in the early 1930s programmers began to experiment with "open-ended evening comedy" through the introduction of *Amos 'n' Andy*. This program, along with other serial comedies like *The Goldbergs* and *Myrt and Marge*, became popular immediately, proving that the serial form could be a successful mode of radio entertainment.[2]

The present work also adopts, without italics, the common Latin American term novela *as an abbreviation of* telenovela, *not to be confused with English* novel *or* novella.

THE RADIO SERIAL

Serial radio drama at the local level actually preceded open-ended comedy on the networks by over a decade. Although critics disagree on when the soap opera was first introduced, most would concede that the earliest prototype for serial drama appeared on Chicago radio in the 1920s—Irna Phillips's *Painted Dreams*, a mosaic of fanciful stories involving heroes, villains and helpless victims. *Painted Dreams* did not do very well on local radio initially, but neither Phillips nor two other Chicago writers with similar aspirations, Frank and Anne Hummert, were discouraged by their failures. Frank Hummert, an advertising executive, was convinced that the successful serial format in newspapers and magazines could translate well to radio. Although his first attempt, *Stolen Husband*, did not go far, he knew that serial drama had a future in radio.[3]

Within a short time Phillips and the Hummerts were proven right: *The Smith Family*, premiering nationally in 1925, became an instant hit. The program was built around two vaudevillians, Jim and Marion Jordan (who later became *Fibber McGee and Molly*). Later, *The Smith Family* was joined by *Clara, Lu 'n Em, Vic and Sade, Just Plain Bill, The Romance of Helen Trent, Ma Perkins* and *Betty and Bob*. Soap operas had begun to take off.

Hence, along with other visionaries of their time, Irna Phillips and Frank and Anne Hummert actually built an institution that had been unforeseen by most programmers—and certainly advertisers—at the time. In fact, the networks' first impulse was to reject the notion of any type of serial drama targeting women. They thought such programming foolhardy and unprofitable. Their concerns centered on the seemingly unattractive listening population of unpaid workers (housewives) during the afternoon time block, as well as the questionable cost efficiency of providing serious drama in continuing segments. Despite these reservations, the networks decided to experiment with several 15-minute "episodes," provided at discounted prices, to interested sponsors in the early 1930s. Most advertising support for these daytime dramas came from corporations like Colgate Palmolive-Peet and Procter and Gamble, who sold household products to interested female listeners. Thus, the term "soap opera" was developed to describe the melodramatic plotlines sold by detergent companies.[4]

In retrospect, those who "gambled" on the success of radio soap operas need not have worried; the format seemed to be a perfect complement to the medium. Relying completely on sound, radio producers had inadvertently developed into twentieth-century "troubadours," spreading news, information, musical entertainment and folktales. In minstrel tradition narrators could easily set the stage for radio drama, providing descriptions of characters and settings for the stories. Within minutes listeners (mostly women) were ushered into an imaginary world (guided by the narrator) with friends and enemies they might never encounter otherwise. In short, they became participants in a place more exciting, dramatic and compelling than the home from which they listened. As Robert C. Allen notes, "The economic and ideological confinement of most women to their homes reinforced the notion, already deeply engrained in American culture, of two separate social spheres defined by sex: the 'outside world,' which was the province of the male provider, and the home, toward which women were expected to orient their talents, energies, and desires."[5]

With this in mind it should come as no surprise that the introduction of daytime drama met with as immediate a success as it had with its evening serial counterpart. Devoted listeners faithfully followed the lives and loves of their favorite soap opera characters. And much to the networks' surprise, housewives were not an unattractive listening demographic to possess. In fact, programmers soon discovered that housewives, although not directly in the labor force, often controlled the purse strings of the household economy. By 1939 advertising revenue for the popular serials had exceeded $26 million.[6] Less than 10 years later Procter & Gamble was spending over $20 million each year on radio serials.[7] Housewives had indeed found an alluring substitute for previous programming fare (such as hygienic information, recipe readings and household tips) and were demonstrating their consumer power as well. Network programmers and advertisers had inadvertently stumbled onto an undiscovered gold mine. Thus, creative programming was not the only reason for the immediate popularity of radio soap operas. To better understand the success of daytime drama in the '30s it is important to look at two additional factors: the story formula and its relationship to post–Depression America.

Serial Drama and the Cultural Landscape of 1930s America

The assembly-line approach to developing the soap opera genre we know today began in the early '30s, through many of the first serials created by Frank and Anne Hummert. They originated many of the popular early daytime dramas like *Just Plain Bill*, *The Romance of Helen Trent* and *Ma Perkins*.[8] The Hummerts set most of their stories in the Midwest—an ideal setting for several reasons. First of all, the Hummerts' ad agency was located in Chicago. Practically speaking, they felt their soap operas should be produced there to cut expenses and to allow them more creative control.[9] Further, because most of the Hummerts' life experience came from the Midwest, they were more confident of the authenticity of their ideas. Finally, the Hummerts felt that the Midwest carried with it an accurate reflection of American values, attitudes and lifestyles. It seemed to be an ideal part of the country for audiences to associate the familiar themes of daytime drama, known as the "Hummert formula."

The Hummerts' story formula was really quite simple. They combined fantasies of exotic romance, pathos and suspense with a familiar environment of everyday life in a small-town or rural setting. Combined with an identifiable hero or heroine, this formula produced an overwhelming audience response. For example, each episode of *Our Gal Sunday* began accordingly:

(Voiced over the song, "Red River Valley"):

> Our Gal Sunday—the story of an orphan girl named Sunday from the little mining town of Silver Creek, Colorado, who in young womanhood married England's richest, most handsome lord, Lord Henry Brinthrope. The story asks the question: Can this girl from a mining town in the west find happiness as the wife of a wealthy and titled Englishman?[10]

Listeners flocked to hear the adventures of the small-town girl they "knew" and "loved" in predicaments they might only experience vicariously. And although the settings and characters varied from soap to soap, the underlying premise in the Hummerts's daytime dramas was always the same: people everywhere share common needs, common values, common problems.

In early radio most of the main soap opera characters were considered economically middle class. Their homes, their dress and the towns in which they lived were usually described by radio announcers as plain, simple and not overly impressive. And, as Rudolph Arnheim noted in his 1944 study, "The World of the Daytime Serial," homemaking and professional occupations continued to be most prevalent in serial drama during the early '40s.[11] The large number of characters portraying housewives was easy to explain: the listening audience identified easily with them. However, the presence of characters with professional careers was more difficult to understand; although most of the professional characters featured (doctors, lawyers, businessmen, politicians and artists) were probably better off economically than most listeners, they were generally not rich enough to be considered "dream" objects. Conversely, the "social elite" often served as foils for the "common folk" to exhibit wisdom, knowledge and expertise. Thus, housewives and small shopkeepers often succeeded in their endeavors when those most qualified were unable.[12]

This elevation of "common folk" was especially important during the post–Depression era, when poverty, unemployment and general political pessimism threatened the very fiber of American family life. Women, in particular, felt threatened—although most were not themselves laid off from jobs, they found themselves demoralized as those around them, one by one, lost work. Household incomes declined markedly, and women were forced to feed, clothe and shelter their families with far fewer resources than before. Amid their discouragement, listeners relied on soap opera characters such as Ma Perkins and "Just Plain Bill" Davidson—common folks who could survive despite overwhelming odds. Their victories over the trials and tribulations of daily living gave many Americans the feeling that they, too, could and would survive. Author Seli Groves offers insight into both the desperate times and the development of serial drama in the early 1930s:

In 1933, with the Great Depression raging, and war clouds gathering in Europe, Irna Phillips, the prolific writer some call the Mother of Soap Operas ... created and starred in her first serial on NBC. Called "Today's Children," its epigraph gives us a definite impression of how much radio soaps were beginning to close in on the more modern effort, to wit—"And today's children with their hopes and dreams, their laughter and tears, shall be the builders of a brighter world tomorrow." (This epigraph is loaded with future buzz words that would become part of soapdom's glossary: "brighter world..." "tomorrow..." "hopes..." "children...").[13]

By 1936 soap operas began to dominate the daytime radio dials. *The Goldbergs* moved from its primetime perch to afternoons (followed in 1937 by *Myrt and Marge*); several Hummert dramas premiered (including *David Harum, Rich Man's Darling, Love Song* and *John's Other Wife*; and a soon-to-be-famous soap writer, Elaine Carrington, debuted her first work, *Pepper Young's Family*. In 1937, more daytime drama appeared, some worthy of note (like *Guiding Light*, the oldest running soap opera in radio/television history), some better forgotten. However, the total impact of radio serials had finally been realized—both negatively and positively—and, as such, became open for sniper's fire from womens' groups like the "Auntie Septics," who argued that story lines with suggestive sex, faulty marriages and subsequent divorces threatened the survival of the American family unit.[14] Moreover, these political action groups were supported by male doctors who charged that "the soaps made men look weak in comparison to women, and *as everyone knows*, men are physically, mentally, and maybe even morally stronger than women."[15] Ultimately, the moral proselytizers faded away, due in large part to network and advertiser resistance. Soap operas had survived, even flourished, at a time when most everything else in the nation had diminished.

As daytime drama entered the 1940s several characteristics of serial writing emerged. First, characterization was simple, straightforward and easily recognizable.[16] A good example of a character description in the '40s was Ma Perkins:

> a woman whose life is the same, whose surroundings are the same, whose problems are the same as those of thousands of other women in the world today. A woman who spent all her life taking care of her home, washing and cooking and cleaning and raising her family. And now, her husband's death pitched her head foremost into being the head of the family as well as the mother.[17]

Because most daytime radio listeners were women, they could identify with a woman who led a simple life yet was also a solid citizen and model for others in her mythical community.

Second, characters found themselves in predicaments that were easily identifiable by their listeners, with settings easily imaginable to those who had never traveled far beyond their home environment. As scholar Rudolf Arnheim discovered, soap opera characters seemingly preferred common-day occurrences in their own home town to problems in an unknown environment.[18] And when circumstances necessitated travel, the new setting invariably took place in the United States. Arnheim surmised that soap opera producers refrained from international travel because they felt that listeners would not enjoy a foreign setting, which would demand that they imagine a place outside their own realm of experience.[19]

Third, most of the action centered on strong, stable female characters who were not necessarily professionals but community cornerstones nonetheless. Men were very definitely the weaker sex in soap opera life—a direct reflection on the primary listening audience during daytime hours.

Finally, daytime drama was often used as a vehicle for moral discussions or rededication to American beliefs and values. Soap opera heroines often voiced the platitudes of the Golden Rule as well as the rewards that would come to those who could endure the trials and tribulations of living in a troubled society. Take, for example, Ma Perkins's philosophy in 1938: "Anyone of this earth who's done wrong, and then goes so far as to right that wrong, I can tell you that they're well on their way to erasing the harm they did in the eyes of anyone decent."[20]

Thus, the success of daytime drama during the 1930s can be tied in part to creative programming skills and advertiser support, but one must also acknowledge the importance of the creation of a "cultural landscape" of America (through plot and characterization) that both reflected and shaped radio listeners' beliefs, attitudes and values. This broadcast unity of beliefs and attitudes was especially important during the post–Depression era, when poverty, unemployment, crime and political disarray threatened the very fiber of American family life. Audiences found courage through such characters as *Just Plain Bill*, *Ma Perkins* and *Our Gal Sunday*.

Soap Operas and Postwar America

After World War II, "happy days" were here once again economically, and soap operas reflected this boom with more career-oriented characters (especially women). But negative postwar elements also emerged, such as postwar mental stress and alcoholism. All these and more were discussed on Ma Perkins's doorstep—often with easy solutions—keeping the "painted dream" of America alive and well.

Career women became more numerous on soap operas in the 1940s because of writers like Irna Phillips. Phillips also introduced mental problems and amnesia to daytime drama to reflect America's postwar interest in psychology. Usually a central character suffered some type of emotional malady, such as memory loss, a nervous breakdown, alcoholism or shell-shock, as a result of wartime stress. Also, psychosomatic paralysis was a common affliction to the long-suffering soap opera heroes and heroines.

Toward the end of the '40s crime emerged as an important plotline theme, especially in the area of juvenile delinquency. This direction also reflected the times, for Americans were becoming increasingly concerned about youth crime in this country. Criminal story lines continued throughout the early '50s and remain an important theme in daytime drama on television (although the situations have been updated considerably).

THE MOVE FROM RADIO TO TELEVISION ... AND A NEW CULTURAL LANDSCAPE

In the early 1950s most soap operas moved from radio to television, and the resulting change in technology was felt at all levels, including script writing, acting and production. Author and soap opera writer Jean Rouverol shows great sympathy for those early days of "passage":

> Those radio actors who had made the transition to television struggled to adapt. They could no longer read their parts with script in hand but now had to memorize them, often on only a few hours' notice, and perform without benefit of [the] TelePrompTer, which was not yet in general use. Writers, too, coped with the new medium, wistfully remembering the infinite versatility of radio's sound people (storms at sea, crying babies, auto crashes, etc.) as they wrestled with the problems of a visual medium and the restrictions imposed on them by live tape production.... A director would not interrupt a scene if the roof were falling in. Establishing shots were unheard of and shooting on location was an impossible dream.[21]

The visual medium of television allowed for a wider choice in soap opera settings because writers were not forced to limit themselves to the experiential world of radio listeners. Rather, they could take their characters anywhere, as long as they visually established the appropriate setting. However, the visual element in television also had distinct limits, for soap writers could no longer rely on "imagination" to set a scene. Irna Phillips was among those who doubted, at first, that radio serials could "translate" to television: "I have had very little interest in television from a daytime standpoint, and unless a technique could be evolved whereby the auditory could be followed without the constant attention to the visual ... I see no future for a number of years in televising the serial story.[22] Phillips later recanted, adjusting herself to the new medium with more reality based stories, such as *Guiding Light* (which moved from radio to television in 1952), *As the World Turns* (with Agnes Nixon), *Another World* (with Bill Bell), *Days of Our Lives* and *Love Is a Many Splendored Thing*. Phillips's stories, along with those of other serial writers like Roy Winsor (*Search for Tomorrow*, *Love of Life*, *The Secret Storm*) and Irving

Vendig (*The Edge of Night*), were lauded by viewers and critics alike: ratings skyrocketed and scholars now asserted that daytime drama was entertaining as well as informative.[23]

In the mid–1950s some soap operas became 30 minutes in length as compared to the 15-minute capsules of the '30s and '40s. *As the World Turns* (another Irna Phillips vehicle) and *The Edge of Night* (created by Irving Vendig) pioneered this trend, and it soon became the formula for all soaps (until *As the World Turns* created a new, hour-long template). Because viewers could now see their characters, plotlines became more slowly paced to capitalize on all the advantages of the visual medium, such as character reactions and new locales. In fact, a common plotline, such as a marriage proposal, could last for weeks in a 1950s television soap. After the male character "popped the question" in *The Secret Storm*, for example, several days of programming would be spent learning the reactions of principal and supporting characters for this event: the bride-to-be, her mother, her old boyfriend, his old girlfriend or ex-wife, his secret admirer, her secret admirer, etc. The possibilities were endless. Thus, one major plotline could sustain itself much longer on television than would have been possible on radio, despite the added 15 minutes of programming each day.

Most of the soap operas in the '50s and early '60s followed the same mating-marriage-baby cycle,[24] although from time to time, someone chose to take an imaginary leap from the norm. One such example was Irving Vendig's *The Edge of Night*, which often featured crime detection and courtroom drama. The main character was Mike Karr (a former assistant district attorney turned private eye), whose wife died while saving their small daughter's life. He was left to balance the daily life of single fatherhood and crime stopping. The early demise of Sarah Lane Karr (Mike's wife) so shocked viewers that CBS had to announce that the actress had not actually died. Soon after the show's ratings rose, the creative direction of adventuresome plotlines also met its demise, and *The Edge of Night* settled in as yet another teary-eyed sudser, with Mike Karr as a romantic interest rather than a relentless investigator. *The Edge of Night* ultimately rode into the sunset—perhaps a bit ahead of its time, compared to soaps just five or six years later.

Along with *The Edge of Night*, another soap, *General Hospital*, seemed to be "ahead of its time" in the early to mid–1960s. Created by Agnes Nixon, *GH* soon became, however, a beacon for change rather than a fatality from good intentions. Nixon, among other things, included different racial and ethnic groups (Jews, Blacks, Irish and Polish) in her soaps (including *All My Children* and *One Life to Live*, in addition to *General Hospital*), and these characters were often confronted with societal problems of drug addiction, child abuse and venereal disease, as well as the more traditional fare of love, marriage and children. Sex was freer, women were more independent, and community problems were addressed more directly than in the past. Two ground-breaking story lines during this time involved a light-skinned African American woman's dilemma between an identity with white coworkers and pride for her darker-skinned family and a woman's battle against spousal abuse (both featured on *One Life to Live*).[25]

Nixon also waged awareness "campaigns" on ecological issues, SIDS (Sudden Infant Death Syndrome) and the importance of getting yearly Pap tests. In the 1970s her characters in *All My Children* addressed the pain of the Vietnam conflict, voicing both pro- and antiwar sentiment. Two of Nixon's most memorable characters during this period included a mother whose son was missing in action and a prisoner of war who had returned to a very different America than he'd remembered.[26]

Agnes Nixon (along with her executive producer at ABC, Gloria Monty) thus paved the way for character and plotline innovations on all the networks. CBS and NBC began to revamp their older, more traditional shows, appealing to the demographics of a changing American daytime audience. According to author, teacher and social critic Karen Lindsey, some of the more interesting plotlines from these networks in the 1980s and 1990s included:

Hank's Homosexuality (*As the World Turns*): The show explored homophobia through Hank's troubled teenage friend Paul and Paul's caring but misguided stepfather, Hal.

White Supremacy (*Days of Our Lives*): Dr. Marcus Hunter [was revealed as] a danger to a corrupt government official because as a boy, Marcus had witnessed the bombing of a black church in which three little girls were killed.

Casey's Right to Die (*As the World Turns*): Casey, paralyzed and dying, begged his friend/stepdaughter Margo to promise she would pull the plug when he was brain-dead.

Native American Sacred Ground (*As the World Turns*): Lyla Peretti's friendship with a young Indian woman who boards in her home.[27]

Viewers were now younger, more male, more educated, more career-oriented and more ethnically and racially diverse than before. However, without a visionary (in the form of Nixon), this rather startling fact may have gone unnoticed for a very long time.

By the late 1970s and through the 1980s, the social strata found in soap operas began to expand, as had the racial/ethnic mix and relevant story lines several years before. More blue-collar and lower-income families entered the world of soaps, along with fashion designers and business scions. And, as Christopher Schemering noted in *The Soap Opera Encyclopedia*, "every adult female on 'Ryan's Hope,' set in New York City, held down a job—from barmaid to doctor—to support herself or her family."[28]

Despite these trends, soap operas in the '90s are still identified by their stories of love, family, health and security—much like their radio predecessors. Serious issues may appear more often, and they are addressed by more racially and socially mixed character groups, but their "tape life" and importance are related directly to the popularity pulse of the viewing public. In short, a character can project his/her storyline to last no longer than the next ratings sweep— a time of conclusion or a time of renewal.

Actually, the only major difference between soap operas then and soap operas now may be the existence of a "global village" and its related technology. Today, American serials are transmitted worldwide, reaching across geographical boundaries and carrying images of American values ... or at least someone's perception of them. The cultural landscape of America now reaches around the globe, spreading images and icons that define who we are to millions of people. A frightening concept at best.

Cultural Studies and the British Soap Opera

Before transmitting programs directly to other cultures, American soap operas were influential in a more obtuse way. Serial drama in Great Britain, for example, actually began in 1942, as a means to show U.S. soldiers stationed in London and its environs that the English were keeping a "stiff upper lip" during the height of World War II.[29] *Front Line Family*, a story about the rather dull life of the Robinson family, became an instant hit for soldiers who missed the continuing sagas of *Ma Perkins*, *Our Gal Sunday* and *Just Plain Bill*. The BBC was surprised to find that British listeners were equally enthralled, and *Front Line Family* not only survived the war but thrived until 1947 under its postwar title, *The Robinsons*.

In 1948 another middle-class radio serial, *Mrs. Dale and Her Diary*, became an audience favorite, and two years later a family-agricultural soap (*The Archers*) began its decades-long run.[30] The Archer family worked hard on their farm, and many listeners could identify with the difficult postwar life they endured. Often, amid the standard plotlines of love, romance and marriage, scriptwriters would insert helpful hints to cope with food shortages or tight budgets. This met the BBC's goal of blending education with entertainment.

Nineteen fifty-four marked the year for TV soaps in Britain. *The Grove Family*, produced and distributed by the BBC, established a model for most serials to follow—that of struggling, working-class blue-collar characters living in an urban environment.[31] This setting became so popular that by the time ITV's[32] *Coronation Street* (originally titled *Florizel Street*)[33] debuted to television audiences in 1960, many British plays, films and novels had also focused on the struggles of ordinary people trying to make a life in the city. According to Christine Geraghty, the setting in these dramas was always important, focusing on the "community" of individuals rather than on the individual within a nondescript neighborhood.[34] Geraghty also notes that the early years of *Coronation Street* were very character driven, despite the emphasis on locale, until the 1980s, when soap operas like Channel 4's *Brookside* (1982) and the BBC's *EastEnders* (1985) premiered. *Coronation Street* only then began to follow the trend of de-emphasizing the individual in favor of the culture. She explains: "In doing so, the new programs sought to engage an audience which included those not normally attracted to soaps—young people, men, those concerned about political and social issues."[35] The move to broaden the audience was bold ... and successful. By December 1986 *EastEnders* had become one of the most popular shows in Great Britain (claiming a viewership of 30 million on Christmas Day alone),[36] having proved itself enough to inspire plans for international distribution in continental Europe, North America and Australia.

Not long after the immense popularity of *EastEnders* and *Brookside*, other soap "hopefuls" emerged, most notably the multimillion-dollar effort, *Little England* (later retitled *Eldorado* to avoid ill will from Ireland, Scotland and Wales).[37] Unfortunately, none have fared so well as *EastEnders* and *Coronation Street*. In fact, most soap viewers in Great Britain these days prefer the sun-soaked serials from Australia, like *Neighbours*. Barry Brown, a BBC executive, once explained the British fascination for soaps from "Down Under": "The world of 'Neighbours' clearly is far away from the infamous damp and drizzle that constitutes the British climate. That, I *know*, is a clear fantasy for the British. In America, people aspire to wealth and power. Here in Britain, people aspire to good weather."[38] But the British are not the only folks to favor Aussie soap operas—Australia is one of the most prolific and prestigious soap distributors in the world today. And they continue to grow.

Serial Drama in Australia— From "Down Under" to "On Top"

In 1996 Greg Stevens, a Grundy Organization production executive and creator of *Neighbours* and other soaps, became embroiled in a real-life soap opera of his own—responding to multiple charges of underage sexual offenses.[39] This abominable disclosure marred indelibly the career of one of Australia's most respected television producers. It also affected the Grundy Organization, heretofore reaping substantial rewards from serial dramas like *Neighbours*, which has aired in more than 60 countries since its 1985 debut.

Ironically, Stevens's debacle would have been an unlikely plotline for one of his dramas, which usually feature sunny weather, casual talk and healthy lifestyles.[40] In fact, one of the secrets of Australia's success in the international soap opera market has been the lack of sinister story lines. "There may be sex, intrigue and murder," says Nick Lazaredes, an executive at Angst (an Australian film/TV company), "but it is done in a more wholesome way."[41] In addition, Lazaredes notes, "There is a certain reality to it—it's not the kind of glitzy, romance-driven soap opera,"[42] as evidenced by some of the older serials like *The Sullivans, Prisoner in Cell Block H, Country Practice*, and *E Street*.

In general, producers like the Australian soap model because it uses English dialogue (the world's most spoken language), is comparatively inexpensive to produce and appeals to a teenage market.[43] In addition to *Neighbours*, Aussie soaps such as *Home and Away, Echo Point* and *Paradise Beach*, have found varied success either at home or abroad.[44] In fact, one of the most recent releases, *Pacific Drive*, was contracted by several overseas distributors before the first episode was ever produced. And with shows like *Pacific Drive* and *Paradise Beach*, tourism thrives—people come in droves to experience firsthand the beach culture.

It should also be noted that beaches are not the only attraction in Australia. A 1995 survey in *Good Food Vegetarian Magazine* extolled the foods eaten by characters on *Home and Away* and *Neighbours*. Their diets of "fruit, vegetables, fish and brown bread" clearly rose above the "fry-ups and alcohol" featured on *Coronation Street*.[45]

In short, Australia is enjoying an international recognition previously unknown. This recognition is due in part to its soap opera dominance throughout the world, a dominance that does not appear to be diminishing anytime soon.

The Latin American Telenovela and Its Migration

Unlike the American/British/Australian soap opera models (rooted in domestic novels and screenplays), telenovelas derive from nineteenth-century serialized stories and novels found in European newspapers and magazines and are intended specifically for theatrical presentation.[46] As journalist Anne Valdespino explains,

> In Britain and the United States, traditional theatrical genres splintered in different directions; opera stayed traditional, operetta developed into the Broadway musical. Nonmusical theater split into drama and light comedy, from which came television and movie writing. Vaudeville had a short-lived history on television in the form of the variety show. In the 1950s, playwrights such as Paddy Chayefsky, Arthur Miller, William Inge and Clifford Odets wrote for television or the movies.... By contrast, in Latin America, cinema and television stayed much closer to their theatrical roots. The palette of theatrical origins ranges from zarzuela (a type of Spanish opera-operetta) and Spanish melodrama to carpa (a traveling theater in Mexico and the Southwest, drawing stock characters and broad gestures from Italian commedia dell'arte) and vaudeville, from which came slapstick comedian-film star Cantinflas. (Mexico's most influential comic actor, he was Charlie Chaplin, Jim Carrey and Jerry Lewis rolled into one.)[47]

As a result, traditional works by authors like Charles Dickens and Eugene Sue were enjoyed by men and women alike and thus judged to be both popular and respected enough to be presented to mass audiences through the new, twentieth-century technology.

By most accounts, this adaptation of print novela form to the electronic media was first heard in Cuba, where the serial drama (*El Direcho de Nace/The Right to Be Born*) became an immediate radio hit in 1948. Before long the genre became immensely popular, helping to establish Cuban broadcasters as front-runners in creative media programs. Between 1951 and 1958 Brazil, Mexico and Venezuela also brought telenovelas to their viewing audiences, but Cuba still reigned as the dominant "storyteller" during this decade throughout Latin America and in Spanish-speaking parts of the United States—everywhere within earshot of the small island in the Gulf of Mexico. Ten years later, after Castro's 1959 Revolution, Cuban novela form was transported throughout Central and South America quite literally, with large emigrations of political fugitives from the country. It was through this emigration (of writers, directors and producers) that telenovelas developed in Argentina, Peru and Colombia (and increased in Brazil, Venezuela and Mexico). From there the genre developed characteristics specific to each individual culture.

Like their U.S. counterparts, Latin American radio- and telenovelas told heart-wrenching stories of unrequited love, family difficulties and forbidden romance. Unlike American soaps many of these serials took place in previous historical eras rather than contemporary times. Also, the early Latino plotlines differed in their attitudes toward sex, featuring "the furies of passion, abortion and illegitimacy,"[48] with nudity or seminudity as a common accompaniment to a steamy story line (especially in Brazil).[49]

Despite the emphasis on sexual passion in some telenovelas, others were used as vehicles for education and social acculturation. In the mid–1970s and early 1980s, Mexico's Televisa, led by novelist Miguel Sabido, became an agency for change, instructing viewers on such issues as family planning, health, literacy, drug abuse, political corruption and women's rights.[50] Sabido, a scholar as well as a popular writer, persuaded Televisa to produce six telenovelas, incorporating themes of family planning, sexual equality and adult education. He theorized that market-driven entertainment could also be instructive and even socially redemptive.

Sabido's first piece, *Ven Conmigo* (*Come with Me*) proved his point dramatically. *Ven Conmigo* featured five characters—ranging from single mothers to subsistence farmers—who contemplated the value of joining a state-run literacy program. The telenovela averaged a 32.6 household rating during its 13-week run (beginning November 1975) and was credited with persuading almost one million Mexicans to enroll in the program.[51] Sabido's subsequent works were equally successful and later were exported to 47 pan–American markets.[52]

Some critics have argued that Sabido's entertainment-education achievements on Televisa were due, in part, to the social needs in the country at that time. David Poindexter (executive director of Population Communications International) explains:

> Mexico was the logical place because the government realized quite early on the need to do something about population growth. I argued with them from the beginning that no country can develop properly until the fertility rate drops to 2.3 children per woman, or below that.... Telenovelas can entertain and educate at the same time, and their impact can be truly astonishing. If properly done, they can be used to reinforce desirable social behavior.[53]

The results of qualitative studies on Sabido's programs could not be denied. In fact, other nations, notably India and Brazil, subsequently followed Mexico's example in their telenovela programming and were equally pleased with the outcome of their "campaigns." They have since tackled other informational needs as well.

In addition to consumer education, telenovelas have often been a "safe" way to reflect societal changes in a country. One such example was the Mexican novela, *Los Ricos También Lloran* (*The Rich Also Cry*), in which an impoverished young woman overcomes her low social status by marrying into an aristocratic family. After giving birth to a beautiful son, she discovers to her dismay that her wealthy husband has been cheating on her. In desperation she gives her son to a poor street woman selling gum in the park. The husband finally reunites with his wife, but they must now spend the rest of their lives finding their lost child.[54] Although Mexico's population is highly Catholic and hierarchically structured, the message was clear, according to novela fan Veronica Villanueva: "They show that you don't have to be a virgin to get married, it's OK not to be one if you love and accept one another. And a divorce is OK. And if you get remarried and have kids from another family join your new family, that's OK. In the past, those were big no-nos."[55] Incidentally, although *Los Ricos También Lloran* was first produced in 1979, it still enjoys great popularity at home and abroad. As recently as January 1997, the *Financial Times* reported that "Veronica Castro [the show's star], Mexico's answer to Joan Collins, was in Moscow ... to put a little cheer into Boris Yeltsin's life. He is a big fan."[56]

Los Ricos También Lloran is not the only story of success for Latin American serial drama. Other examples abound, as shown by a brief chronology of some of the most popular telenovela influences in the last twenty years[57]:

- 1976   Brazil's TV Rede Globo produces *A Escrava Isaura* (*Isaura, the Slave Girl*), which later becomes its first major export to Europe, the USSR and China.
- 1985   TV Globo airs *Roque Santeiro*, which earns a 98 percent share of its broadcast audience.

- 1987 Mexico's Televisa launches a global sales arm in Los Angeles.

- 1989 Argentine and Mexican novelas become primetime television fare for Mediaset's Rete-4 network in Italy.

- 1990 Venezuelan RCTV makes a big impression in Spain with its hit, *Cristal*, capturing an 80 percent share of 11 million Spanish viewers.

- 1992 Mexico's *Los Ricos También Lloran* sets a ratings record in Russia with an estimated viewing audience of 100 million.

- 1994 RCN (Colombia) airs *Café con Aroma de Mujer* (*Coffee with a Scent of Woman*), which quickly becomes a domestic hit, as well as the biggest export in Latin America.

- 1994 Mexico's Televisa teams with Fox Network to coproduce its first English-language novela, *Empire*.

- 1995 *Acapulco Bay* is Televisa's first English-language serial to air in the United States, by three Fox-affiliated stations.

- 1996 President Boris Yeltsin arranges a special airing of Brazil's TV Globo hit, *Tropicalmiente*, to persuade Russians against leaving town on polling day.

America may have been "conquered" by Old World explorers centuries ago, but through the medium of the telenovela, the process seems to have reversed itself.

A "World" of Telenovelas

In 1991 a merger between Warner Bros. and Venezuela's Marte TV expanded resources to include telenovela coproduction in the United States, creating yet another cross-cultural corporate venture between South America and "El Norte."[58] This agreement was no doubt due in part to the changing "face" of America—by 2010, the U.S. Latino population is expected to reach 41.5 million, 13.9 percent of the total population.[59] However, statistics show that Latin American influences are not limited to the U.S. market. In 1993 Mexico's Grupo Televisa teamed with Rupert Murdoch's News Corp. (each with an initial commitment of $5 million) in a joint venture to produce "500 hours of identical bilingual programming," mostly telenovelas, for similar ethnic reasons.[60] Even before these expensive coproduction agreements were drawn, Latin American novelas had been exported to the United States and Canada, Spain, Portugal, Italy, Greece, Israel, Turkey, Poland, Russia, Romania, parts of Scandinavia and Germany.[61] The genre had also been copied and culturally adapted extensively in Japan, India, Pakistan, Korea, China, Thailand, South Africa, Kenya, Egypt and several other countries in Asia and Africa, as demonstrated by the following story synopses:

> *Humraahi* (India)—Angoori is a beautiful, lively 14-year-old Indian girl, eager for life and desperate for an education. But she comes from a poor

family that drives her into an arranged—and unhappy—marriage. Bowing to pressure from her mother-in-law, Angoori becomes pregnant, eventually dying in childbirth....[62]

Tushauriane (Kenya)—the life of a beautiful young woman, a veterinarian, who [goes] out with a young man from another tribe.... The heroine's friends resent her "abandoning" her tribe and [cause her] needless pain.[63]

Mind-boggling investments by international corporate giants have set new goals and territories for program production, export and distribution. They have also catapulted the telenovela genre into an entirely new direction, as demonstrated by the new all-telenovela satellite channel.

In January 1997 Venevision announced the formation of the Telenovela Channel in Eastern Europe—a joint venture between Vision Europe (Venevision's European distribution company) and Zone Vision (a British company). Programming will be beamed through Israel's Amos satellite and funded by subscription fees and advertising.[64] According to Zone Vision president and CEO Chris Wronski,

> ...the new service will at first be cable-exclusive and target a potential audience of three million in Poland, Hungary and Romania. However, it will soon afterwards increase its airtime from eight to between 15–23 hours daily and add Russian and Czech-language soundtracks. This, along with a possible place on MultiChoice's digital package and the extension of its coverage to Mediterranean countries such as Spain and Italy, should see the channel's viewership rise considerably.[65]

With international distribution at the forefront and increasingly sophisticated domestic audiences, what seems to be the future of the telenovela? According to Mexican telenovela producer-director Raul Araiza, there will be more realism: "They will portray deeds, institutions, groups, trends, defects in our society. And when it affects these groups and institutions, there will be objections."[66]

Araiza's assessment of current novela trends was demonstrated quite graphically in *Nada Personal* (*Nothing Personal*), produced by Television Azteca in 1996–1997. According to the London *Financial Times*,

> Instead of the usual lachrymose melodrama, the producers—two former war correspondents and the publisher of a left-wing daily—set "Nothing Personal" against the violent backdrop of modern Mexico. "We wanted to give viewers a modern drama, with real flesh-and-blood characters immersed in the complexities of daily life," says Alberto Barrera, a member of the script-writing team. "Latin American telenovelas cannot continue repeating the same old formula in which the maid marries the boss's son and lives happily ever after."[67]

Maybe. Maybe not. Only time will tell.

Notes

1. The serial form of drama was certainly not new to radio or television. In fact, it's been around since preliterate troubadours sang tales of sorrow and bereavement, of fantasy and high adventure. However, when adapted for the electronic media, the genre took on a new form, which became an entity of its own.

2. Robert LaGuardia, *Soap Opera World* (New York: Arbor House, 1983), 9.

3. Jean Rouverol, *Writing for Daytime Drama* (Stoneham, MA: Focal Press, 1992), 3.

4. Muriel Cantor and Suzanne Pingree, *The Soap Opera* (Beverly Hills, CA: Sage, 1983), 36–37.

5. Robert C. Allen, *Speaking of Soap Operas* (Chapel Hill: University of North Carolina Press, 1985), 135.

6. J. Fred MacDonald, *Don't Touch That Dial: Radio Programming in American Life from 1920 to 1960* (Chicago: Nelson-Hall, 1979), 233.

7. Jeff Kisseloff, *The Box: An Oral History of Television* (New York: Viking, 1995), 430.

8. LaGuardia, 12.

9. *Ibid.*, 20.

10. MacDonald, 235.

11. Rudolph Arnheim, "The World of the Daytime Serial," in *Radio Research: 1942-1943*, ed. Paul F. Lazarsfeld and Frank N. Stanton (New York: Essential, 1944), 38–85.

12. *Ibid.*, 64.

13. Seli Groves, *The Ultimate Soap Opera Guide* (Detroit: Visible Ink Press, 1995), 3.

14. *Ibid.*, 8.

15. *Ibid.*

16. MacDonald, 241–243.

17. *Ibid.*, 243.

18. Arnheim, 38–85.

19. *Ibid.*, 38–39.

20. MacDonald, 243–244.

21. Rouverol, 7.

22. Quoted in Kisselhoff, 432.

23. Rouverol, 7.

24. Edith Efron, "The Soaps—Anything But 99-44/100 Percent Pure," in *Television*, 4th ed., ed. Barry G. Cole (New York: Free Press, 1973), 156–162.

25. Gerard J. Waggett, quoting social critic Karen Lindsey in *The Soap Opera Book of Lists* (New York: HarperCollins, 1996), 150.

26. Rouverol, 8.

27. In Waggett's *Soap Opera Book of Lists*, 151–152.

28. Christopher Schemering, *The Soap Opera Encyclopedia* (New York: Ballantine, 1985), 3.

29. Laurie Werner, "Working Class Heroes," *Northwest Portfolio* (July 1989), 24.

30. *Ibid.*

31. *Ibid.*

32. "ITV" stands for the "Independent Television Authority."

33. Nicholas Hellen, "Sky Launches Bid to Wrest 'Coronation Street' from ITV," *Sunday Times* (September 24, 1995) [database on-line]; available from Lexis-Nexis.

34. Christine Geraghty, "Social Issues and Realist Soaps: A Study of British Soaps in the 1980/1990s," in *To Be Continued... Soap Operas Around the World*, ed. Robert C. Allen (London: Routledge, 1995), 66.

35. *Ibid.*, 66–67.

36. Werner, 23.

37. Lester Middlehurst, "Why the BBC Needs Eldorado," *Daily Mail* (July 4, 1992), 33 [database on-line]; available from Lexis-Nexis.

38. Werner, 73.

39. "Hit TV Soap Producer Admits Child Sex Charges," Agence France Presse (December 18, 1996) [database on-line]; available from Lexis-Nexis.

40. Belinda Goldsmith, "Australians Mold Soap Operas for Overseas Markets," Reuters North American Wire (September 11, 1995) [database on-line]; available from Lexis-Nexis.

41. Genine Babakian, "'Neighbours' Hoping to Send 'Maria' Packing," *Moscow Times* (February 11, 1995) [database on-line]; available from Lexis-Nexis.

42. *Ibid.*

43. Goldsmith (September 11, 1995).

44. Ironically, Australian soaps are now enjoyed by international audiences more than those within the country. The pendulum of change may swing back, but at present no one seems concerned, given the healthy revenues overseas.

45. *Ibid.*

46. Heidi Noel Nariman, *Soap Operas for Social Change: Toward a Methodology for Entertainment-Education Television* (Westport, CT: Praeger Publishers, 1993), 13.

47. Anne Valdespino, "A Novela Approach: Spanish-Language Soap Operas, the Highest-Rated Programming in Latin America, Are Gaining Fans in the United States," *Orange County Register* (September 29, 1996), F12 [database on-line]; available from Lexis-Nexis.

48. Ana M. Lopez, citing Reynaldo Gonzalez, *Llorar es un Placer* (Havana: Editorial Letras Cubanas, 1988) in "Our Welcome Guests: Telenovelas in Latin America," *To Be Continued... Soap Operas Around the World*, ed. Robert C. Allen (London: Routledge, 1995), 271.

49. "Brazilian Soaps—Popular, Racy and High-Budgeted," *Video Age International* (January 1992), 18 [database on-line]; available from Lexis-Nexis.

50. Fred Hift, "Seeing the Issue in Black and White: Telenovelas Created for Audiences from Rio to Bombay Are Prompting Big Changes," *Worldpaper* (January 1994), 10 [database on-line]; available from Lexis-Nexis.

51. Andrew Paxman, "Instruments of Change," *Variety* (October 7–13, 1996), 63 [database on-line]; available from Lexis-Nexis.

52. *Ibid.*

53. Hift, 10.

54. Nariman, 14.

55. Valdespino, F12.

56. "Skullduggery Behind the Soap," *Financial Times, London Edition* (January 10, 1997), 11 [database on-line]; available from Lexis-Nexis.

57. This chronology has been excerpted from a "Special Report" in *Variety* (October 7–13, 1996), 64 [database on-line]; available from Lexis-Nexis.

58. Meredith Amdur, "Cable Networks Head South: Latin America Ripe with Program Opportunities," *Broadcasting & Cable* (January 24, 1994), 118.

59. Janet Purdy Levaux, "Univision Communications, Inc.: The New America," *Investor's Business Daily* (November 26, 1996), A6 [database on-line]; available from Lexis-Nexis.

60. Amdur, 118.

61. John Hopewell, "Novelas Still a Staple but Waning," *Variety* (September 25, 1995), 90 [database on-line]; available from Lexis-Nexis.

62. Hift, 10.

63. *Ibid.*

64. "From Venezuela with Love," *Television Business International* (January 1997), 16 [database on-line]; available from Lexis-Nexis.

65. *Ibid.*

66. S. Lynne Walker, "Mexico's 'Telenovelas' Breaking Their Traditional Themes," Copley News Service (February 20, 1997) [database on-line]; available from Lexis-Nexis.

67. "Skullduggery Behind the Soap," 11.

North America

Countries included

Bermuda, Canada, Greenland, St.-Pierre et Miquelon, United States[1]

Stations/Networks

Bermuda

Population: n/a (see United Kingdom)
(TV sets—n/a; radios—n/a)
Bermuda Broadcasting Company
VSB-TV (Channel 11)

Canada

Population: 29,123,194—8 per sq. mi.
(TV sets—1:1.5 persons; radios—
1:1 persons)
Canadian Broadcasting Corporation/
Société Radio-Canada (publicly
owned)
CITY-TV
Canwest Global System
CTV Television Network Limited
Le Réseau de Télévision (TVA)
Télévision Quatre Saisons
Société de Radio-Télévision du
Quebec
TV Ontario

Greenland

Population: n/a (see Denmark)
(TV sets—n/a; radios—n/a)

Kalaallit Nunaata Radios
AFRTS (U.S. Air Force)

St.-Pierre et Miquelon

Population: n/a (see France)
(TV sets—n/a; radios—n/a)
Société Nationale de Radio Télévision
Française d'Outre Mer (RFO)

United States

Population: 267,954,767—73 per
sq. mi.
(TV sets—1:1.2 persons; radios—
1:0.5 persons)
AF Diego Garcia Television (AFRTS)
American Broadcasting Company
(ABC)
American Forces Antarctic Network
(AFAN McMurdo)
Columbia Broadcasting System, Inc.
(CBS)
National Broadcasting Company (NBC)
PBS
The Fox Television Network
TV Marti

Satellite Channels Available in This Region[2]

Action Pay-per-View (USA)
AFRTS (USA)
Airport News and Transportation
   Netw. (USA)
Alaska Satellite TV Project
America's Collectibles Netw. (USA)
America's Talking (USA)
America-1 (USA)
American Collectibles Netw. (USA)
American Movie Classics (USA)
American One (USA)
American TV News (USA)
APNA TV (India)
Arab Netw. America (USA)
Argentina TV a Color (USA)
Around the World after Dark (USA)
Arts & Entertainment TV (USA)
Atlantic Satellite News Halifax
   (Canada)
Automotive Sat. Training Netw. (USA)
BBC Breakfast News (UK)
BBC World (UK)
Black Entertainment TV (BET) (USA)
Bravo (USA)
C-Span (USA)
C-Span 1/2 (USA)
Cable Health Club (USA)
Cal-Span (USA)
Canadian Exxxstacy (Canada)
Canal 13 (XHDF-TV) (Mexico)
Canal France Int.
Canal Sur (Peru)
Cartoon Network (USA)
CBC Newsworld (Canada)
CBC North (Canada)
CBCM (Canada)
CBMT Montreal/CBC
CCC (Chinese Commercial Channel)
   (USA)
Channel 1 Moscow (Russia)
Cinemax East I/II (USA)
Cinemax East 2 (USA)
Cinemax West (USA)
Classic Sports Network (USA)
CNN (USA)
CNN Airport Channel (USA)
CNN Headline News (USA)

CNN Int. (USA)
CNN International (USA)
CNN Newsource (USA)
Comedy Central (USA)
Computer Television Netw. (USA)
Consumer News & Business Channel
   (CNBC) (USA)
Cornerstone TV (USA)
Country Music TV (USA)
CTV Television Netw. (Canada)
CycleSat Comm. (USA)
Deutsche Welle TV (Germany)
Deutsche Welle TV (foreign)
   (Germany)
Discovery Channel (USA)
Disney Channel (USA)
E! Entertainment (USA)
ECO-Televisa (Mexico)
Encore (USA)
Encore 2 (USA)
Encore 8 (USA)
ESPN (USA)
ESPN 2 (USA)
ESPN Blackout Channel (USA)
ESPN International (USA)
Estación Montello (USA)
Eternal Word TV (USA)
Europlus/Teleplus (Italy)
Eurotica (USA)
Exxxstacy 2 (Canada)
Exxxtreme/Climaxxx Promo Chan.
   (USA)
Fantasy Cafe TV (USA)
FLIX movie services (USA)
FOXNet PrimeTime (USA)
fX Movies (USA)
G.O.P. TV (USA)
Game Show Network (UK)
GEMS TV (USA)
Georgia Public TV (GPTV) (USA)
Global Shopping Netw. (USA)
Global TV (Canada)
Gospel Music TV (USA)
HBO East 2/3 (USA)
HBO II East/West (USA)
HBO III East (USA)
HBO West 2 (USA)

HBO/Cinemax (USA)
Hispavisión (Spain)
Home and Garden TV Netw. (USA)
Home Box Office East/West (USA)
Home Shopping Club 2 (USA)
Home Shopping Netw. 1 (USA)
Home Sports Entertainment (USA)
Hong Kong TVB Jade Channel
  (Hong Kong)
Hospitality TV (USA)
HRT Croatia
HSE2 (USA)
HTV Hispanic music videos (USA)
Independent Film Channel (USA)
Infomercial Channel (USA)
Infomerica TV (USA)
KCNC, Denver (USA)
KDVR, Denver (USA)
KMGH, Denver (USA)
KNBC-TV, L.A. (USA)
Knowledge TV (USA)
KOMO-TV, Seattle (USA)
KPIX-TV, San Francisco (USA)
KRMA, Denver (USA)
KTLA, L.A. (USA)
KWGN, Denver (USA)
La Cadena de Milagro (USA)
La Chaîne French (Canada)
Lifetime East/West (USA)
Madison Square Garden (USA)
MCET Educational Netw. (USA)
Merchandise and Entertainment TV
  (MET) (USA)
Midwest Sports Channel (USA)
MOR Music Television (USA)
Movie Channel (West) (USA)
MTV (West) (USA)
MuchMusic (Canada)
Music Television (West) (USA)
Music TV (East) (USA)
Muslim Television (USA)
Muslim TV (Russia)
NASA Select Channel (USA)
Nat. Empowerment TV Network (USA)
National Weather Netw. (USA)
NBC (USA)
Nebraska Educational TV (USA)
Network One (N1) (USA)
New England Sports Channel (USA)

Newsport (USA)
NewsTalk Television (USA)
NHK Tokyo (Japan)
Nickelodeon (USA)
Nostalgia Channel (USA)
Nustar (USA)
Odyssey Network (USA)
Ontario Legislature (Canada)
ORT TV-1 (Russia)
Panda America (Home Shopping)
  (USA)
PBS (schedules C/D) (USA)
Perú TV (Argentina)
Perú TV Ch. 13 (Peru)
Perú TV Ch. 2 (Peru)
Perú TV Ch. 4 (Peru)
Perú TV Ch. 5 (Peru)
Playboy at Night (USA)
PrevuGuide (USA)
Prime Network (USA)
Prime Sports Intermountain (West)
  (USA)
Prime Sports Northwest (USA)
Prime Sports Showcase (USA)
Prime Ticket, California (USA)
Pro-Am sports, Detroit (USA)
Public Broadcasting Sce. (PBS) (USA)
Q-CVC (Mexico)
Quorum multi-level marketing (USA)
QVC Fashion Channel (USA)
QVC Home Shopping Netw. (USA)
RAI (Italy)
RCTV (Venezuela 7)
Real Estate TV Network (USA)
Request TV 1 (USA)
RTP Internacional (Portugal)
RTV Beograd (Croatia)
Russian TV Network (USA)
S. Carolina Educational TV (USA)
Satellite City TV (USA)
Sci-Fi Channel (USA)
Sellevision (USA)
Shepherd's Chapel (USA)
Shop at Home (USA)
Shop-at-Home (USA)
Shop-at-Home Network (USA)
Showtime East/West (USA)
Skyvision Home Shopping Ch.
  (USA)

Skyvision Promo Channel (USA)
Space (Argentina)
Sport South (USA)
SportsChannel alternatives (USA)
SportsChannel Chicago (USA)
SportsChannel Chicago Plus (USA)
SportsChannel Cincinnati (USA)
SportsChannel Florida (USA)
SportsChannel Hawaii (USA)
SportsChannel New England (USA)
SportsChannel New York (USA)
SportsChannel New York Plus (USA)
SportsChannel Ohio (USA)
SportsChannel Pacific (USA)
SportsChannel Philadelphia (USA)
SRC Educational Netw. (USA)
SSVC (UK)
Sundance Channel (USA)
Sunshine Blackout Channel (USA)
Sunshine Network (USA)
Super Television Channel (USA)
System United for Retransm. (Latin
   America)
TCI Preview Channel UA (USA)
TCI TV (USA)
Telecasa (Mexico)
Telefé (Argentina)
Televisión Boliviana (Bolivia)
TF1 (France)
The Babe Network (USA)
The Baseball Netw. (TBN) (USA)
The Family Channel (USA)
The Filipino Channel (Philippines)
The Golf Channel (UK)
The International Channel (USA)
The Kentucky Netw. (USA)
The Learning Channel (USA)
The Movie Channel (USA)
The Nashville Network (USA)
The New Inspirational Netw. (USA)
The Outdoor Channel (USA)
The People's Network (USA)
The Travel Channel (USA)
The University Netw. (USA)
The X Channel (USA)
Three Angels Broad. (USA)
TNT Internacional (Turkey)
Trinity Broadcasting Network (USA)
Turner Classic Movies (USA)

Turner Network Television (USA)
Turner Vision Promo Channel (USA)
Turner Vision Promo Sce. (USA)
TV 69 (USA)
TV Asia (USA)
TV Erotica (USA)
TV Nacional de Chile (ch. 7) (Chile)
TV Nacional de Chile (ch. 10)
   (Chile)
TV Ontario (Canada)
TV-Japan
TVE Internacional (Spain)
TVN Theatre 1/2/3/4/5/6/7/9/10 (USA)
UAE TV Dubai (UAE)
United Arab Emirates TV (UAE)
United Paramount Network (UPN)
   (USA)
United States Info. Agency (USA)
Univision (USA)
USA Network
USIA WorldNet (USA)
Valuevision (USA)
Venus Adult (Canada)
VH-1 (USA)
Via TV (Inter.) (UAE)
Video Catalog Channel (Canada)
Viewer's Choice (USA)
VTC Satellite Network (Canada)
WABC, New York (USA)
Weather Channel (USA)
Westerns Encore 3 (USA)
WFLD-TV, Chicago (USA)
WGN, Chicago (USA)
WHDH-TV, Boston (USA)
Wholesale Shopping Netw. (USA)
WJLA, Washington (USA)
WMNB (USA)
WMNB Russian Lang. Station (USA)
WNBC New York (USA)
World Harvest TV (USA)
Worldnet (USA)
Worship TV (USA)
WPIX, New York (USA)
WRAL, Raleigh, NC (USA)
WSBK, Boston (USA)
WTBS, Atlanta (USA)
WUSA-TV, Washington, DC (USA)
WWOR-TV (USA)
WXIA, Atlanta (USA)

XEIPN-TV, Canal 11, Mexico City (Mexico)
XEQ-TV 9 (Mexico)
XEW-TV, Mexico City (Mexico)

XHGC-TV (Canal 5) (Mexico)
XHIMT, Canal 22 (Mexico)
XXXPlore (USA)
Z-Music (USA)

Overview of Cultural Patterns and Audience Trends

North America stands out as a region of stark contrast for study in soap opera/telenovela production and distribution. The two largest nations in this group—Canada and the United States—have assumed totally different strategies of cultural identity through television. Ironically, although Canada has stringent program import quotas for its primetime schedule, it does not (with the exception of Quebec)[3] produce any daytime dramas but imports liberally from distributors in the United States, the United Kingdom and Australia. *Coronation Street* and *Neighbours*, for example, have legions of Canadian fans. *General Hospital, All My Children, Days of Our Lives* and *The Young and the Restless* are equally popular.

The rationale for this strategy is actually quite sound, both economically and culturally. As in every other country around the world, station managers in Canada are given limited funding for unlimited, "round-the-clock" programming. As such, budgets must be prioritized, reserving the most ambitious expenditures for the most-watched, primetime hours. A careful look at sample 1997 TV schedules reveals that, indeed, network executives in Canada spend most of their reserves for nighttime programs, focusing on subjects of specific interest to Canadians. Other time slots are not as important and therefore warrant less funding. As for the choice in program imports, it is important to remember that Canadian history also includes English, American, Australian and French elements, either through geographic proximity, economic partnership or political necessity. Thus, the inclusion of television series from these cultures doesn't necessarily detract from the Canadian identity— especially during nonprimetime hours.

Further south, however, Americans are quite different. Aside from relatively recent forays into telenovelas to address the rising domestic Latino population, most stations are reluctant to program serial dramas that are not "homegrown." Viewers seem to prefer the technological "glitz" of higher production values and more glamorous actors and actresses than those found in serial dramas in other countries. They also seem reluctant to learn more about other cultures, leading to a certain ethnocentrism and xenophobia. At a time when America's cultural diversity is expanding, this course of action may not be very wise. Clearly, the United States continues to reign as one of the major players in the global soap opera/telenovela market, but the lack of program imports, although building a national identity, limits a very valuable resource to encourage learning about other cultures at home, as well as in the "global village."

This chapter is unique because it focuses on only one country—the United States—for the reasons stated above. But even though the United States is the only serial producer in North America, this region is one of the most important areas of study, for American influences extend far beyond the geographic borders. They, above most others, penetrate the cultures of almost every other nation in the world.

Focus: United States

As mentioned in the previous chapter, daytime soap operas in the United States have experienced a ratings decline in the last 10 years. Journalist Curt Schleier provides this profile comparison—1987 vs. 1997:

> "General Hospital," the top-rated soap a decade ago with an 8.3 rating, has averaged around 4.2 this season. "The Young and the Restless" is down from 8.0 to 6.7 over the period. "Days of Our Lives," "All My Children," and "As the World Turns," which all had about a 7.0 rating 10 years ago, now average 5.4, 4.4 and 4.2 respectively. (Each rating point represents a percent of TV households.)[4]

Despite the seeming lag, networks are still willing to bet that many American fans continue to follow their "stories" with loyalty, dedication and enthusiasm—as can be seen from the number of serial program choices available. As Susan D. Lee (vice president of NBC Daytime Programming) says, "I think what we've learned is that talkshows [the other major daytime genre] have a limited shelf life. They may be cheaper but they have a very limited run."[5] To back this statement, one need only look at TV Guide. Currently, there are 11 daytime soaps on the air (including two relatively new entries), with literally hundreds more that have had some previous airtime.

In 1997 the daytime soap operas found on American television included the following[6]:

All My Children (January 5, 1970–)—Originally the series featured three families (the Tylers, the Martins and the Brents), who were the major forces behind the daily happenings in Pine Valley (a fictional community near New York City). The Tylers clearly overpowered the other houses, though, and became the only surviving character group by the end of the first decade. Phoebe, the strong matriarch of the Tyler clan, was portrayed as an elegant socialite, forever concerned with her family reputation within the community. As a result, she meddled in everyone's affairs ... although she nearly always meant well while she was meddling. (ABC)

Another World (May 4, 1964–)—The first episode of this drama opened by introducing one of Bay City's most respectable families (the Matthewses) mourning the loss of brother William (who had been quite wealthy, and even more arrogant). As the serial progressed, the less fortunate Matthewses had to endure William's widow and her children. Created by Irna Phillips, *Another World* was the first daytime drama to give rise to not only one spinoff, but two: *Somerset* and *Texas* (which will be described later in this chapter). (NBC)

As the World Turns (April 2, 1956–)—Another Irna Phillips creation, this soap took place in the fictitious town of Oakdale (allegedly near Chicago) and focused on two families (the Hugheses and the Lowells). Although the Lowells were better off financially and somewhat more glamorous, the middle-class Hughes clan was clearly more interesting and has ultimately survived as the primary family 40 years later. *ATWT* was one of the first existing half-hour soaps to expand to an hour and celebrated its ten thousandth episode in 1995. (CBS)

The Bold and the Beautiful (March 23, 1987–)—Like most of the newer soap operas, this drama was set in the "real" city of Los Angeles. Originally titled *Rags*, it featured the airbrushed lives and loves of the Forrester family, owners of an upscale design house. Between the cutthroat competition of the fashion industry and the fierce passions of the Forresters (amongst themselves as well as others), *B&B* has become one of the most popular serial dramas throughout the world, although the show title changes with the country—In Scandinavia, it's known as *Glamour*; in Belgium and the Netherlands, it's *Top Models*; and in France, it's known as *Love, Fame and Beauty*. In Italy, it's simply *Beautiful*. (CBS)

Days of Our Lives (November 8, 1965–)—When MacDonald Carey first invited audiences to look through the sand-filled hourglass, the trials and tribulations of the Horton family comprised the predominant story lines. For over 30 years the Hortons have sustained their place in the drama, although now the grandchildren and great-grandchildren are the major characters. *Days* is particularly popular with college students (especially men), which may account for the large percentage of action-adventure story lines and "drop-dead" gorgeous actors and actresses. (NBC)

General Hospital (April 1, 1963–)—As mentioned in chapter one, this soap opera has been a major force in redefining audience tastes, story lines and character diversity for the last three decades. Created by Agnes Nixon, it featured the intricate professional and personal lives of the medical staff of a Port Charles city hospital. Ironically, *GH* began airing on the same day as NBC's medical drama *The Doctors*, but it has continued to top daytime ratings for almost twenty years after Hope Memorial closed its doors ... and looks likely to continue into the next millennium. (ABC)

The Guiding Light (June 30, 1952–)—Enjoying the distinction of the longest continuous run, *GL* was perhaps the only radio soap to translate well to the medium of television. Created by Irna Phillips, the radio version (premiering in 1937) at first featured the lives of a preacher and his congregation in a small town in Five Points. Within a decade, however, the setting moved to a new location (Springfield) with a new focus (the Bauer family). Suffering from anemic ratings in the mid–1990s, the fate of this drama has seemed nebulous from time to time; but in 1997 it was still hanging on to the CBS daytime schedule and enjoying popularity throughout the world, especially in Malta, Italy, France, Germany, Turkey, Japan and the Philippines. (CBS)

One Life to Live (July 15, 1968–)—Set in Llanview, this story originally focused on the prominent Lord family, owners of the local newspaper. Victor (the widower father) tried to raise his two daughters (Victoria and Meredith) by himself while maintaining the legacy of the paper (through chosen daughter Victoria). Neither was very easy, as viewers followed Victoria's schizophrenia and Meredith's blood disorder. These story lines in *OLTL* (another Agnes Nixon creation) pale when compared to the soap's focus on different ethnic and racial characters (as well as important social issues). Without a doubt, this emphasis on *OLTL* (and in other Agnes Nixon vehicles) has proven that social responsibility in broadcasting can also pay off in advertising revenues. (ABC)

Port Charles (June 1, 1997–)—Premiering in a two-hour Sunday night made-for-television movie, this drama has tried to establish its own identity, while enjoying immediate viewer interest as a spinoff from *General Hospital*. The series began with the return of Scotty Baldwin (a character who had disappeared on *GH*), which caused immediate distress between Lucy Coe (his previous love) and her current boyfriend, Kevin Collins. From there, new characters have emerged, seeming to take hold with new audiences as well as the *GH* crossovers. (ABC)

Sunset Beach (January 7, 1997–)—The first daytime drama produced by Aaron Spelling is set in a small Pacific coast town, where locals gather either at the local watering hole (The Deep) or the cyber coffeehouse (Java). Although the characters are middle class (police officers, lifeguards, newsreporters, cafe owners, etc.), the lushly photographed scenes and beautiful stars are surely not. At first, *Sunset Beach* was recorded on film (unlike other daytime soaps). Shortly after its premiere, producers decided to go to videotape. U.S. audiences were slow to "warm up" to *Beach*, but foreign sales were gigantic—before the soap was ever aired, Worldvision Enterprises (Spelling Productions' export subsidiary) had already sold 260 episodes to the U.K., France, Germany, Sweden, Norway, Denmark, Belgium, Greece, the Middle East, North Africa and Latin America.[7] (NBC)

The Young and the Restless (March 26, 1973–)—To better compete with the culturally diverse, youth-oriented ABC soaps of the 1960s, CBS hired William J. Bell and Lee Phillip Bell to create a slick drama featuring young, attractive actors who face contemporary problems. *Y&R* took place in fictional Genoa City and originally featured two families: the wealthy Brooks clan and the lower-class Fosters. Class differences were only the beginning of the problem: family feuds, social-climbing manipulation, love triangles and marital infidelity dominated the story lines. The Brooks and Foster clans were later dropped, but new families of power (the Abbotts and Chancellors) have since moved into Genoa City, as have middle-class families (like the Williamses) and those of different race (the Winterses and Voliens). The same themes are popular with viewing audiences, but within the last two decades, social issues such as date rape, eating disorders and recently discovered illegitimate children fathered by American servicemen in Vietnam have also been explored. (CBS)

This list, although substantial, pales when compared to prior decades. Since the early 1930s, many daytime heroes, heroines, hussies and housewives have lived their "lives" in front of millions of listeners or viewers. In the 1940s radio schedules abounded with serial drama, sometimes airing as many as 45 soaps during one programming season. Television soap opera production has never been quite as prolific since that time, but daytime drama continues to be a network staple nevertheless. Some samples of earlier TV soap opera series include the following[8]:

Another Life (1981–1984)—Set in the town of Kingsley, this serial served up the usual menu for daytime (illicit love, alcohol abuse, divorce) but from a different perspective: a Christian one. Produced by the Christian Broadcasting Network, the message throughout each crisis underscored the need for Judeo-Christian faith and love. (Syndicated)

The Best of Everything (March–September 1970)—Based on a film about young career women, this short-lived soap featured three idealistic females living in New York City and trying to make their mark in the publishing industry. (ABC)

Bright Promise (1969–1972)—This drama was clearly conceived after network executives discovered the profitable daytime audience of young adults. Taking place at a small midwestern college, the story focused on the transition from student to successful adult. Unfortunately, it was cancelled before its first class could graduate. (NBC)

The Brighter Day (1954–1962)—One of Irna Phillip's creative radio dramas, this serial crossed over to television quite successfully. Most of the major characters were members of the Dennis family and their marital mates. As in radio, each TV episode lasted only fifteen minutes at first; the program later expanded to a half hour. (CBS)

Capitol (1982–1987)—Set in Washington, D.C., this drama featured two warring political families, the McCandlesses and Cleggs. In a plot twist straight out of *Romeo and Juliet*, one of the McCandless sons soon fell in love with a Clegg daughter. This provided enough grist for a five-year run at the soap mill. (CBS)

Dark Shadows (1966–1971)—An immediate cult hit, this serial captured young audiences for its Gothic undertones. One of its main characters, Barnabas Collins, was a 200-year-old vampire. The rest of the Collins family (including a werewolf), who lived on the brooding shores of Maine, was equally unique. Despite its 25-year absence from the daytime schedule, fans still talk about the episodes and can see repeats either through video or on some cable channels from time to time. (NBC)

The Doctors (1963–1982)—One of the earlier TV soaps that featured a professional "family" (as compared to the traditional biological family), this drama took place in Hope Memorial Hospital. Orin Tovrov (best known for his popular radio soap, *Ma Perkins*) was the show's creator. Tovrov originally envisioned the show as an anthology (with story lines beginning and ending during one episode), but within a year the format changed to a continuous drama—a wise decision, considering that *The Doctors* was the first daytime series to be awarded an Emmy. (NBC)

The Edge of Night (1956–1975)—Premiering the same day as *As the World Turns*, *Edge* was named (in part) for its late-afternoon time slot; the title was also suggestive of the crime/courtroom stories which were featured. Later, however, this drama moved in the direction of its competitors, focusing on investigator Mike Karr's personal life more than his crime-fighting ambitions. *The Edge of Night* was the first soap opera to jump networks after a few seasons of declining ratings on CBS. (CBS/ABC)

The First Hundred Years (1950–1952)—The first soap opera aired on CBS, this show was a fairly light-hearted portrayal of a newly married couple and their in-laws. Perhaps because of its lack of angst, it later gave way to *Guiding Light*, which clearly has been able to provide at least enough angst for the past 45 years ... and then some. (CBS)

First Love (1954–1955)—Airing live from Philadelphia, this 15-minute soap concentrated on the ups and downs of newlywed life. (NBC)

Follow Your Heart (1953–1954)—Another product from Philadelphia, this drama was created by Elaine Carrington, who reprised her earlier radio soap, *When a Girl Marries*. The story featured a wealthy young socialite who fought her mother's suggested marital choice. (NBC)

Generations (1989–1991)—Continuing in the soap opera tradition of family-centered drama, this story departed from the norm by featuring a black family among its major characters. Taking place in Chicago, the main dramatic tension took place between a socially established white family and an upwardly mobile black one. Although cancelled by NBC less than two years after its inception, the reruns have since been shown on the BET Network. (NBC)

Love Is a Many Splendored Thing (1967–1973)—A derivation of a popular film by the same name, creator Irna Phillips envisioned this drama's major initial theme to be interracial love. However, after a few episodes, network executives balked at the idea. Phillips then quit, but the serial survived with a new emphasis on political machinations. (CBS)

Love of Life (1951–1980)—Like several of its contemporaries, this serial began as a 15-minute capsule and was later expanded to 30 minutes. The location of the soap changed as well over the years, moving from the town of Barrowsville to a nearby community named Rosehill. The drama focused on the opposing personalities of two sisters for the first several years of its run. And later, although younger characters dominated the major storylines, one of the sisters (Meg) still returned from time to time. (CBS)

Loving (The City) (1983–1997)—ABC was confident that this daytime drama which premiered in a Sunday night made-for-television movie would soon find itself in a league with *All My Children* and *General Hospital*. And with producers like Agnes Nixon and Douglas Marland, success seemed inevitable. Unfortunately, even though the story formula was proven—four major families living in the college town of Corinth—audiences never really warmed up to the "hot" love triangles in the drama. After 14 years of trying to boost ratings, the network finally gave up *The City* on March 28, 1997, replacing the haggard soap with a *General Hospital* spinoff called *Port Charles*. The soap still enjoys great popularity in several countries, including Israel, Turkey, Morocco, Cameroon, the U.K. and New Zealand. (ABC)

Return to Peyton Place (1972–1974)—Spinning off of the popular primetime serial, this drama continued the saga of romance in a small New England town. Viewers were not as interested in the "new" version, perhaps because the daytime vehicle did not include any of the primetime stars cast in the original series. (NBC)

Ryan's Hope (1975–1989)—Created by Claire Labine and Paul Avila Mayer as a reproduction of some of Irna Phillips's earlier radio soaps, the story was set in New York City and featured the Ryan family (proprietors of a saloon). This large, lower-middle-class Irish American clan took great pride in hard work and strong family values. When away from the tavern, most of the other major script action took place at Riverside Hospital, where caring and crisis were never mutually exclusive. (ABC)

Santa Barbara (1984–1993)—Focusing on four families—the wealthy Capwells and Lockridges, the middle-class Perkinses and the lower-class Latino Andrades—this soap achieved only moderate success in the United States in the 1980s. It has proven to be a tremendous hit overseas. In the late 1980s, *SB* was one of the most watched shows in the world—a close competitor of *The Bold and the Beautiful* and *Baywatch*. According to Jim Fuller, a spokesman for New World Entertainment (the show's distributor), some of the most telling comments come from Croatian fans, who write, "We are being bombed, but we still find time to tune in to *Santa Barbara*."[9] (NBC)

Search for Tomorrow (1951–1986)—Switching from radio to television in 1951, this serial was the longest-running television soap (surpassing *Guiding Light*) prior to its demise in 1986. The central character, Joanne Gardner Barron, was a young military housewife who tried to cope with the daily trials of raising a small daughter amid the seemingly never-ending interference of her in-laws. As time went on, Jo eventually became a widow, and her in-law problems increased—they now wanted custody of the daughter. Through it all Jo survived and remained a major character throughout the entire run of the series. In 1982 CBS hinted that Jo may have experienced her last trauma ... as they announced the soap's anticipated cancellation. NBC acquired the show shortly after the announcement and ran it for another four years. By 1986 ratings were among the lowest in *SFT* broadcast history; subsequently, the writers created a huge flood and wiped out most of the existing characters. The new "facelift" didn't take—within months, the longest-running TV soap was cancelled. (CBS/NBC)

The Secret Storm (1954–1974)—Created by Roy Winsor (best known for his work on *Search for Tomorrow* with Gloria Monty), this soap was a typical 1950s serial. Featuring a central family (the Ameses) in the fictional town of Woodbridge, it was originally 15 minutes long and later expanded to a half hour. The love-marriage-baby-divorce cycle was the major theme, and its popularity lasted until the youth-oriented ABC soaps offered fierce competition. Writers tried to breathe new life into the serial by killing off the Ames family in the late 1960s but only succeeded in alienating the old audience without attracting a new one. It was cancelled one week after celebrating its twentieth anniversary. (CBS)

Somerset (1970–1976)—Originally entitled *Another World/Somerset*, this spinoff quickly lost its *Another World* identity and developed its own. Rather than focusing on the themes of love and interpersonal dilemma found on *AW*, *Somerset* developed the story lines of crime and action/adventure similar to those on *The Edge of Night*. (No surprise here—the first head writer, Henry Slesar, had also worked on *Edge*.) Ultimately, *Somerset* may have made a bad decision to diverge from *Another World*, which continues to be very successful. (NBC)

Texas (1980–1982)—Another spinoff of *Another World*, this serial tried to cash in on the popularity of *Dallas*. Set in Houston, the story followed *AW* character Iris Bancroft's relocation to be with her son. Unfortunately, viewer apathy over a daytime *Dallas*, along with fierce scheduling competition with ABC's *General Hospital* caused the soap's demise before it ever really started. Ironically, the show has done fairly well on reruns (most likely due to its actors) and has since been shown on many American cable stations. (NBC)

In 1997 soap opera producers (like all TV producers) adopted a rating system to suggest the appropriate maturity level for viewers. To protect younger audiences from growing numbers of sexually suggestive story lines and possible violence, the recommended viewing age for daytime serials was 14. Although this seems to be a good and responsible move, it may affect future audience numbers. Based on most research, people are introduced to soap operas in several ways.[10] Their first experiences are incidental, either through

1. an experience as a small child, usually because a mother, grandmother or babysitter is tuned in to the drama;

2. an experience as a junior high or high school student (after school) because their friends watch;

3. an experience as a college student, in a common viewing area (either in a suite with several roommates or in a large lounge with a TV);

4. an experience at work or at lunch in a restaurant/bar with the TV set on; or

5. an experience where the viewer is suddenly homebound (due to unemployment, illness, family problems, etc.).

Although the "TV14" rating would not apply in the last three categories, it certainly would apply in the first two—in times of our lives when viewing habits are established. Of course, no one can know the possible effects of the rating system at this point, but it certainly is a question for future research.

American Soaps Abroad

The United States has served as one of the major models for serial drama around the world. Great Britain's first radio soap, *Front Line Family*, was developed, for the most part, to bring a bit of "home" to American GIs who had come to their country to fight in World War II. Castro was so intrigued with American soaps that Cuba became a pioneer for Latin America's telenovela form. Even today, while daytime soaps appear to be in some domestic ratings decline,[11] the genre remains popular (and profitable) in most other areas of the world. For example, through satellite television the Procter & Gamble soaps (*Guiding Light*, *As the World Turns* and *Another World*) have dedicated fans in the Middle East as well as in Europe, Asia and the Pacific. (See fig. 2.1 for the country/station list.)

The Bold and the Beautiful (*B&B*) reaches at least 350 million viewers worldwide each day. In 1997 it aired in 90 countries, including Australia, the Bahamas, Bophuthatswana, Belgium, Brazil, Canada, China, Denmark, Egypt (where the love scenes are censored), France, Finland, Germany, Greece, Great Britain, Italy, Jordan, Luxembourg, New Zealand, South Africa, Singapore, Spain, Switzerland and Taiwan.[12] *Santa Barbara*, out of production since 1989, remains popular on all continents outside of North America, especially in Europe, the Caribbean and the Pacific Rim.

In truth American soap operas are embraced by many overseas networks because the format appeals to both programmers and audiences. First of all, the cost to air these shows is relatively minimal (especially for satellite distributors, who send their signal to millions of people at one time). Second, many of these contracts allow the shows to be run several times each day, taking up the slack for otherwise dead air space. Third, the number of series episodes is large and can be used either once a week for a long time or several times during that same week.

Viewers, on the other hand, can feed their seemingly insatiable hunger for American culture. More important, they can enjoy watching story lines filled with glamor, sex, adventure and opulence, as well as actors and actresses who also represent glamor, sex, adventure and opulence. The latter is no small joke.

Figure 2.1
Contract Details of Procter and Gamble
Daily Series Currently on Air
(April 1997)*

Soap Opera	*Country*	*Station*
Guiding Light	France	TMC
	Romania	Antena 1
	Italy	Rete 4
	England	Bsky B
	Asia	Superchannel
	Iceland	Icelandic American
	Germany	TM3/RTL+
As the World Turns	England	Bsky B
	Holland	RTL 4
	Asia	Superchannel
	Lithuania	Baltic TV
Another World	England	Sky One/Soap
	Australia	FOXTEL
	Middle East	Abu Dhabi TV/ Qatar T.V.

*This list was contributed by D'Arcy Masius Benton & Bowles, Inc. The author is especially grateful to Barbara A. Brady, Syndication Supervisor for Daytime Program Services at DMB&B, for her time and consideration in putting it together.

Some American daytime stars rise to become movie/primetime television celebrities (see fig. 2.2). They can also become primetime icons in other countries. For example, several years ago two stars from *B&B* (Jeff Trachta [Thorne Forrester] and Bobbi Eakes [Macy Alexander Forrester]) actually starred in a successful European concert tour and recorded several songs based on their singing performances on the soap. In Italy *Beautiful* (the Italian translation for *B&B*) fans anxiously watch the episodes on primetime and often press Americans for story updates (the soap has a two-year time delay on RAI-TV).

Ironically, the American soaps that are best-sellers overseas are not necessarily those most popular in the United States. *The Young and the Restless* and *B&B* seem to be universally popular because of their gilt-edged images (similar to the *Dallas* and *Dynasty* models). On the other hand, those soaps featuring more middle- or working-class characters, or those addressing more culturally (or politically) specific topics (like *General Hospital, All My Children* and *One Life to Live*) tend to be less popular in the international marketplace.

Americans and the Telenovela

Within the past decade the rise of American interest in multinational media corporations has spawned the development of joint ventures and export

Figure 2.2: Famous Soap Opera "Graduates" to Primetime/Film*

Kevin Bacon (in the role of Tim Werner, *Guiding Light*)
John Beck (David Raymond, *Santa Barbara*)
Corbin Bernsen (Ken Graham, *Ryan's Hope*)
Yasmine Bleeth (Ryan Fenelli, *Ryan's Hope*)
Ellen Burstyn (Dr. Kate Bartok, *The Doctors*)
Dixie Carter (Brandy, *The Edge of Night*)
Ted Danson (Tom Conway, *Somerset*)
Kim Delaney (Jenny Gardner, *All My Children*)
Sandy Dennis (Alice Holden, *Guiding Light*)
Olympia Dukakis (Dr. Barbara Moreno, *Search for Tomorrow*)
Patty Duke (Ellen Dennis, *The Brighter Day*)
Rob Estes (Glenn Gallagher, *Days of Our Lives*)
Morgan Freeman (Roy Bingham, *Another World*)
Larry Hagman (Ed Gibson, *The Edge of Night*)
Mark Hamill (Kent Murray, *General Hospital*)
Jackee Harry (Lily Mason, *Another World*)
David Hasselhoff (Snapper Foster, *The Young and the Restless*)
Catherine Hicks (Faith Coleridge, *Ryan's Hope*)
Lauren Holly (Julie Chandler, *All My Children*)
Finola Hughes (Anna Scorpio, *General Hospital*)
Kate Jackson (Daphne Harridge, *Dark Shadows*)
Tommy Lee Jones (Mark Toland, *One Life to Live*)
Kevin Kline (Woody Reed, *Search for Tomorrow*)
Judith Light (Karen Wolek, *One Life to Live*)
Hal Linden (Larry Carter, *Search for Tomorrow*)
Audra Lindley (Liz Matthews, *Another World*)
Ray Liotta (Joey Perrini, *Another World*)
Tony LoBianco (Dr. Joe Corelli, *Love of Life*)
Nia Long (Kat Speakes, *Guiding Light*)

George Maharis (Bud Gardner, *Search for Tomorrow*)
A Martinez (Cruz Castillo, *Santa Barbara*)
Rue McClanahan (Caroline Johnson, *Another World*)
Donna Mills (Rocket, *Secret Storm*)
Demi Moore (Jackie Templeton, *General Hospital*)
Kate Mulgrew (Mary Ryan, *Ryan's Hope*)
Luke Perry (Ned Bates, *Loving*)
Brad Pitt (day player, *Another World*)
Sheryl Lee Ralph (Laura McCarthy, *Search for Tomorrow*)
Phylicia Rashad (Courtney Wright, *One Life to Live*)
Christopher Reeve (Ben Harper, *Love of Life*)
Meg Ryan (Betsy Andropolous, *As the World Turns*)
Anthony Sabato, Jr. (Jagger Cates, *General Hospital*)
Emma Samms (Holly Sutton Scorpio, *General Hospital*)
Tom Selleck (Jed Andrews, *The Young and the Restless*)
John Stamos (Blackie Parrish, *General Hospital*)
Beatrice Straight (Vinnie Phillips, *Love of Life*)
Marisa Tomei (Marcy Thompson, *As the World Turns*)
John Travolta (Spence Andrews, *General Hospital*)
Janine Turner (Laura Templeton, *General Hospital*)
Kathleen Turner (Nola Dancy, *The Doctors*)
Cicely Tyson (Martha Frazier, *Guiding Light*)
Jack Wagner (Frisco Jones, *General Hospital*)
Christopher Walken (Mike Bauer, *Guiding Light*)
Sigourney Weaver (Julie Murano, *Love of Life*)
Michael T. Weiss (Mike Horton, *Days of Our Lives*)
Billy Dee Williams (Dr. Jim Frazier, *Guiding Light*)
JoBeth Williams (Carrie Wheeler, *Somerset*)
Robin Wright (Kelly Capwell, *Santa Barbara*)

*This list was compiled through information from Christopher Schemering's *The Soap Opera Encyclopedia* (New York: Ballantine, 1985), 315–317; *Daytime TV* (September 1997), 10–23; and Gerard J. Waggett's *Soap Opera Book of Lists* (New York: HarperCollins, 1996), 187, 191–192.

syndication. A 1994 *Business Week* article noted the following directions in international mass communication:

- Time Warner was operating in over 70 countries, with 40% of its $14 billion revenues coming from outside the United States. Time Warner was also building relationships with Japan's Toshiba and Itochu.
- Sixty-four percent of Asia's Star TV and 50% of British Sky Broadcasting was owned by News Corp.
- Viacom's MTV channel reached over 239 million households in 63 countries, while two of its other networks, VH-1 and Nickelodeon, were expanding in Europe and parts of Asia.[13]

Closer to home, U.S. broadcasters are recognizing the viewer potential of a growing Hispanic population. According to the 1990 census, 77 percent of the country's 20 million Latinos over the age of five speak Spanish at home. Further, 22 percent of Latinos over the age of five speak no English at all or speak it poorly.[14] And according to a report distributed by DRI/McGraw-Hill (consultants for the Spanish language Univision network):

- The number of Hispanics that speak Spanish at home will grow from 15.3 million in 1990 to 21 million in 2000 and 26.7 million by 2010. This represents an average annual increase of 3.2% during the 1990s and 2.4% during 2000–2010.
- The Spanish-speaking Hispanic market is distributed across all income groups. Two-thirds of Hispanics with incomes over $80,000 speak Spanish at home; 43% of Hispanics that use Spanish in the home are in households with incomes of $30,000 or more.
- Major Hispanic state and metro-area markets differ substantially in the extent to which Spanish is used in the home—from a low of 47% in Denver to a high of 94% in Miami—variations that are traceable to differences in the demographic characteristics of the Hispanic population, which are analyzed in this study.[15]

Based on this data, as well as the fact that other countries (notably Venezuela and Mexico) had already created program export bureaus in Miami and Los Angeles (in 1982 and 1987 respectively),[16] American entrepreneurs decided that the Latino viewing audience was both solid and attractive. Fox Television, for example, has emerged as the mainstream network leader of Hispanic programming in the United States. In 1994 Fox embarked on a successful co-production effort with Mexico's Grupo Televisa, resulting in an English-language telenovela, *Empire*, which is still shown in markets throughout the Americas. In 1995 Fox again teamed up with Televisa, airing *Acapulco Bay* (Mexico's first English-language novela) on three of its affiliates in the United States.[17] Other English-speaking Televisa ventures include *The Shadow* (a tale of a psychotherapist and his evil deeds) and *Only You* (the story of step-sibling rivalry). Both have high production values and multi-tiered viewer appeal.[18]

In addition to Fox's efforts, two North American Latino networks have emerged and are now particularly popular in the Southwest (as well as in other areas with large Hispanic populations). They are Telemundo and Univision (along with its cable partner, Galavision). In 1996 Denver-based Telecommunications, Inc., (TCI) also entered into the Latino market through Sky Entertainment—a joint satellite TV venture with Rupert Murdoch's News Corp., Mexico's Grupo Televisa SA and Brazil's TV Globo.[19]

A partial list of American-made telenovelas[20]

Empire—(co-produced with Mexico) (no date known)
Loba Herida/Wounded She-Wolf—1994
El Magnate/The Rich Magnate—(no date known)
Marielena—1994
Morelia—1996
Piel/Skin—(no date known)
Tres Destinos/Three Destinies—1993

Telenovelas currently aired in the United States (2/1/97)[21]

Aguejetas de Color de Rosa/Pink Shoelaces—Galavision
Alcanzar Una Estrella II/To Reach a Star, Part II—Galavision
Baila Conmigo/Dance with Me—Galavision
Bajo Un Mismo Rostro/Beneath the Same Face—Univision
Bendita Mentira—Univision
Caminos Cruzados/Crossed Roads—Galavision
Chiquititas/Little Girls—Telemundo
Con Toda el Alma/With All My Soul—Telemundo
Divina Obsesión/Divine Obsession—Univision
Dos Mujeres, Un Camino/Two Women, One Road—Univision
La Dueña/The Owner—Galavision
Fabiola—Galavision
María Celeste—Galavision
María la del Barrio—Univision
Marimar—Galavision
Mi Adorable Mónica—Galavision
Nada Personal/Nothing Personal—Telemundo
Por Amarte Tanto/Because I Love You So—Galavision
Simplemente María/Simply Maria—Galavision
Tu y Yo/You and I—Univision

In November 1997 the Hispanic Institute of Radio & TV created a new era of Latino novela production in the United States—the bilingual soap opera.[22] *Love without Boundaries* (*Amor sin Fronteras*) attempts to address actual problems faced by middle-class Hispanics in America. According to the show's producers, it shows "how a majority of Latinos in the US (25 million) really live, in lifestyles that are completely different from the Hollywood and media stereotypes wrongly depicting Latinos as descendants of 'West Side Story' and other similar ghettos, and Mexicans as wetbacks, welfare dependents, drug dealers, alcoholics or people with evil habits and customs."[23] Given the increasing popularity of Spanish novelas among English-speaking Americans, the bilingual *Love without Boundaries* fills an "enormous cultural gap,"[24] while presenting quality serial entertainment. More soaps of this type are most certainly in the planning stages.

Thus, whether it be through traditional American soaps, co-produced telenovelas or a new trend in bilingual serials, the United States should continue to be a world leader in soap opera distribution. Given the growing global popularity of telenovelas, as well as burgeoning domestic interest and increased ventures in crosscultural (and bilingual) co-production, American soaps are likely to compete successfully by continuing to include more international settings, foreign intrigue and interculturally diverse characters.

Notes

1. Station/network information taken from *World Radio TV Handbook, 1997 Edition*, ed. Andrew G. Sennitt (New York: Billboard Books, 1997). Television/radio set information and population figures taken from *The World Almanac and Book of Facts 1998* (Mahwah, NJ: K-III Reference Corporation, 1997).

2. This listing is compiled from *WRTH Satellite & TV Handbook,* 4th edition, ed. Andrew G. Sennitt (New York: Billboard Books, 1997). It represents the *available* stations on satellite dishes through a transponder in Region II of the world satellite map. Although it is difficult to tell how many people have access to these channels, it is important to acknowledge the variety of cross-national program content on them.

3. Unlike the rest of its Canadian neighbors, the province of Quebec has a long and colorful history of locally produced *téléromans* (the French equivalent of the telenovela). In fact, in December 1996 Quebec's Museum of Civilization featured a two-year interactive exhibition, honoring the 40-year tradition of téléromans. Among the viewer favorites: *La Famille Plouffe* (the very first soap); *La Petite Vie* (Quebec's highest rated teleroman in history); *Cormoran* (1990–1994); *Le Temps d'une Paix* (1980–1986); and *Entre Chien et Loup* (1984–1992). Further information available on the Museum of Civilization's Web site <http://www.mcq.org/presse/aateleron.html> [database on-line].

4. Curt Schleier, "In a Lather: Ratings Drop, but Die-Hard Fans Keep Their Soaps Afloat," *Detroit News* (May 24, 1997), 6C.

5. Quoted in Chris Pursell, "Webs Lather Up with New Soaps," *Variety* (August 29, 1997), 44.

6. The information for these summaries and comments has been gathered from: Alex McNeil, *Total Television: The Comprehensive Guide to Programming from 1948 to the Present* (New York: Penguin Books, 1996); Marilyn J. Matelski, *The Soap Opera Evolution: America's Enduring Romance with Daytime Drama* (Jefferson, NC: McFarland, 1988); Rachelle Berlatsky-Kaplan, "Surprise! Our Soaps Are Taking the World by Storm," *National Enquirer* (n.d.); and the daytime Web sites of CBS, NBC and ABC.

7. Elizabeth Guider, "Foreign Sales in the *Sunset*," *Variety* (December 2–8, 1996), 82.

8. Information for these summaries and comments has been gathered from Alex McNeil, *Total Television: The Comprehensive Guide to Programming from 1948 to the Present* (New York: Penguin Books, 1996); and Rachelle Berlatsky-Kaplan, "Surprise! Our Soaps Are Taking the World by Storm," *National Enquirer* (n.d.).

9. Rachelle Berlatsky-Kaplan, "Surprise! Our Soaps Are Taking the World by Storm."

10. Many scholars—including Muriel Cantor, Suzanne Pingree, Bradley S. Greenberg and Wilbur Schramm—have explored daytime drama and its audiences. In 1986 the author attempted to replicate some of this research (in *The Soap Opera Evolution*) and came up with results similar to those previously described.

11. Schleier, "In a Lather," 1C, 6C.

12. "B & B Background," part of *The Bold and the Beautiful* homepage <http://www.cbs.com/daytime/bb> [database on-line].

13. Mark Landler, Joyce Barnathan, Geri Smith and Gail Edmondson, "Think Globally, Program Locally," *Business Week* (November 18, 1994) [database on-line]; available from Lexis-Nexis.

14. "The Use of Spanish Language in the U.S.," Univision home page [database on-line].

15. *Ibid.*

16. "A Brief History," *Variety* (October 7–13, 1996), 64.

17. *Ibid.*

18. "Series/Novelas at Mipcom '95," *Television Business International* (October 1995) [database on-line]; available from Lexis-Nexis.

19. Michael Molinski, "Sky Entertainment Starts Brazil Satellite TV," *Bloomberg Business News* (October 30, 1996) [database on-line].

20. Telenovela Web site, Yolette Nicholson <yoletten@site.net> [database on-line].

21. *Ibid.*

22. "Hispanic Institute of Radio & Television: "Love Without Boundaries," Press Release (November 6, 1997) [database on-line].

23. *Ibid.*

24. *Ibid.*

Central America and the Caribbean

Countries included

Antigua & Barbuda, Aruba, Bahamas, Barbados, Belize, Costa Rica, Cuba, Dominica (Commonwealth of), Dominican Republic, El Salvador, Grenada, Guadeloupe, Guatemala, Haiti, Honduras (Republic of), Jamaica, Martinique, Mexico, Montserrat, Netherlands Antilles, Nicaragua, Panama, Puerto Rico, St. Kitts & Nevis, St. Lucia, St. Vincent, Trinidad & Tobago, Virgin Islands (American), Virgin Islands (British)[1]

Stations/Networks

Antigua & Barbuda
Population: 66,175—387 per sq. mi.
(TV sets—1:2.7 persons; radios—1:2.3 persons)
ABS-TV (Antigua and Barbuda Broadcasting Service)
CTV Entertainment Systems

Aruba
Population: n/a (see Netherlands)
(TV sets—n/a; radios—n/a)
Tele Aruba

Bahamas
Population: 262,034—49 per sq. mi.
(TV sets—1:4.4 persons; radios—1:1.4 persons)

Broadcasting Corporation of the Bahamas

Barbados
Population: 257,731—1,553 per sq. mi.
(TV sets—1:3.6 persons; radios—1:1.1 persons)
Caribbean Broadcasting Corporation

Belize
Population: 224,663—25 per sq. mi.
(TV sets—1:6 persons; radios—1:1.7 persons)
CTV (ch-9)
Tropical Vision

Costa Rica
Population: 3,534,174—179 per sq. mi.

(TV sets—1:7 persons; radios—1:3.8
persons)
Corporación Costaricense de Televisión

Cuba
Population: 10,999,041—257 per sq.
mi.
(TV sets—1:5.8 persons; radios—1:2.9
persons)
Cubavison
Instituto Cubano de Radiodifusión
Tele Rebelde
AFRTS

Dominica (Commonwealth of)
Population: 83,226—287 per sq. mi.
(TV sets—1:13 persons; radios—n/a)
Dominica Broadcasting Corporation
Marpin-TV

Dominican Republic
Population: 8,226,151—438 per sq. mi.
(TV sets—1:11 persons; radios—1:5.8
persons)
Radio Televisión Dominica

El Salvador
Population: 5,661,827—697 per sq.
mi.
(TV sets—1:12 persons; radios—1:2.3
persons)
Televisión Cultural Educativa

Grenada
Population: 95,537—718 per sq. mi.
(TV sets—1:3 persons; radios—1:1.7
persons)
Grenada Broadcasting Corporation

Guadeloupe
Population: n/a (see France)
(TV sets—n/a; radios—n/a)
RFO-Guadeloupe
Archipel 4
Canal Antilles
TCI Guadeloupe

Guatemala
Population: 11,558,407—275 per sq.
mi.
(TV sets—1:19 persons; radios—1:15
persons)
Televisión Cultural Educativa
Radio-Televisión Guatemala

Haiti
Population: 6,611,407—618 per sq. mi.
(TV sets—1:208 persons; radios—1:20
persons)
Télé-Haiti (S.A.)
Télévision Nationale d'Haiti

Honduras (Republic of)
Population: 5,751,384—132 per sq. mi.
(TV sets—1:13 persons; radios—1:2.5
persons)
Compañía Televisora Hondureña

Jamaica
Population: 2,615,582—616 per sq. mi.
(TV sets—1:7 persons; radios—1:2.3
persons)
Jamaica Broadcasting Corporation

Martinique
Population: n/a (see France)
(TV sets—n/a; radios—n/a)
ATV Antilles Television
Canal Antilles
TCI Martinique/Télé Caraibes Interna-
tional
Société Nationale de Radio-Télévision
d'Outre Mer (RFO)

Mexico
Population: 97,563,374—129 per sq.
mi.
(TV sets—1:6.1 persons; radios—1:3.9
persons)
Grupo Televisa SA de CV
Instituto Mexicano de Televisión
(IMEVISION) (Ch 7 &13)

Montserrat

Population: n/a (see United Kingdom)
(TV sets—n/a; radios—n/a)
Antilles TV Ltd.
Radio Montserrat

Netherlands Antilles

Population: n/a (see Netherlands)
(TV sets—n/a; radios—n/a)
Tele Curaçao (Cable)
Leeward Broadcasting Corporation-
  Television

Nicaragua

Population: 4,386,399—86 per sq. mi.
(TV sets—1:15 persons; radios—1:3.8
  persons)
Sistema Sandinista de Televisión

Panama

Population: 2,693,417—92 per sq. mi.
(TV sets—1:5.9 persons; radios—1:4.4
  persons)
Televisora Nacional

Puerto Rico

Population: n/a (see United States)
(TV sets—n/a; radios—n/a)
AFRTS

St. Kitts & Nevis

Population: 41,803—401 per sq. mi.
(TV sets—1:4.7 persons; radios—n/a)
ZIZ Radio & Television

St. Lucia

Population: 159,639—670 per sq. mi.
(TV sets—1:5.3 persons; radios—1:1.3
  persons)
Cablevision
Helen TV

St. Vincent

Population: 119,092—793 per sq. mi.
(TV sets—1:6.3 persons; radios—1:1.5
  persons)
St. Vincent & the Grenadines Broadcasting Corporation Ltd.

Trinidad & Tobago

Population: 1,273,141—643 per sq.
  mi.
(TV sets—1:3.2 persons; radios—1:2
  persons)
International Communications Network Ltd.

Virgin Islands (American)

Population: n/a (see United States)
(TV sets—n/a; radios—n/a)
WBNB-TV
Caribbean Comm. Corp.
Virgin Islands Public TV System

Virgin Islands (British)

Population: n/a (see United Kingdom)
(TV sets—n/a; radios—n/a)
Television West Indies Ltd.
BVI Cable TV

Satellite Channels Available in This Region[2]

Action Pay-per-View (USA)
AFRTS (USA)
Airport News and Transportation
  Netw. (USA)
Alaska Satellite TV Project
America's Collectibles Netw. (USA)
America's Talking (USA)
America-1 (USA)
American Collectibles Netw. (USA)

American Movie Classics (USA)
American One (USA)
American TV News (USA)
APNA-TV (India)
Arab Netw. America (USA)
Argentina TV a Color (USA)
Around the World after Dark
  (USA)
Arts & Entertainment TV (USA)

Atlantic Satellite News Halifax (Canada)
Automotive Sat. Training Netw. (USA)
BBC Breakfast News (UK)
BBC World (UK)
Black Entertainment TV (BET) (USA)
Bravo (USA)
C-Span (USA)
C-Span 1/2 (USA)
Cable Health Club (USA)
Cal-Span (USA)
Canadian Exxxstacy (Canada)
Canal 13 (XHDF-TV) (Mexico)
Canal France Int.
Canal Sur (Peru)
Cartoon Network (USA)
CBC Newsworld (Canada)
CBC North (Canada)
CBCM (Canada)
CBMT Montreal/CBC
CCC (Chinese Commercial Channel) (USA)
Channel 1 Moscow (Russia)
Cinemax East I/II (USA)
Cinemax East 2 (USA)
Cinemax West (USA)
Classic Sports Network (USA)
CNN (USA)
CNN Airport Channel (USA)
CNN Headline News (USA)
CNN Int. (USA)
CNN International (USA)
CNN Newsource (USA)
Comedy Central (USA)
Computer Television Netw. (USA)
Consumer News & Business Channel (CNBC) (USA)
Cornerstone TV (USA)
Country Music TV (USA)
CTV Television Netw. (Canada)
CycleSat Comm. (USA)
Deutsche Welle TV (Germany)
Deutsche Welle TV (foreign) (Germany)
Discovery Channel (USA)
Disney Channel (USA)
E! Entertainment (USA)
ECO-Televisa (Mexico)
Encore (USA)

Encore 2 (USA)
Encore 8 (USA)
ESPN (USA)
ESPN 2 (USA)
ESPN Blackout Channel (USA)
ESPN International (USA)
Estación Montello (USA)
Eternal Word TV (USA)
Europlus/Teleplus (Italy)
Eurotica (USA)
Exxxstacy 2 (Canada)
Exxxtreme/Climaxxx Promo Chan. (USA)
Fantasy Cafe TV (USA)
FLIX movie services (USA)
FOXNet PrimeTime (USA)
fX Movies (USA)
G.O.P.-TV (USA)
Game Show Network (UK)
GEMS TV (USA)
Georgia Public TV (GPTV) (USA)
Global Shopping Netw. (USA)
Global TV (Canada)
Gospel Music TV (USA)
HBO East 2/3 (USA)
HBO II East/West (USA)
HBO III East (USA)
HBO West 2 (USA)
HBO/Cinemax (USA)
Hispavisión (Spain)
Home and Garden TV Netw. (USA)
Home Box Office East/West (USA)
Home Shopping Club 2 (USA)
Home Shopping Netw. 1 (USA)
Home Sports Entertainment (USA)
Hong Kong TVB Jade Channel (Hong Kong)
Hospitality TV (USA)
HRT Croatia
HSE2 (USA)
HTV Hispanic music videos (USA)
Independent Film Channel (USA)
Infomercial Channel (USA)
Infomerica TV (USA)
KCNC, Denver (USA)
KDVR, Denver (USA)
KMGH, Denver (USA)
KNBC-TV, L.A. (USA)
Knowledge TV (USA)

KOMO-TV, Seattle (USA)
KPIX-TV, San Francisco (USA)
KRMA, Denver (USA)
KTLA, L.A. (USA)
KWGN, Denver (USA)
La Cadena de Milagro (USA)
La Chaîne [French] (Canada)
Lifetime East/West (USA)
Madison Square Garden (USA)
MCET Educational Netw. (USA)
Merchandise and Entertainment TV
  (MET) (USA)
Midwest Sports Channel (USA)
MOR Music Television (USA)
Movie Channel (West) (USA)
MTV (West) (USA)
MuchMusic (Canada)
Music Television (West) (USA)
Music TV (East) (USA)
Muslim Television (USA)
Muslim TV (Russia)
NASA Select Channel (USA)
Nat. Empowerment TV Network
  (USA)
National Weather Netw. (USA)
NBC (USA)
Nebraska Educational TV (USA)
Network One (N1) (USA)
New England Sports Channel (USA)
Newsport (USA)
NewsTalk Television (USA)
NHK Tokyo (Japan)
Nickelodeon (USA)
Nostalgia Channel (USA)
Nustar (USA)
Odyssey Network (USA)
Ontario Legislature (Canada)
ORT-TV-1 (Russia)
Panda America (Home Shopping)
  (USA)
PBS (schedules C/D) (USA)
Perú TV (Argentina)
Perú TV Ch. 13 (Peru)
Perú TV Ch. 2 (Peru)
Perú TV Ch. 4 (Peru)
Perú TV Ch. 5 (Peru)
Playboy at Night (USA)
PrevuGuide (USA)
Prime Network (USA)

Prime Sports Intermountain (West)
  (USA)
Prime Sports Northwest (USA)
Prime Sports Showcase (USA)
Prime Ticket, California (USA)
Pro-Am Sports, Detroit (USA)
Public Broadcasting Sce. (PBS)
  (USA)
Q-CVC (Mexico)
Quorum multi-level marketing (USA)
QVC Fashion Channel (USA)
QVC Home Shopping Netw. (USA)
RAI (Italy)
RCTV (Venezuela 7)
Real Estate TV Network (USA)
Request TV 1 (USA)
RTP Internacional (Portugal)
RTV Beograd (Croatia)
Russian TV Network (USA)
S. Carolina Educational TV (USA)
Satellite City TV (USA)
Sci-Fi Channel (USA)
Sellevision (USA)
Shepherd's Chapel (USA)
Shop at Home (USA)
Shop-at-Home (USA)
Shop-at-Home Network (USA)
Showtime East/West (USA)
Skyvision Home Shopping Ch.
  (USA)
Skyvision Promo Channel (USA)
Space (Argentina)
Sport South (USA)
SportsChannel alternatives (USA)
SportsChannel Chicago (USA)
SportsChannel Chicago Plus (USA)
SportsChannel Cincinnati (USA)
SportsChannel Florida (USA)
SportsChannel Hawaii (USA)
SportsChannel New England (USA)
SportsChannel New York (USA)
SportsChannel New York Plus (USA)
SportsChannel Ohio (USA)
SportsChannel Pacific (USA)
SportsChannel
Philadelphia (USA)
SRC Educational Netw. (USA)
SSVC (UK)
Sundance Channel (USA)

Sunshine Blackout Channel (USA)
Sunshine Network (USA)
Super Television Channel (USA)
System United for Retransm. (Latin
   America)
TCI Preview Channel UA (USA)
TCI-TV (USA)
Telecasa (Mexico)
Telefé (Argentina)
Televisión Boliviana (Bolivia)
TF1 (France)
The Babe Network (USA)
The Baseball Netw. (TBN) (USA)
The Family Channel (USA)
The Filipino Channel (Philippines)
The Golf Channel (UK)
The International Channel (USA)
The Kentucky Netw. (USA)
The Learning Channel (USA)
The Movie Channel (USA)
The Nashville Network (USA)
The New Inspirational Netw. (USA)
The Outdoor Channel (USA)
The People's Network (USA)
The Travel Channel (USA)
The University Netw. (USA)
The X Channel (USA)
Three Angels Broad. (USA)
TNT Internacional (Turkey)
Trinity Broadcasting Network (USA)
Turner Classic Movies (USA)
Turner Network Television (USA)
Turner Vision Promo Channel (USA)
Turner Vision Promo Sce. (USA)
TV 69 (USA)
TV Asia (USA)
TV Erotica (USA)
TV Nacional de Chile (ch. 7) (Chile)
TV Nacional de Chile (ch. 10)
   (Chile)
TV Ontario (Canada)
TV-Japan
TVE Internacional (Spain)
TVN Theatre 1/2/3/4/5/6/7/9/10 (USA)

UAE-TV Dubai (UAE)
United Arab Emirates TV (UAE)
United Paramount Network (UPN)
   (USA)
United States Info. Agency (USA)
Univision (USA)
USA Network
USIA WorldNet (USA)
Valuevision (USA)
Venus Adult (Canada)
VH-1 (USA)
Via TV (Inter.) (UAE)
Video Catalog Channel (Canada)
Viewer's Choice (USA)
VTC Satellite Network (Canada)
WABC, New York (USA)
Weather Channel (USA)
Westerns Encore 3 (USA)
WFLD-TV, Chicago (USA)
WGN, Chicago (USA)
WHDH-TV, Boston (USA)
Wholesale Shopping Netw. (USA)
WJLA, Washington (USA)
WMNB (USA)
WMNB Russian Lang. Station (USA)
WNBC New York (USA)
World Harvest TV (USA)
Worldnet (USA)
Worship TV (USA)
WPIX, New York (USA)
WRAL, Raleigh, NC (USA)
WSBK, Boston (USA)
WTBS, Atlanta (USA)
WUSA-TV, Washington, DC (USA)
WWOR-TV (USA)
WXIA, Atlanta (USA)
XEIPN-TV, Canal 11, Mexico City
   (Mexico)
XEQ-TV 9 (Mexico)
XEW-TV, Mexico City (Mexico)
XHGC-TV (Canal 5) (Mexico)
XHIMT, Canal 22 (Mexico)
XXXPlore (USA)
Z-Music (USA)

Overview of Cultural Patterns and Audience Trends

Central America is known for its significant influence on the development of the telenovela form. Beginning with the "invention" of the genre in Castro's Cuba, and growing through the educational-entertainment serials developed by Mexican scholar Miguel Sabido, Central America pioneered many of the soap opera conventions used today throughout South America and the rest of the world. Although some nations in this region (like Dominica) import most of their television programs, others like Jamaica, Mexico and Puerto Rico have become large global exporters.

Here are some titles/summaries of novelas that have been very popular both at home and abroad[3]:

Marisol (Mexico, 1994)—Centers on the life of Marisol, a young woman who has suffered through a life of poverty and facial disfigurement, all the while unaware that her true father is a wealthy man. Her mother dies without telling her this secret, and she mistakenly falls in love with a painter who shares the same grandfather.

Pobre Niña Rica/Poor Little Rich Girl (Mexico, 1995)—Paralleling the story of Cinderella, little Consuelo is a slave to her mother and two selfish brothers. Her father, who loved her very much, dies, leaving her his fortune, but her family keeps this secret from her. Later, Consuelo meets Julio, who makes her feel beautiful both inside and out.

Al Son del Amor/To the Sound of Love (Puerto Rico, 1995)—Features Gabo, a poor stable boy, who falls in love with his boss's daughter, Vicky. At first Vicky is pampered and spoiled, but they ultimately find happiness ... at least until Helen, a jealous schemer, interferes.

Natalia (Puerto Rico, 1992)—Recounts the pain of a woman (Isabel), who seeks revenge after being raped. Unfortunately, she later finds out that the daughter conceived from the rape (Natalia) is in love with a man who is the grandson of her attacker.

Several of the titles listed above are discussed in other chapters of this book. Loyal fans in parts of Europe, Africa, Asia and South America follow them with great fanaticism, often "celebritizing" the actors and actresses far more strongly than fans in the country of origin. In addition, these soaps (and others) are often used as models for indigenous drama development in other countries.

Focus: Dominica

Like several of its island neighbors, the Commonwealth of Dominica does not at present have great resources for indigenous TV production. Aside from news and information shows, much of Dominica's programming is imported from other countries and specifically from the United States and the

United Kingdom. In serial drama the United States has a virtual monopoly, airing *All My Children, Another World, As the World Turns, The Bold and the Beautiful, Days of Our Lives, General Hospital, Guiding Light, One Life to Live, Port Charles, Sunset Beach* and *The Young and the Restless.* Great Britain's *EastEnders* was the only other soap opera seen by Dominicans in 1997.

According to Anestine Lafond, programming/production director of Marpin (a cable TV company), things may change within the next several years. For example, in 1996 Marpin Cable ran its 24-hour cable service with 21 channels. In 1997 they expanded the system to 28 channels. The advent of DBS has also been anticipated, affecting the overall television scene.[4] With the recent amount of technological development in this small island federation, Dominicans may soon need more programming. And because serial drama is both inexpensive and a proven popular commodity, the possibility for a "home-grown" soap is a realistic one.

Focus: Jamaica

Jamaica has been a leader in soap opera production for more than three decades, providing motivational programming for its African neighbors as well as for its domestic audience. Like serial drama in many other countries, Jamaican serial drama began in radio, where scholar Vibert C. Cambridge asserts that national identity—as well as agricultural, economic and cultural reform—could be promoted effectively. Cambridge goes on to describe the state of the nation in the early 1960s:

> Jamaica's colonial legacy had left a stratified society with the majority of society—Jamaicans of African descent—at the bottom of the social and economic ladder. The majority of the African population was marginalized and was concentrated on poor lands, and oriented to resolving problems through internal and external migration. A concomitant of this legacy was a high illiteracy rate (in excess of 35% at independence in 1962.[5]

As a result, all efforts (including serial drama) were geared to changing these demographics.

Jamaican radio soaps usually fell into four categories: (1) historical, (2) slice-of-life, (3) developmental, and (4) folkloric or myth-based.[6] Their production quality and content value made them well known both within the country and on other continents. As technology developed, Jamaican radio soaps moved to television, although serial drama can be found on both media these days.

According to Angela Patterson, Jamaica Broadcasting Corporation's director of marketing and planning,[7] much of Jamaica's TV serial drama today is imported either from Australia (*Home and Away,* twice weekly), South Africa (*Suburban Slice,*[8] *Generations,* weekly) or the United States (*Santa Barbara, The Bold and the Beautiful,* twice daily). As for indigenous programming, JBC (the only network on the island) produces two soap operas for domestic and international broadcast—*Lime Tree Lane* (airing twice weekly during prime-time for 30 minutes) and *Pullet Hall* (airing weekly during primetime for 30 minutes). *Lime Tree Lane* is a look at life in a typical urban working-class environment; Pullet Hall deals with the impact of urban migration on a rural farming family. Both serials target middle- to low-income males and females, 24–45 years old, and both are exported to the United States and the United Kingdom.

Focus: Cuba

Cuba's history with serial drama is long and respected, even though few indigenous shows are now produced there. In 1948 *El Derecho de Nacer*, the first radionovela ever made, aired in the country; in 1952 newly developed Cuban television broadcast its first telenovela, which, incidentally, was also the first telenovela ever made anywhere.[9]

One of serial drama's biggest fans in Cuba during this time was Fidel Castro, who had seen the power of soap operas during his stay in the United States. Castro also recognized that beliefs, attitudes and values could be subtly transmitted through serial drama, and in the early stages of his revolution he encouraged writers to use this genre to persuade audiences toward a "new order" within their country. In 1959 these same creative artists could no longer accept the consequences of Castro's proposed vision. Hundreds fled the country and began to write for Latino broadcast programmers in Mexico, Venezuela and Brazil. One result of this painful emigration was the spread of indigenous radio- and telenovelas throughout Central and South America. Cuba's loss had indeed become Latin America's gain.

For at least two decades after the historic writers' flight, Cuba's reputation for creative media programming was understandably diminished. But creativity was clearly not the highest priority during this era. Propaganda, pure and simple, was. From time to time outside signals sneaked through powerful governmental jamming equipment, providing another view of the world. Radio Marti, for example, was highly effective in sending American music, news—and telenovelas—to underground listeners.[10] Overall, though, broadcast censorship was complete and effective.[11]

Fortunately, in 1993 government media regulations seemed to become a bit more relaxed for Cubans. Imported TV programming, for example, became more accessible; and viewers were once again reunited with their beloved novelas. *La Hora de la Telenovela* (or *The Hour of the Telenovela*) became the new "opium of the people."[12] One of the first features on *La Hora* was *Vale Tudo*, from Brazil's TV Rede Globo. Like most Brazilian novelas, this story featured "passion, ambition and drama,"[13] a welcome change from political oratory and information. In fact, viewer response was so overwhelming, local meetings for political nominations had to be rescheduled around the next episode. Journalist Pascal Fletcher describes the audience fervor even more dramatically in this 1993 report:

> [*Vale Tudo*] is as much a daily talking point as the availability of food, currently tightly rationed because of Cuba's crippling economic recession. Fictional personalities from the soap opera have even found their way into popular idiom on the island. Such is the unremitting malevolence of the character called Fatima, played by actress Gloria Pires, that "Fatima" is the tag applied to the latest strain of flu doing the rounds in Cuba. Flu-stricken Cubans who go to work racked by coughs and with a running nose are likely to be greeted by their colleagues with "What, has Fatima got hold of you then?" Communist Youth leader Roberto Robaina invoked the character of Fatima in a speech last December 30 when he blasted recent U.S. legislation tightening a 30 year-old U.S. economic embargo against the island. He said the so-called Torricelli Bill was "a creation alongside which even Fatima's evil appears small in comparison."[14]

As in South America and Europe (see chapters four and five), even some of the most influential political leaders in Cuba are often devoted soap fans.

Another Cuban favorite from TV Globo has been *Mujeres de Arena* (*Women of Sand*), which first aired in 1995. Audiences were so enamored with the setting and characters of this drama that anything associated with it was an instant money-maker for ambitious entrepreneurs. As a result, almost 1,000 "paladares" (family-run restaurants) named after the popular eatery from the Brazilian telenovela opened throughout the country to rave reviews.[15] According to reporter Marie Sanz, "Roast pork and other Cuban delicacies often figure in the menu, which is served in the living room, the dining room, the garden or even the garage. Many establishments charge in US dollars.... The atmosphere is relaxed and meals are often accompanied by classical music."[16] Although still heavily restricted (compared to restaurants in other countries), these "paladares" offered a freedom and release unknown to many Cubans for several decades.

Today, Brazilian telenovelas (especially from TV Globo), as well as serials from other Latin American countries, continue to be heavily watched by Cuban viewers.[17] And even though they might prefer more quality "home-grown" dramas, Cubans can always claim to be the "creators" of the novela form—a contribution that has truly been appreciated throughout the world.

Focus: Puerto Rico

The last hundred years of Puerto Rico's history have been influenced greatly by the United States—its government, its economy, its education and its television. For the most part Puerto Ricans have complete access to all U.S. programming, but they have comparatively little opportunity to view shows emphasizing their Spanish heritage.

According to Zona Latina, TV sets can be found in almost all (99 percent) Puerto Rican homes.[18] For the 29 percent who are connected to cable, the choices for American programming are seemingly endless, including WABC (New York), WGN (Chicago), WNBC (New York), WOR (New York), WPIX (New York), WRAL (Raleigh), WSBK (Boston), the Discovery Channel, USA Network and ESPN. Programs on these channels are usually dubbed in Spanish but are clearly intended for American audiences. On the other hand, only three Spanish-language stations exist to give viewers a taste of their own culture—GEMS Television, Univision and Galavision—but even these broadcasts emanate from the United States. The search for indigenous programming is not an easy one.

One very effective means to spread culture (and at the same time please advertisers) has been through telenovelas, which start in the morning and run (off and on) throughout the early afternoon and evening. The actors are the major attraction for both Puerto Ricans and Hispanic Americans—beautiful women and men are always the lead characters. However, despite Puerto Rico's highly diverse population, blacks or mulattos are rarely, if ever, represented. This has been especially troublesome for minority groups, who are offended by the obvious slight.[19]

Most Puerto Ricans believe that the best soaps are from Mexico, Colombia and Venezuela because of their high production budgets and special effects, as well as quality acting. A July 1997 program sampling of popular telenovelas aired in Puerto Rico illustrates this point[20]:

Las Aguas Mansas/Calm Waters (Colombia)
El Árbol Azul/The Blue Tree (Argentina)
Bendita Mentira/Blessed Lie (Mexico)
Cadenas de Amargura/Chains of Bitterness (Mexico)
Chispita/Little Spark (Mexico)
La Dama de Rosa/The Lady in Pink (Venezuela)
La Dueña/The Owner (Venezuela)
En Cuerpo Ajeno/The Foreign Body (Colombia)
Esmeralda (Mexico)
Kassandra (Venezuela)
Luz Clarita/Pale Light (Mexico)
Mala Mujer/Bad Woman (Peru)
María Mercedes (Mexico)
Mi Querida Isabel (Mexico)
Pantanal de Amor (Brazil)
Pueblo Chico, Infierno Grande/Small Town, Big Hell (Mexico)
Te Sigo Amando/I Still Love You (Mexico)

Some "homegrown" novelas are also aired, but they really can't compete with those from other Latin American countries. This is ironic, considering that Puerto Rico was once known as a major distributor of quality serial drama. Some of its most popular soaps included the following[21]:

Alejandra—(no date known)
Al Son del Amor/To the Sound of Love—1995
Angélica, Mi Vida/Angelica, My Life (co-produced with the U.S.)—(no date known)
Aventurera/The Adventurous One—(no date known)
Coralito—(no date known)
Cristina Bazan—(no date known)
Hijos de Nadie/Children of No One—1997
Karina Montaner—(no date known)
Pasión de Vivir/Sin of Love—(co-produced with Spain)—1993
Soledad—(no date known)

Today, the number of locally produced novelas is modest. Still, viewers remain loyal to any dramas with Puerto Rican actors and themes in them, as evidenced by a 1997 poll that addressed viewer preferences in TV programming.[22]

Specifically, researchers wanted to know if cultural imperialism (through program imports) was of serious concern to audiences. They asked respondents about TV programs produced in a) the United States, b) Puerto Rico, and c) other Latin American countries. On a five-point scale (1 = not interested; 5 = very interested) subjects were asked to rank their preferences. The results were quite astonishing. Although no one could dispute that overall production quality was higher in the United States and in other areas of Latin America, people were still most interested in locally-produced programs. In short, if available, most audiences would prefer indigenous shows, despite inferior technical quality, to program imports—something for young Puerto Rican novela producers to think about for the future.

Focus: Mexico

Mexico has been a true pioneer in telenovela programming, beginning in 1951–1952, with the nation's first telenovela.[23] By 1959 Mexico had become fairly well known in the field of drama, and this reputation lured many exiled Cubans to work in the broadcast industry. Less than a decade later Mexico reigned as one of the most prolific and respected soap opera distributors.

With its finances stable, one of Mexico's major networks, Televisa, began a significant project that would soon build an even stronger reputation for Mexican novelas. The project—an entertainment-education pilot called *Ven Conmigo* (*Come with Me*)—was proposed by coauthors Miguel Sabido and Celia Alcantara (an Argentine best known for *Simplemente María*). Within its dramatic portrayal of the lives of five major characters (including a servant, a farmer and a single mother) was a strong message promoting adult literacy. *Ven Conmigo* lasted for 13 months and averaged a 32.6 rating in its early evening time block.[24] The soap (along with *Acompañame/Come with Me* and *Vamos Juntos/We Go Together*, novelas on family planning) soon became a model for success in other countries, and Miguel Sabido began to consult with producers on similar projects around the world, especially in developing countries in Asia, Africa and nations from the former Soviet Union (see chapter one). By 1981 Sabido's "motivational" novelas, although still heralded around the world, received little domestic support and thus disappeared. In a 1996 *Variety* article, reporter Andrew Paxman explains why: "The answer has much to do with the jealousy of government officials, who were loath to admit that Sabido's novelas were more effective than their own pamphlets."[25] For fifteen years after Sabido's last educational novela, most Mexican soaps became known for porcelain-skinned, doe-eyed women who yearned for fantasy romances, like *Las Tres Marías—María Mercedes*, *Marimar* and *María la del Barrio*—stories of illiterate peasants who were poor in material wealth but capable of great love and spirit.

Another example of this type of novela was Televisa's *Los Ricos También Lloran* (*The Rich Also Cry*), the most famous Mexican soap of all time. Not only did the classic plotline of love and loss capture the fantasy of domestic audiences, it also made Mexico's mark as a successful novela exporter. One of the most successful international syndication efforts was in Russia, where in 1992 the novela set an all-time ratings record with an average 100 million viewers per episode.[26] Loyal fans (including President Boris Yeltsin) stopped all other activities to follow the exploits of a character similar to *Dynasty's* Joan Collins (see chapter five). In 1994 Mexican soap operas continued to fuel a fanatic Russian fervor, when more than 140 million viewers regularly followed the travails of *Simplemente María* (*Simply Maria*). As one *María* aficionado told *New York Times* reporter Alessandra Stanley: "It's for people with a very low level of culture. But for me it's psychotherapy. We live in hard times, in a gray, difficult country. It's like a fairy tale. I enjoy the bright colors, the bright interior decor."[27] The brilliant colors and warm sunshine of Mexico may serve as a welcome contrast to Russia's dark, dismal landscape. But in fact Russians and Mexicans have far more in common than they may think, according to the Mexican embassy's cultural attaché, Zarina Martínez Borresen (when interviewed by Stanley): "We are similar in temperament. Russians are also very emotional."[28] Still, the success of *Simplemente María* was a surprise to everyone, especially considering that its ratings were even higher in Russia than at home; similar viewer numbers were registered later in other export markets as well.

Simplemente María, and its popularity abroad, only heightened the demand for Mexico's export business, which had been brisk since the 1980s. Networks like Televisa, for example, began to open subsidiary distribution centers in other countries, including the United States. Joint ventures between Mexico and other nations also became commonplace, such as the 1989 contract between Mediastat's Rete-4 Italian network or Televisa's 1994 co-production deal with America's Fox Television for the English-language novela, *Empire*.

At home, Mexicans seemed to be tiring of the same romantic formula during this time. TV Azteca's 1996 novela *Nada Personal* (*Nothing Personal*) dared to be different by taking a political stance, to expose police corruption and Mexico's mounting crime rate. The result turned out to be well worth the risk: the serial pulled in record-high viewer numbers.

More docudrama than outright fiction, *Nada Personal* paralleled the real-life drama of the assassination of a Mexican presidential candidate and a ruling party leader. Even one of the major villains in the novela looked hauntingly similar to former president Carlos Salinas de Gortari.[29] Although the government was not pleased with the production, TV audiences were, and the audiences ultimately won. Rival networks TV Azteca and Televisa were soon in hot pursuit of the "reality" novela.

In 1997 TV Azteca followed its success from *Nada Personal* with *Mirada de Mujer* (*A Woman's Gaze*), a story about a 50-year-old mother of three who starts an affair with a younger man after she discovers her husband has been cheating on her, and *Demasiado Corazón* (*Too Much Heart*), a sequel to *Nada*, in which an honest cop tries to rise above Mexico's underworld of drugs and corruption.[30] Televisa, Mexico's largest broadcast conglomerate, also began to depart from its previous romantic "Cinderella" reputation, opting instead for political intrigue, illegal border crossings, the HIV virus, cancer, abortion and financial peril.[31] This was no small gesture, considering that the Televisa conglomerate controls more than 80 percent of the audience market[32] and produces 18 novelas each year (each airing for about six months in Mexico and then being dubbed in 50 languages for distribution to some 108 countries worldwide).[33]

Because of Televisa's huge investment in global program syndication, this change in the network's traditionally successful novela formula surprised many. Most often, soap operas (and other program genres) "travel" best to other countries when they are devoid of indigenous political issues, local idioms and ephemeral topics. Televisa (TV Azteca's chief competitor) realized that its primary audience, Mexicans, were becoming more demanding. When interviewed by reporter Lynne Walker, Raul Araiza, a novela producer-director for Televisa, explained:

> We offer what the public wants.... [And] what is the most important thing to people in Mexico? The novela.... [Until recently,] we always did the same soap opera. Mexican television is just starting to take steps toward more realistic programming.... Soap operas must tell realistic stories so people do not dream foolishly.... If we talk about AIDS in soap operas, or other medical problems, and people see positive examples, it shows them how to deal with these situations.[34]

Incurable romantics needn't despair. Araiza goes on to say that novelas should never completely lose their ability to provide fantasy and escape from reality: "We cannot throw in people's faces day after day the struggle and stress of the world in which they live. If they have problems with debts, with not having enough to eat, reality does not entertain them. It worries them."[35]

Below is a sampling of some Mexican telenovelas that have been well received by both domestic and global audiences. The titles, production years and brief summaries are also provided[36]:

Acapulco Cuerpo y Alma/Acapulco Body and Soul (1995)—Focuses on the main character, David Montalvo, whose successes are marred by jealousy and hatred in his family. This conflict becomes even worse after David and his half-brother, Marcelo, both fall in love with the beautiful Lorena.

Agujetas de Color de Rosa/Pink Shoelaces (1994)—Reveals the pain endured by a widow (Elisa) after her mother-in-law tries to deprive her and her children (Paola, Daniel and Anita) of their rightful inheritance. They survive the ordeal as best they can, and Elisa also meets Gonzalo David, a single father, along the way.

Alondra (1995)—Features a young, idealistic woman who tries to escape her horrific family to find love and happiness with the man of her dreams.

Azul/Blue (1996)—Set in an amusement park, this story tells of love between an idealistic man and woman, both of whom care about humanitarian causes as much as they do for each other.

Con Todo el Alma/With All My Soul (1995)—Recounts the rather dismal life of Daniel Linares, who has been cut out of his family's will, loses his actress girlfriend to her leading man, and barely survives a helicopter crash as he tries to win back his inheritance at his grandfather's ranch. Daniel's luck turns when he meets a poor peasant girl and falls in love.

Corazón Salvaje/Wild Heart (1993)—Recounts the hardships of Juan del Diablo, the illegitimate son of a wealthy landowner, Don Francisco (who is unaware Juan belongs to him). Shortly before his death, the landowner discovers the secret and acknowledges Juan's birthright. Unfortunately, Don Francisco's widow hides this letter, and for years afterward Juan must try to fend for himself in an unfriendly world. His suffering turns to bitterness, until he finally falls in love with Monica, the daughter of a poor aristocrat, who has been in a convent to hide from the humiliation of being left at the altar by Don Francisco's legitimate son.

La Culpa/The Blame (1996)—Features two young lovers who must solve a murder mystery before they can find true happiness together.

María la del Barrio (1995)—Follows the travails of a 15-year-old waif, Maria, who tries to fight her way out of the ghetto by working for a wealthy landowner (Don Fernando). Along the way Maria is abused by Don Fernando's wife and niece but is hopeful all will turn out well when she falls in love with Don Fernando's son, Luis. Unfortunately, a great misunderstanding occurs after Maria and Luis are married, and unwittingly she gives away their newborn baby. Once the couple is reunited, Maria lives in the hopes of seeing her young son once more.

María Mercedes (1992)—Victimized by a poor, unloving family, Maria grows to be a manipulative young woman on the streets. She will stop at nothing to keep her family fed and clothed. One day she meets a wealthy landowner named Santiago del Olmo, who falls in love with her (even though he is dying). Del Olmo's evil sister-in-law will have none of this and tries to throw Maria out of the house before she is named as a major heir in his will.

Marimar (1994)—The story of a young (apparently orphaned) girl who lives with her destitute, elderly grandparents on a beach, Marimar is forced to steal to feed her family. One day, as she tries to pinch some vegetables and eggs from a hacienda, she's caught by the foreman, who threatens to turn her in if she doesn't kiss him. As she screams for help, the wealthy, spoiled son of the house rushes to her rescue and later offers to marry her to humiliate his parents. Little does Marimar know that her real father (a wealthy man in his own right) is not dead and is looking for her to make her his heir.

Los Parientes Pobres/The Poor Relatives (1993)—Tells the story of Margarita Santos, a young woman who has lost her family fortune as well as the man she loves. Because of her bitterness, she decides never to trust anyone again and to gather as much wealth as possible. While striving for her new goals, she meets Chucho, a poor but honest man, and the two fall in love. The love is then challenged by outsiders.

Triángulo/Triangle (1992)—Centers on the very complicated life of Sara, a young, idealistic nurse who unwittingly becomes pregnant by David (a spoiled son of the wealthy Villafranca family). David's brother Ivan then forces him to move to Brazil (without Sara). She then talks to Ivan about David's return, but when they call their contact in Brazil, they are told David is dead. In the meantime Sara's father has committed suicide in his jail cell, having been falsely arrested for allegedly killing David's father. Ivan then feels sorry for Sara and the unborn child, falls in love with her, and asks her to marry him. Shortly after, David reappears.

In contrast, here are some examples of the newer, "more realistic" novelas[37]:

Los Hijos de Nadie/No One's Children (1997)—Addresses the problems of homeless children.[38]

Lagunilla/The Little Lagoon (1997)—Focuses on street peddlers in the barrio and the city government's distaste for them.[39]

Al Norte del Corazón/North of the Heart (1997)—Deals with the horrors of being an undocumented immigrant, including being beaten by the U.S. border patrol.[40]

Tijuana (1997)—Uses illegal immigration, drug trafficking, discrimination, gun running and xenophobic U.S. politicians as a backdrop for dramatizing the difficulties of city life.[41]

Finally, here are some of the most popular telenovelas aired in Mexico in 1997[42]:

Alguna Ve Tendremos Alas/Someday We'll Have Wings—Canal 2
El Alma No Tiene Color/The Soul Has No Color—Canal 2
Al Norte de Corazón/North of the Heart—Canal 13
El Amor Tiene Cara de Mujer/Love Has the Face of a Woman—Canal 4
Aprendiendo a Vivir/Learning to Live—Canal 4
Café con Aroma de Mujer/Coffee with the Scent of Woman—Canal 13
Carrusel—Canal 9
La Casa de las Dos Palmas/The House of the Two Palms—Canal 13
Cuando Llega el Amor/When Love Comes—Canal 4
Esmeralda—Canal 2
Gente Bien/Good People—Canal 2

La Jaula de Oro/The Golden Age—Canal 2
Marimar—Canal 2
Peligrosa/Dangerous—Canal 4
Pueblo Chico, Infierno Grande/Small Town, Big Hell—Canal 2
Sueños y Espejos/Dreams and Mirrors—Canal 13
Teresa—Canal 4

This profile indicates that Mexican novelas have come full circle—from Sabido's 1970s "motivational" drama to the 1990s emphasis on political and social "realism." But as producer Raul Araiza warns, serials should also recognize their power to "[help people] escape from the cruel reality that they live."[43]

Notes

1. Station/network information taken from *World Radio TV Handbook, 1997 Edition*, ed. Andrew G. Sennitt (New York: Billboard Books, 1997). Television/radio set information and population figures taken from *The World Almanac and Book of Facts 1998* (Mahwah, NJ: K-III Reference Corporation, 1997).
2. This listing is compiled from *WRTH Satellite & TV Handbook,* 4th edition, ed. Andrew G. Sennitt (New York: Billboard Books, 1997). It represents the *available* stations on satellite dishes through a transponder in Region II of the world satellite map. Although it is difficult to tell how many people have access to these channels, it is important to acknowledge the variety of cross-national program content on them.
3. These summaries have been created through information in the "archives link" on a comprehensive telenovela Web site created and maintained by Yolette Nicholson <yoletten@site.net> [database on-line]. The author is extremely grateful to her for this useful information.
4. Written correspondence with Mrs. Anestine Lafond, Program/Production Director, Marpin T.V. Company Limited (August 1996).
5. Vibert C. Cambridge, "Radio Soap Operas in Global Africa: Origins, Applications, and Implications," in *Staying Tuned: Contemporary Soap Opera Criticism*, ed. Suzanne Frentz (Bowling Green, OH: Bowling Green State University Popular Press, 1992), 115.
6. *Ibid.*
7. Written correspondence with Mrs. Angela Patterson, Director of Marketing & Planning at Jamaica Broadcasting Corporation (September 1996).
8. According to the SABC-TV Schedule ([database on-line] <http://www.sabc. co.za>), *Suburban Slice* is actually known as *Suburban Bliss* in South Africa.
9. "A Brief History," *Variety* (October 7–13, 1996), 64.
10. One example of this was the 1985 airing of *Esmeralda*, the story of a poor blind girl who finds romance and happiness with a rich young man and his family. This novela was produced in Miami in the 1970s.
11. "Pull Plug on a Wasteful Program: TV Marti Accomplishes Nothing," *Sun Sentinel* (October 18, 1993), 6A.
12. Pascal Fletcher, "Brazilian TV Soap Opera Is Cuba's Opium of the People," The Reuter Library Report (February 12, 1993) [database on-line]; available from Lexis-Nexis.

    13. *Ibid.*
    14. *Ibid.*
    15. Marie Sanz, "Private Restaurants Booming," Agence France Presse (March 23, 1996) [database on-line]; available from Lexis-Nexis.
    16. *Ibid.*
    17. Mark Landler, Joyce Barnathan, Geri Smith and Gail Edmundson, "Think Globally, Program Locally," *Business Week* (November 18, 1994), 186.
    18. Zona Latina Web site <http://www.zonalatina.com/Zldata18.htm> [database on-line].
    19. This information was provided through interviews with Puerto Rican viewers. The author would like to especially acknowledge Victoria Barges, a colleague at Boston College, for her insights.
    20. Telenovela Web site.
    21. *Ibid.*
    22. Zona Latina Web site.
    23. "A Brief History," *Variety* (October 7–13, 1996), 64.
    24. Andrew Paxman, "Instruments of Change," *Variety* (October 7–13, 1996), 63.
    25. *Ibid.*
    26. "A Brief History," 64.
    27. Alessandra Stanley, "Russians Find Their Heroes in Mexican TV Soap Operas," *New York Times* (March 20, 1994), 12.
    28. *Ibid.*
    29. S. Lynne Walker, "Mexico's 'Telenovelas' Breaking Their Traditional Themes," Copley News Service (February 20, 1997) [database on-line]; available from Lexis-Nexis.
    30. Edward Robinson, "Sex, Drugs and Dinero," *Fortune* (November 10, 1997) [database on-line].
    31. *Ibid.*
    32. Mark Landler, Joyce Barnathan, Geri Smith and Gail Edmondson, "Think Globally, Program Locally," *Business Week* (November 18, 1994) [database on-line]; available from Lexis-Nexis.
    33. Walker, "Mexico's 'Telenovelas' Breaking Their Traditional Themes."
    34. *Ibid.*
    35. *Ibid.*
    36. Telenovela Web site.
    37. *Ibid.*
    38. Sam Quinones, "Suddenly, to the Fantasy Factory Known as the Mexican Telenovela Industry, Reality Matters," *Fort Worth Star-Telegram* (April 23, 1997), 3.
    39. *Ibid.*
    40. *Ibid.*
    41. *Ibid.*
    42. Telenovela Web site. This list reflects the novelas aired on Mexican television up to July 1997.
    43. Walker, "Mexico's 'Telenovelas' Breaking Their Traditional Themes."

South America

Countries included

Antarctica, Argentina, Bolivia, Brazil, Chile, Colombia, Ecuador, Falkland Islands, Guiana (French), Guyana, Paraguay, Peru, Suriname, Uruguay, Venezuela[1]

Stations/Networks:

Antarctica

Population: n/a (see Australia and United Kingdom)
(TV sets—n/a; radios—n/a)
American Forces Antarctic Network (AFAN McMurdo)

Argentina

Population: 35,797,536—33 per sq. mi.
(TV sets—1:4.6 persons; radios—1:1.5 persons)
America (ch 2)
Artear (ch 13)
Asociación de Teleradiodifusoras Argentinas (ATA)
ATC (ch 7)
Channel 9 (Libertad)
Ministerio de Obras y Servicios Publicos Secretaría de Comunicasiones
Pramar SA
SATV
Servicio Oficial de Radiodifusión (SOR)

Telefé (ch 11)
Torneos Network

Bolivia

Population: 7,669,868—18 per sq. mi.
(TV sets—1:8.8 persons; radios—1:1.5 persons)
Televisión Boliviano

Brazil

Population: 164,511,366—50 per sq. mi.
(TV sets—1:4.8 persons; radios—1:2.5 persons)
Associação Brasileira de Emissoras de Radio e Televisão (ABERT)
Central Nacional de Televisão (CNT)
Fundação Roquette Pinto
MTV Brasil
Radio e Televisão Bandeirantes
Sistema Brasileira de Televisão (SBT)
TV Cultura (Fundação Padre Anchieta)
TV Globo

TV Manchete
TV Record

Chile

Population: 14,508,168—50 per sq. mi.
(TV sets—1:4.7 persons; radios—1:2.9
persons)
Chilevisión
Corporación de Televisión Universi-
dad Católica de Chile (ch 13)
RED Televisa Megavisión
Televisión Nacional de Chile (ch 7)
Universidad Católica sw Valparaíso

Colombia

Population: 37,418,290—85 per sq. mi.
(TV sets—1:8.5 persons; radios—1:5.6
persons)
Caracol Televisión
Instituto Nacional de Radio y Televis-
ión Inravisión
Radio Cadena Nacional (RCN)
Radio Televisión Interamericana (RTI)

Ecuador

Population: 11,690,535—111 per sq. mi.
(TV sets—1:11 persons; radios—1:3.1
persons)

Falkland Islands

Population: n/a (see United Kingdom)
(TV sets—n/a; radios—n/a)
British Forces Broadcasting Service
(BFBS)

Guiana (French)

Population: n/a (see France)
(TV sets—n/a; radios—n/a)
RFO-Guyane
Antenne Creole

Guyana

Population: 706,116—9 per sq. mi.
(TV sets—1:26 persons; radios—1:2
persons)
Guyana Television

Paraguay

Population: 5,651,634—35 per sq. mi.
(TV sets—1:12 persons; radios—1:5.8
persons)
Canal 9 TV Cerro Cora S.A.
Teledifusora Paraguayana S.A.

Peru

Population: 24,949,512—50 per sq.
mi.
(TV sets—1:10 persons; radios—1:3.9
persons)
Compañía Latinoamericana de
Radiodifusión S.A.
Compañía Peruana de Radiodifusión,
Cas.
Panamericana de Televisión
Empresa de Cine, Radio y Televisión
Peruana
Andina de Televisión
RBC Televisión
Difusora Universal de Televisión
Empresa Radiodifusora

Suriname

Population: 443,446—7 per sq. mi.
(TV sets—1:7.1 persons; radios—1:1.5
persons)
Alternatieve Televisie Verzorging
(ATV Telesur)
Surinaamse Televisie Stichting
(STVS)

Uruguay

Population: 3,261,707—47 per sq. mi.
(TV sets—1:4.3 persons; radios—1:1.7
persons)

Venezuela

Population: 22,396,407—63 per sq. mi.
(TV sets—1:6.1 persons; radios—1:2.3
persons)
Camara Venezolana de la Televisión
Corporation
Televisora Nacional (TVN)
Venezolana de Televisión ("5")
Venezolana de Televisión ("8")

Satellite Channels Available in This Region[2]

Action Pay-per-View (USA)
AFRTS (USA)
Airport News and Transportation
  Netw. (USA)
Alaska Satellite TV Project
America's Collectibles Netw. (USA)
America's Talking (USA)
America-1 (USA)
American Collectibles Netw. (USA)
American Movie Classics (USA)
American One (USA)
American TV News (USA)
APNA-TV (India)
Arab Netw. America (USA)
Argentina TV a Color (USA)
Around the World after Dark (USA)
Arts & Entertainment TV (USA)
Atlantic Satellite News Halifax
  (Canada)
Automotive Sat. Training Netw. (USA)
BBC Breakfast News (UK)
BBC World (UK)
Black Entertainment TV (BET) (USA)
Bravo (USA)
C-Span (USA)
C-Span 1/2 (USA)
Cable Health Club (USA)
Cal-Span (USA)
Canadian Exxxstacy (Canada)
Canal 13 (XHDF-TV) (Mexico)
Canal France Int.
Canal Sur (Peru)
Cartoon Network (USA)
CBC Newsworld (Canada)
CBC North (Canada)
CBCM (Canada)
CBMT Montreal/CBC
CCC (Chinese Commercial Channel)
  (USA)
Channel 1 Moscow (Russia)
Cinemax East I/II (USA)
Cinemax East 2 (USA)
Cinemax West (USA)
Classic Sports Network (USA)
CNN (USA)
CNN Airport Channel (USA)

CNN Headline News (USA)
CNN Int. (USA)
CNN International (USA)
CNN Newsource (USA)
Comedy Central (USA)
Computer Television Netw. (USA)
Consumer News & Business Channel
  (CNBC) (USA)
Cornerstone TV (USA)
Country Music TV (USA)
CTV Television Netw. (Canada)
CycleSat Comm. (USA)
Deutsche Welle TV (Germany)
Deutsche Welle TV (foreign) (Ger-
  many)
Discovery Channel (USA)
Disney Channel (USA)
E! Entertainment (USA)
ECO-Televisa (Mexico)
Encore (USA)
Encore 2 (USA)
Encore 8 (USA)
ESPN (USA)
ESPN 2 (USA)
ESPN Blackout Channel (USA)
ESPN International (USA)
Estación Montello (USA)
Eternal Word TV (USA)
Europlus/Teleplus (Italy)
Eurotica (USA)
Exxxstacy 2 (Canada)
Exxxtreme/Climaxxx Promo Chan.
  (USA)
Fantasy Cafe TV (USA)
FLIX movie services (USA)
FOXNet PrimeTime (USA)
fX Movies (USA)
G.O.P.-TV (USA)
Game Show Network (UK)
GEMS-TV (USA)
Georgia Public TV (GPTV) (USA)
Global Shopping Netw. (USA)
Global TV (Canada)
Gospel Music TV (USA)
HBO East 2/3 (USA)
HBO II East/West (USA)

HBO III East (USA)
HBO West 2 (USA)
HBO/Cinemax (USA)
Hispavision (Spain)
Home and Garden TV Netw. (USA)
Home Box Office East/West (USA)
Home Shopping Club 2 (USA)
Home Shopping Netw. 1 (USA)
Home Sports Entertainment (USA)
Hong Kong TVB Jade Channel (Hong
   Kong)
Hospitality TV (USA)
HRT Croatia
HSE2 (USA)
HTV Hispanic music videos (USA)
Independent Film Channel (USA)
Infomercial Channel (USA)
Infomerica TV (USA)
KCNC, Denver (USA)
KDVR, Denver (USA)
KMGH, Denver (USA)
KNBC-TV, L.A. (USA)
Knowledge TV (USA)
KOMO-TV, Seattle (USA)
KPIX-TV, San Francisco (USA)
KRMA, Denver (USA)
KTLA, L.A. (USA)
KWGN, Denver (USA)
La Cadena de Milagro (USA)
La Chaîne [French] (Canada)
Lifetime East/West (USA)
Madison Square Garden (USA)
MCET Educational Netw. (USA)
Merchandise and Entertainment TV
   (MET) (USA)
Midwest Sports Channel (USA)
MOR Music Television (USA)
Movie Channel (West) (USA)
MTV (West) (USA)
MuchMusic (Canada)
Music Television (West) (USA)
Music TV (East) (USA)
Muslim Television (USA)
Muslim TV (Russia)
NASA Select Channel (USA)
Nat. Empowerment TV Network
   (USA)
National Weather Netw. (USA)
NBC (USA)

Nebraska Educational TV (USA)
Network One (N1) (USA)
New England Sports Channel (USA)
Newsport (USA)
NewsTalk Television (USA)
NHK Tokyo (Japan)
Nickelodeon (USA)
Nostalgia Channel (USA)
Nustar (USA)
Odyssey Network (USA)
Ontario Legislature (Canada)
ORT-TV-1 (Russia)
Panda America (Home Shopping)
   (USA)
PBS (schedules C/D) (USA)
Perú TV (Argentina)
Perú TV Ch. 13 (Peru)
Perú TV Ch. 2 (Peru)
Perú TV Ch. 4 (Peru)
Perú TV Ch. 5 (Peru)
Playboy at Night (USA)
PrevuGuide (USA)
Prime Network (USA)
Prime Sports Intermountain (West)
   (USA)
Prime Sports Northwest (USA)
Prime Sports Showcase (USA)
Prime Ticket, California (USA)
Pro-Am sports, Detroit (USA)
Public Broadcasting Sce. (PBS)
   (USA)
Q-CVC (Mexico)
Quorum multi-level marketing
   (USA)
QVC Fashion Channel (USA)
QVC Home Shopping Netw. (USA)
RAI (Italy)
RCTV (Venezuela 7)
Real Estate TV Network (USA)
Request TV 1 (USA)
RTP Internacional (Portugal)
RTV Beograd (Croatia)
Russian TV Network (USA)
S. Carolina Educational TV (USA)
Satellite City TV (USA)
Sci-Fi Channel (USA)
Sellevision (USA)
Shepherd's Chapel (USA)
Shop at Home (USA)

Shop-at-Home (USA)
Shop-at-Home Network (USA)
Showtime East/West (USA)
Skyvision Home Shopping Ch. (USA)
Skyvision Promo Channel (USA)
Space (Argentina)
Sport South (USA)
SportsChannel alternatives (USA)
SportsChannel Chicago (USA)
SportsChannel Chicago Plus (USA)
SportsChannel Cincinnati (USA)
SportsChannel Florida (USA)
SportsChannel Hawaii (USA)
SportsChannel New England (USA)
SportsChannel New York (USA)
SportsChannel New York Plus (USA)
SportsChannel Ohio (USA)
SportsChannel Pacific (USA)
SportsChannel Philadelphia (USA)
SRC Educational Netw. (USA)
SSVC (UK)
Sundance Channel (USA)
Sunshine Blackout Channel (USA)
Sunshine Network (USA)
Super Television Channel (USA)
System United for Retransm. (Latin
   America)
TCI Preview Channel UA (USA)
TCI-TV (USA)
Telecasa (Mexico)
Telefé (Argentina)
Televisión Boliviana (Bolivia)
TF1 (France)
The Babe Network (USA)
The Baseball Netw. (TBN) (USA)
The Family Channel (USA)
The Filipino Channel (Philippines)
The Golf Channel (UK)
The International Channel (USA)
The Kentucky Netw. (USA)
The Learning Channel (USA)
The Movie Channel (USA)
The Nashville Network (USA)
The New Inspirational Netw. (USA)
The Outdoor Channel (USA)
The People's Network (USA)
The Travel Channel (USA)
The University Netw. (USA)
The X Channel (USA)

Three Angels Broad. (USA)
TNT Internacional (Turkey)
Trinity Broadcasting Network (USA)
Turner Classic Movies (USA)
Turner Network Television (USA)
Turner Vision Promo Channel (USA)
Turner Vision Promo Sce. (USA)
TV 69 (USA)
TV Asia (USA)
TV Erotica (USA)
TV Nacional de Chile (ch. 7) (Chile)
TV Nacional de Chile (ch. 10)
   (Chile)
TV Ontario (Canada)
TV-Japan
TVE internacional (Spain)
TVN Theatre 1/2/3/4/5/6/7/9/10 (USA)
UAE-TV Dubai (UAE)
United Arab Emirates TV (UAE)
United Paramount Network (UPN)
   (USA)
United States Info. Agency (USA)
Univision (USA)
USA Network
USIA WorldNet (USA)
Valuevision (USA)
Venus Adult (Canada)
VH-1 (USA)
Via TV (Inter.) (UAE)
Video Catalog Channel (Canada)
Viewer's Choice (USA)
VTC Satellite Network (Canada)
WABC, New York (USA)
Weather Channel (USA)
Westerns Encore 3 (USA)
WFLD-TV, Chicago (USA)
WGN, Chicago (USA)
WHDH-TV, Boston (USA)
Wholesale Shopping Netw. (USA)
WJLA, Washington (USA)
WMNB (USA)
WMNB Russian Lang. Station (USA)
WNBC New York (USA)
World Harvest TV (USA)
Worldnet (USA)
Worship TV (USA)
WPIX, New York (USA)
WRAL, Raleigh, NC (USA)
WSBK, Boston (USA)

WTBS, Atlanta (USA)
WUSA-TV, Washington, DC (USA)
WWOR-TV (USA)
WXIA, Atlanta (USA)
XEIPN-TV, Canal 11, Mexico City
   (Mexico)

XEQ-TV 9 (Mexico)
XEW-TV, Mexico City (Mexico)
XHGC-TV (Canal 5) (Mexico)
XHIMT, Canal 22 (Mexico)
XXXPlore (USA)
Z-Music (USA)

Overview of Cultural Patterns and Audience Trends

In 1996 the global telenovela industry was estimated to be worth more than $1 billion.[3] Most of this industry is centered in South America, especially in Brazil, Colombia, Venezuela and Argentina. Here are some titles and summaries of novelas that have been very popular both at home and abroad[4]:

Deus Nos Acuda/God Help Us (Brazil, no date known)—Portrays Brazil as an inferno that only God can save.

A Escrava Isaura/Isaura, the Slave Girl (Brazil, no date known)—Focuses on a young white girl, born into slavery in nineteenth-century Brazil. From her childhood, Isaura yearns for freedom and will not be satisfied until she has realized her dream.

Pantanal (Brazil, no date known)—A fantasy, featuring characters from Brazilian folklore, including a jaguar-woman and other river spirits.

Azúcar/Sugar (Colombia, 1990)—A tale of wealth, power and mistaken parentage, all taking place on a large sugarcane plantation.

Café con Aroma de Mujer/Coffee with the Scent of Woman (Colombia, 1994)—Centers on a powerful romance between the son of a wealthy ranch owner (Sebastian Vallejo) and one of the coffee-bean pickers on the property (Gaviota). After a single night of love-making, Sebastian travels to Europe to finish his studies, and Gaviota realizes she's pregnant and sets out to find him. Along the way, she falls onto hard times and is trapped in a prostitution ring. Sebastian hears that she is a prostitute and will not have anything to do with her ... until she takes on a new identity (Carolina), and he falls in love with her all over again.

Celeste (Argentina, no date known)—Follows the life of a young woman named Celeste as she tries to make a life for herself and her dying mother. In the midst of her sorrow, she meets a "mystery" man (Franco), with whom she immediately falls in love. Through a series of twists and turns (including some nasty business with Franco's mother, Teresa), Celeste comes to live with the family only to discover later that Franco is the mystery man in her life. They fall in love ... and should live happily ever after ... but they still live under a veil of secrecy that could destroy them.

Celeste, Siempre Celeste/Celeste, Always Celeste (Argentina, no date known)—The sequel to *Celeste*, the story picks up after Celeste and Franco prepare for their wedding and leave for their honeymoon. However, Franco's mother, Teresa, continues to wreak havoc by having Celeste kidnapped. Celeste escapes but is injured in the process and is hospitalized with pneumonia. In the meantime Clara, Celeste's heretofore unknown twin sister, surfaces in the hospital. Confusion with each woman's identity occurs ... especially with Franco, who at first believes Clara is Celeste and later must continue this charade when he learns that Clara will put Celeste in greater peril if he tells the truth.

Chiquititas/Little Girls (Argentina, 1995)—Opens with a character named Martin Moran, who while on a business trip to Argentina learns that his sister is mentally ill. He gives up his job and moves back home to help her. After finding a new job in a factory, Martin meets and falls in love with Belen. In the meantime Martin also develops a special friendship with Mili, an orphan who lives in his family-owned orphanage. From there, complications develop between these three and, of course, Martin's sister Gabriela.

Nano (Argentina, 1994)—Features a young man named Nano (short for "Manuel") who decides, against his father's wishes, to leave his aristocratic heritage and open an oceanarium. By day he is the curator; by night he plays a sort of "Robin Hood," taking risks to help people who have been victimized by upper-class corruption. Nano is not happily married but finds love with a deaf mute named Camila. His wife, however, will have none of it ... and proceeds to make his life even more difficult than before.

Cristal (Venezuela, no date known)—Starts with a woman's (Victoria Ascano) search for the daughter she abandoned years ago. At the same time, a young woman, Cristina, leaves her orphanage home to pursue a career in modeling and meets Victoria, the owner of a fashion house. As the story develops, Cristina falls in love with Victoria's stepson (Luis Alfredo), but Victoria separates them and forces Luis to marry his old girlfriend. In the meantime Cristina discovers she's pregnant.

La Dama de Rosa/The Lady in Pink (Venezuela, no date known)—Gabriela, an ambitious, enterprising girl, works hard to help her family. She takes a job at a carwash and has a romance with its owner (Tito), only to find out later that Tito has set her up to appear guilty of drug trafficking. Subsequently, she is taken to court and put in jail. As she awaits her freedom, Gabriela plots to change her appearance and get even with Tito.

Quirpa de Tres Mujeres (Venezuela, 1996)—A remake of a former hit, *Las Amazonas,* the story of a multi-generational family feud over love and an unfair land deal.

Señora (Venezuela, 1987)—Eugenia, a young woman sent unfairly to prison, vows revenge on the man who put her there. She encounters several people along the way—some helpful, some harmful—but she cannot truly find love and contentment until she has gotten over her obsession.

Other nations, like Chile and Peru, have had fairly successful track records in serial drama production as well. In recent years, given the unstable political and economic conditions in these areas, TV networks have had to prioritize news and informational programming over drama.

In some of the lesser-developed South American countries, indigenous novelas are few and often are sponsored by outside organizations and intended for instructional use. Population Services International (PSI) has been a leader in this area, recognizing the edifying potential of serial drama: "Soap operas around the world have captured the imagination of large viewing audiences, and are thus an excellent medium for educational messages. PSI is using a traditional commercial entertainment tool, the TV 'soap,' for a social good—the prevention of AIDS—in the same way that it uses brand specific advertising to promote Prudence, through social marketing."[5]

Viewers in Bolivia have benefited greatly from PSI's commitment to social marketing through motivational novelas, specifically in birth control issues. An especially popular serial, for example, featured a young woman successfully practicing sexual abstinence. Another drama advanced the discussion of condom use and its role in preventing HIV and AIDS.[6]

The emphasis on serious social issues, along with high production standards and a strong sense of viewer preferences, has cemented South America's place as the world's most respected novela producer. The magnitude and diversity of serial drama are as overwhelming as the countries that are a part of this great continent.

Focus: Chile

Although Chile is not as avid a novela producer as some of its South American neighbors, its record in serial drama production is representative of most South American nations. Like Bolivia, Ecuador, Paraguay, Suriname and Uruguay, Chile produces at least one or two novelas each year. In 1997 there were no telenovelas produced in Peru, given the unstable political situation of the country. However, in previous years this nation, too, had a respectable reputation for novela production.

According to Valerio Fuenzalida, program director of Televisión Nacional de Chile,[7] and Yolette Nicholson's "Telenovelas en Mundo,"[8] some of the Chilean novela titles include the following:

Pero Sigo Siendo el Rey/But I'm Still the King—no date known (number of episodes unavailable)
El Milagro de Vivir/The Miracle of Life—1990 (80 episodes)
Volver a Empezar/To Return to the Beginning—1991 (109 episodes)
Trampas y Caretas/Lies and Masks—1992 (105 episodes)
Jaque Mate—1993 (95 episodes)
Rompecorazón/Heartbroken—1994 (98 episodes)
Rojo y Miel/Red and Honey—1994 (90 episodes)
Estupido Cupido/Stupid Cupid—1995 (112 episodes)
Juegos de Fuego—1995 (89 episodes)
Sucupira—1996 (108 episodes)
Loca Piel/Crazy Skin—1996 (number of episodes unavailable)
Oro Verde/Green Gold—1997 (number of episodes unavailable)

On the other hand, Chilean viewers love novelas with the same passion as audiences in other countries. A 1996 sampling of serial drama aired on Chilean television is shown below (including each soap's country of origin and the local network where it can be found)[9]:

Cara Sucia/Dirty Face—Chilevisión (Venezuela)
Con Toda el Alma/With All My Soul—TVN (Mexico)

Eternamente Manuela/Eternally Manuela—TVN (Colombia)
Kassandra—Megavision (Venezuela)
Lazos de Amor/Ties of Love—Megavision (Mexico)
Pecado de Amor/Sin of Love—Chilevisión (Venezuela)
Perla Negra/Black Pearl—UCC (Argentina)
El Premia Mayor/The Best Prize—Megavision (Mexico)
Quirpa de Tres Mujeres—Chilevisión (Venezuela)
Sucupira—TVN (Chile)

Focus: Brazil

Journalist di Donato Dinapiera, in a 1992 *UNESCO Courier* article, describes Brazil as "a country where, according to a 1984 survey, television serials are more important to the national economy than the motor industry, and where the two leading TV networks, Rede Globo and Manchete, arguably have more impact on illiterates than the millions of reading manuals distributed by the national literacy campaign."[10]

Since the early 1950s, Brazilian television has been a major force in unifying its culturally (and educationally) diverse population. Serial drama has shown itself to be an important means to this end. The success of this genre is complicated yet clear according to Dinapiera:

> The Brazilian telenovela is the product of a favourable set of circumstances that, without forcing it to eschew such conventions of the serial form as fragmented plotlines, suspense, love interest and emotional drama, prevents it from becoming too far-fetched or from portraying a world divided simplistically into goodies and baddies, and instead encourages humour and an interest in the ups and downs of everyday life. It is also the fruit of teamwork, benefiting from the combined efforts of the country's best dramatists, authors, actors, composer-musicians, directors and documentary film-makers. This is rarely the case in North America, where the television serial is regarded as a minor genre left to be semi-improvised by B-movie directors. The limitations of the serial format are the same in Brazil as elsewhere, but Brazilian programme-makers have long since learned how to overcome them and give free rein to their creativity.[11]

As early as 1951 Brazil began producing its first telenovelas,[12] including *Eu Compro Essa Mulher* (*I'll Buy That Woman*)[13]—a stunning success, which, in turn, provided incentive for other dramatists (including Cuban exiles in the late 1950s) to contribute to the genre. By 1964 advertisers had begun to recognize the potential power of soap opera viewers, opting to sponsor *O Direito de Nascer,* a Brazilian remake of the Cuban novela, *El Derecho de Nacer* (*The Right to Be Born*).[14]

After the success of *El Derecho,* large numbers of novelas were commissioned by the government-sponsored television networks, mostly because the newly established military dictatorship saw serial drama as a safe way to give people an identity without making controversial political statements. In fact, novelas were one of the few genres to face little censorship during this time (although the situation changed from time to time over the next decade.) As a result, some activist groups, like Cinema Novo and the Tropicalists, recruited highly acclaimed dramatists to produce stories of the hardships of contemporary life rather than "safe" period pieces.[15] A good example of this type of novela was TV Tupi's *Beto Rockefeller*, an entertaining serial with humor as well as a social message.[16]

By the mid 1970s Brazilian soap operas like Rede Globo's *A Escrava Isaura* (*Isaura, the Slave Girl*) were highly regarded throughout the world.[17] Within Brazil, however, a novela "war" of sorts broke out between the TV networks. Rede Globo (or TV Globo) ultimately emerged as the leader of the pack and dominated soap opera production and distribution for the next 25 years. A brief chronology of Rede Globo is described below:

- 1965   Rede Globo airs its first program.

- 1970s   Considered to be TV Globo's "golden age," when some novela episodes actually receive 100 percent ratings.[18]

- 1985   TV Globo airs *Roque Santeiro*, which gets a 98 percent audience share.[19]

- 1989   TV Globo begins to face stiff competition from another telenovela producer, Manchete, whose *Pantanal* captures high ratings for its beautifully videographed Amazon setting and occasional steamy nude scenes.[20]

- 1995   Ninety-one Globo TV stations dominate 99.84 percent of Brazil's 4,974 municipalities, earning high ratings in all programming blocks (56 percent in the morning, 59 percent in the afternoon, and 69 percent in the evening, with a 74 percent share during prime time hours).[21] This figure is particularly noteworthy when considering that only 20 percent of the adult population is literate at this time, and that the average Brazilian watches more than two hours of TV each day.[22]

- 1996   Globo tries a shorter novela form—in *O Fim do Mundo* (*The End of the World*). It is warmly received, despite some harsh criticism from the Roman Catholic Church.[23]

    Globo inadvertently affects Russia's election day, as Boris Yeltsin capitalizes on the popularity of *Tropicalmiente* (a sultry beach romance between a rich, rebellious girl and a ruggedly handsome fisherman)[24] and airs extra episodes on Russian TV to dissuade voters from going to the polls.

Today, most (80 percent) of TV Globo's programming is produced in its own studios and exported to viewers in over 130 nations (in addition to attracting large domestic audiences). Understandably, global exports are considered as seriously as local programming—multinational syndication accounts for more than $25 million for the corporation each year.[25]

Many of TV Globo's most popular programs—both at home and abroad—are telenovelas designed to accomplish the company's primary mission: "To reflect and stimulate Brazilian culture in all its facets."[26] An example of this type of novela is *A Escrava Isaura* (*Isaura, the Slave Girl*)—perhaps Globo's most popular export—portraying a white girl in nineteenth-century Brazil who fights bravely for her freedom.[27] Even Fidel Castro was enamored of the story, rescheduling the meeting times of his Central Committee to catch all the episodes.[28]

But Rede Globo, although dominant, is not the only globally influential novela producer in Brazil. The Sistema Brasileiro de Televisão (SBT), Brazil's second-largest network, has consistently gained ground on its major competitor for the last several years. In 1993 SBT began producing historical novelas, spending large amounts of money to lure big-name actors and actresses (like Sonia Braga) away from Globo. The SBT also raided two of Globo's top writers, with long-term contracts paying more than $100,000 per month for each writer. This figure was reportedly twice the amount paid by Globo.[29]

In 1995 SBT wanted to expand its international distribution but realized that it was far behind Rede Globo in prestige. The company needed a "creative" way to entice foreign programmers to try an SBT soap rather than one with the more "established" TV Globo logo. The strategy SBT ultimately decided on was "bartering." Instead of selling time on the show, the production company would simply sell multinational rights to novela sponsors in Brazil, who, in turn, would provide free programming to other countries in exchange for commercial airtime.[30] The strategy seemed to work quite well. Within a few months TV Globo reported "below average" ratings of its usual 55–60 percent share of the domestic audience, as well as considerably less success in global exports (compared to previous years).[31]

In 1996 SBT premiered three new novelas—an unprecedented move in Brazilian TV history—including a $20 million teen school drama, *Colégio Brasil/Brazil High School* (à la *Beverly Hills, 90210*); a serial featuring a top singer as a taxidriver; and a story about a struggling single mother. All were aimed at a youth-oriented market.[32] With SBT's rising success, Rede Globo began to change its novela direction to better attract new viewers and to keep its old ones. In short, according to Benedito Ruy Barbosa (a Globo novela scriptwriter): "The genre that has brought Globo its greatest success needs to be overhauled. The telenovela needs to leave the studio and show what Brazil and its people look like. The secret is in the public's identifying with it."[33]

Globo may also be looking over its shoulder at a third network, Machete, which also produces novelas. In the early 1990s this company had neither the resources nor the product to compete very strongly with either Rede Globo or SBT, but it has since been rising rapidly.

Whether on Globo, SBT or Machete, Brazilian viewers have easy access to the novela of their choice almost every day. A partial list of popular Brazilian telenovelas in 1997 includes the following[34]:

Alcanzar Una Estrella I/To Reach a Star, Part I—CNT
O Amor Está No Ar—Rede Globo

Corazón Salvaje/Wild Heart—CNT
Os Ossos do Barão—SBT
A Indômada—Rede Globo
Kananga do Japão—Rede Manchete
María la del Barrio—SBT
A Viagem—Rede Globo
Perdidos de Amor/Lost for Love—Rede Bandeirantes
Prisionera de Amor/Prisoner of Love—CNT
Zaza—Rede Globo
Simplemente María/Simply Maria—CNT
Xica do Silva—Rede Manchete

As for the rest of the world, the list of Brazilian-produced novelas could probably fill this book. Here are the titles of just a few[35]:

O Amor Está No Ar—1997
Antonio Alves, Taxista/Antonio Alves, Taxi Driver—no date known
Barrigo...—no date known
Beto Rockefeller—no date known
O Compeão/The Champ—no date known
Colégio Brasil/Brazil High School—1996
Dancin' Days—no date known
De Corpo e Alma/Body and Soul—no date known
Doña Anja—1997
Doña Beija—no date known
La Escrava Isaura/Isaura, the Slave Girl—no date known
O Fim do Mundo/The End of the World—no date known
A Indômada—1997
Kananga do Japão—1997
Malhacão/Pumping Iron—1996
Mulheres de Areia/Women of Sand—1997
Os Ossos do Barão—1997
Pantanal de Amor—no date known
Perdidos de Amor/Lost for Love—1997
Primeiro Amor/First Love—1996
Razão de Vivir/Reason to Live—1996
Roque Santeiro—no date known
Salsa y Merengue/Hot and Sweet—no date known
Sinha Moça—no date known
Tocaia Grande/The Big Ambush—1995
Vale Tudo—no date known
A Viagem—1997
Xica de Silva—1997
Zaza—1997

Brazil does more than produce novelas for other countries. Another direction taken by Rede Globo and others in recent years has been to sell their serial formats (including scripts, scene and costume descriptions) to countries (especially in Europe) wanting to produce indigenous soaps within their own cultural contexts—yet another dimension to the cultural landscaping of the global village.[36] But those who decide to make their own serial dramas would do well to heed some warnings of the potentially harmful effects experienced by some Brazilian novela producers.

First of all, the choice of characters (and the actors and actresses who play them) on Brazilian soaps often reinforces a "whiter-equals-better" message to viewing audiences.[37] As *Washington Post* reporter Eugene Robinson observes,

> Watching the people on Brazilian television—the soap opera stars, the game-show hosts, the news anchors—you'd think you were in Portugal, given the paucity of black or even brown faces.... The number of truly prominent Brazilians with truly dark skin is limited to just a few, mostly singers and soccer players, topped by the legendary soccer star Pele. The acceptability of racial mixing holds, however, even in the uppermost stratum of celebrityhood.... Once a person becomes successful enough, he is welcomed into full citizenship in the "racial democracy." But to be born dark-skinned in Brazil must be to have an acute and debilitating sense of the limits that society intends to impose.[38]

And nowhere is this more evident than with the distinct absence of "people of color" on Brazilian TV.

Another seemingly inadvertent effect of TV novelas is the tendency to blur the line between fiction and reality, especially when addressing political issues. One soap star was overwhelmed by crowds when she accompanied the Brazilian president on a state visit. An actress from another drama influenced voters in Russia after being invited by Boris Yeltsin to condemn his rivals.[39] Still another drama, after its producers fired an actress for "undisciplined behavior," became the subject of front-page headlines.[40]

One of the most harmful consequences of confusing the fantasy of telenovelas with real life occurred to popular actor Andre Gonçalves (who portrayed the first gay character in the primetime novela, *Explode Coração/Exploding Hearts*). Shortly after the first episode was aired, Gonçalves received some serious death threats and was later beaten by a street gang—even though he isn't gay. The issue was not just homosexuality, according to Verian Terto, Jr. (Project Coordinator for the Brazilian Interdisciplinary AIDS Association), it was the fact that "he played a young man like anybody else ... he wasn't exotic."[41]

Even more dramatic was the 1997 trial of a soap opera star (Guilherme de Padua), accused of the 1992 murder of his on-screen lover by stabbing her 18 times with a pair of scissors. The defendant first confessed to the crime, then pleaded "not guilty," saying the actual culprit was his real-life wife. After the wife's confession, she re-accused de Padua. Months (and a long trial) later, both were declared "guilty" and sent to prison for at least five years.[42]

Focus: Colombia

Although Colombia has not been as prolific at novela production as Brazil, it nonetheless has a solid foothold in the genre, broadcasting stories with high production values and popular actors and actresses. Radio Cadena Nacional (RCN) is perhaps the nation's greatest soap supplier, airing novelas such as 1994's *Café con Aroma de Mujer (Coffee with a Scent of Woman)*, which became an immediate hit among Colombian viewers and later spread to the rest of Latin America as well.[43]

As with most traditional serial drama, Colombian novelas usually feature a Cinderella-like protagonist who wants little more than to find happiness with her true love. Predictably, the road to rapture is often dotted with "potholes," and the heroine must overcome incredible hurdles (discovering unclaimed inheritances, exposing greedy and jealous family impersonators, recognizing one's true parents, etc.) before reaching her goal. Along the way she learns a great deal about life and her own strengths and weaknesses.

Recently, attempting to follow a trend set by novela producers in Brazil, Argentina and Mexico, Colombian writers have tried to introduce more daring story lines to their viewing public. In 1997 *Perfume de Agonía (Perfume of Agony)* featured a lesbian guerrilla falling in love with her female captive. As in the United States, the motivation was economic—producers wanted to grab high ratings points, and based on similar scenes on Latin American television[44] it seemed to be a workable idea. The climactic scene—a romantic kiss between the two women—was anticipated to reap high ratings from viewing households. To the network's surprise, the concept was a dud, perceived by both gay and straight audiences as overly sensational and degrading to same-sex relationships. The novela was ultimately dropped by its major sponsor.[45] This by no means indicates that the Colombian trend in serial drama is less realistic than in other countries, but for the time being it appears that there will be more "Cinderellas" than "Barbarellas" on the Colombian novela schedule.

Some traditional serials made in Colombia during the 1980s and 1990s include the following[46]:

Las Aguas Mansas/Calm Waters—1994
Almas de Piedra/Souls of Stone—1995
Azúcar/Sugar—1990
Café con Aroma de Mujer/Coffee with a Scent of Woman—1994
La Casa de las Dos Palmas/The House of the Two Palms—1991
Clase Aparte/A Class Apart—1995
Copas Amargas/Bitter Cocktails—1997
Detrás de un Ángel/Behind an Angel—1994
Dos Mujeres/Two Women—1997
Dulce Ave Negra/Sweet Black Bird—1993
En Cuerpo Ajeno/The Foreign Body—1992
Escalona/The Shallot—no date known

Eternamente Manuela/Eternally Manuela—no date known
Flor de Oro/Golden Flower—1996
Fuego Verde/Green Fire—1996
Géminis/Gemini—1996
Guajira/Cuban Peasant—1996
Hombres/Men—no date known
Las Juanas—no date known
María—1991
María Bonita/Beautiful Maria—1995
Momposina—no date known
Los Motivos de Lola/Lola's Motives—1992
Otra en Mi/Another in Me—1996
La Otra Mitad del Sol/The Other Half of the Sun—1996
Pasiones Secretas/Secret Passions—1996
Pecado Santo/Sacred Sin—1995
La Potra Zaina/The Chestnut Colored Horse—no date known
Puerta Grande/Big Door—no date known
Señora Isabel—1995
Si Mañana Estoy Vivo/If Tomorrow I Am Alive—1992
Sólo una Mujer/Only a Woman—1996
La Sombra del Deseo/The Shadow of Desire—1996
Sueños y Espejos/Dreams and Mirrors—1995
Vida de mi Vida/Life of My Life—1994
La Viuda de Blanco/The Widow in White—1996
La Vorágine/The Vortex—1990

But Colombian viewers do not limit themselves to indigenous novelas, as demonstrated in this 1997 television "snapshot"[47]:

Marcelina—Canal A
Padres e Hijos/Fathers and Sons—Canal A
Esmeralda—Cadena Uno
Bendita Menura/Blessed Lie—Canal A
Canaveral de Pasiones—Canal A
Lola Calamidades—Cadena Uno
Sentimientos Ajenos/Foreign Feelings—Canal A
Celeste Siempre Celeste/Celeste Always Celeste—Cadena Uno
Pecado de Amor/Sin of Love—Canal A
Morelia—Cadena Uno
Llovizna/Drizzle—Canal A
Te Sigo Amando/I Still Love You—Cadena Uno
Las Juanas—Canal A
Dos Mujeres—Cadena Uno
Perfume de Agonía/Perfume of Agony—Canal A
Prisioneros de Amor/Prisoners of Love—Cadena Uno

Like their Latino neighbors, Colombian audiences are fond of their novelas and are likely to continue spinning "Cinderella" stories (perhaps with one or two controversial twists) well into the next millennium.

Focus: Argentina

Argentina has also been a giant in telenovela production and distribution—especially overseas. In 1989 telenovelas became so popular in Italy that Mediastat's Rete-4 network, hungry for quality primetime programming, negotiated a four-year contract with Argentinian soap opera producers.[48] In 1991 one of Argentina's premiere networks, Telefé, introduced *Celeste,* an immediate ratings smash, elevating its star (Andrea del Boca) to fame and creating audience demand for a sequel. Below is a partial list of Argentinian telenovelas[49]:

Alen do Horizonte—1993
Alen Luz de Luna—1996
Apasionada/The Passionate One—no date known
El Árbol Azul/The Blue Tree—1991
Celeste—no date known
Celeste Siempre Celeste/Celeste Always Celeste—no date known
Chiquititas/Little Girls—1995
Cien Días de Ana/One Hundred Days of Ana—no date known
Como Pan Caliente/Like Hot Bread—no date known
Cosecharás Tu Siembra—no date known
Dejate Querer/Let Yourself Love—(co-produced with Spain) no date known
Días de Ilusión/Days of Hope—1980
Esos Que Dicen Amarse/Those Who Say They Love Each Other—no date known
Estrellita Mia/My Little Star—1987
Habia una Vez un Circo/There Once Was a Circus—1972
Jugar a Morir/Play of Death—1969
Manuela—1991
María de Nadie/Maria of No One—no date known
Mas Allá del Horizonte/Past the Horizon—1994
Milagros/Miracles—1993
Micaela—(co-produced with Italy) 1992
Mi Nombre es Coraje/My Name Is Courage—no date known
Nano—1994
El Oro y el Barro/Gold and Mud—no date known
Papá Corazón—no date known
Perla Negra/Black Pearl—1994
Poliladron—1996
Primer Amor/First Love—(co-produced with Spain) 1993
Princesa—no date known
Rebelde/Rebel—no date known
Sheik—1995
El Último Verano/The Last Summer—1996
Yolanda Lujan—no date known
Zingara—1996

Capitalizing on the worldwide attention garnered by Princess Diana's tragic death, the Telefé network created a bizarre serial in 1997 entitled *Milady: The Story Continues.* Starring one of Argentina's leading models, Florencia Raggi (as Diana's goddaughter), the story focused on Prince William and

Prince Harry as adults. As in other novelas love, romance and wealth were featured, and, similarly, the drama was intended for international distribution as well as domestic broadcast. Given the nature of the story, however, this may have been one global venture that went bust. But this one failure is not likely to dampen the viewers' demands for an Argentinian standard they've come to know and love.

Focus: Venezuela

Venezuela may not have begun its telenovela production until 1958, but the nation's track record in this program genre since that time has been nothing short of extraordinary. After RCTV produced its first soap, *Doña Barbara*,[50] programmers realized the power of serial drama and were anxious to create as much of it as possible. Through the migration of thousands of exiled Cuban writers who came to Venezuela in 1959, their goals were actually recognized sooner than they dreamed possible.

As noted in chapter three, Fidel Castro had encouraged (and subsidized) novela production, realizing the propagandistic potential to unify a nation. After the Cuban Revolution, political repression discouraged free artistic expression, and Cuban writers (many of them experienced telenovelists) sought asylum in other countries. Venezuela, anxious to build its cadre of dramatists, was only too happy to welcome these writers. Subsequently, the nation's growth in dramatic programming rose sharply. By 1970 one of the country's major networks, Venevision, had accumulated enough product inventory to create a sales subsidiary. Its first major export, *Esmeralda*, was warmly received in several countries.

In 1982 RCTV followed Venevision's lead and formed Coral Pictures, an export facility in Miami, Florida. Within 10 years RCTV dominated the Spanish telenovela market after its domestic hits grabbed viewers on the other side of the Atlantic as well. By 1995 the company claimed 11,000 hours of export programming, 70 percent of which were telenovelas.

Following in the footsteps of Mexican icon Miguel Sabido, many of the first Venezuelan soaps were geared toward education and information, especially in the areas of population control, health care and the empowerment of women. Perhaps the most stunning example of a commitment to these "motivational" novelas was *Cristal* (aired in Venuezuela in 1990 and still amassing viewers around the world). This serial focused on a young woman's battle with breast cancer and emphasized the importance of early detection of the disease, as well as the emotional battles that accompany the medical quest for a cure.

In 1992 RCTV attempted more social realism with *Por Estas Calles (In These Streets),* which proved extremely popular among domestic viewers; but its biggest international hit to date (with the exception of *Cristal*) would have to be *Kassandra*, aired shortly after *Por Estas Calles*. In 1994 Coraima Torres, the star of *Kassandra*, visited Indonesia after the program had been aired. Her popularity was so overwhelming that another visiting VIP, U.S. president Bill Clinton, was virtually ignored.

Since 1994 *Kassandra* has played an even greater role in international diplomacy. This time the nation was Bosnia-Hercegovina, where "capturing control of the airwaves is always essential."[51] In August 1997, after Bosnian rebels attempted a power play by taking the Venezuelan novela off the air, the U.S. State Department stepped in to restore programming. The reason for intervention was simple (or so the department thought). *Kassandra* had become a bastion of stability in a war-torn land.

The State Department soon recognized that soap opera addiction can often be as complicated as political diplomacy. After recruiting the help of Coral Pictures (the distributor for *Kassandra*), government officials learned— much to their surprise—that the renowned novela had, in fact, been pirated from another country. A few hours later, Coral Pictures tactfully offered to donate all 150 episodes, providing Bosnian viewers with "a much-demanded visual escape."[52] *Kassandra* stars Coraima Torres and Henry Soto were not surprised about the soap's popularity. As Torres observed, "We are completely different cultures and miles apart, but I think we all [have] a common denominator, which is love."[53] Soto added, "I've always said there isn't a stronger feeling than love. When something can calm fury, it is important."[54] Viewers in Bosnia-Hercegovina would most certainly agree.

Cristal and *Kassandra* are not Venezuela's only claims to novela fame, however. A partial list of Venezuelan serials is given below[55]:

Abigail—1988
Adriana—1985
Alejandra—no date known
Alma Mia—no date known
Alondra—no date known
Amanda Sabater—no date known
Amor de Papel/Paper Love—no date known
Los Amores de Anita Peña/The Loves of Anita Pena—no date known
Anabel—no date known
Ángelito—1981
El Ángel Rebelde/The Rebellious Angel—no date known
Azucena/Annunciation Lily—no date known
Bellisima/Beautiful—no date known
Bienvenida Esperanza/Welcome Hope—1983
Candida—1982
Cara Sucia/Dirty Face—no date known
Caribe/Savage—no date known
Carmen Querida/Carmen, My Love—no date known
Ciao Cristina—1983
Como Tu, Ninguna/Like You, No One—1996

Cristal — 1990
Cruz de Nadie/Cross of No One — 1996
La Dama de la Rosa/The Lady in Pink — no date known
De Mujeres/Two Women — no date known
De Oro Puro/Of Pure Gold — no date known
El Desafío/The Challenge — no date known
El Desprecio/The Hatred — (co-produced with Spain) no date known
Divina Obsesión/Divine Obsession — 1996
Las Dos Dianas — no date known
La Dueña/The Owner — no date known
Dulce María/Sweet Maria — no date known
Dulce Enemiga/Sweet Enemy — no date known
Dulce Ilusión/Sweet Hope — no date known
Elizabeth — no date known
El Engano/Deception — no date known
El Esposo de Anais/Anais's Husband — 1981
Fabiola — 1989
Gardenia — no date known
La Gata Salvaje/The Wild She Cat — no date known
La Goajirita — 1982
La Hija de Nadie/The Daughter of No One — 1982
Ilusiones — no date known
Ines Duarte, Secretaría — no date known
La Inolvidable/The Unforgettable Woman — 1995
La Intrusa/The Intruder — 1987
Jugando a Vivir/Playing Life — 1982
Kaina — 1995
Kapricho, S.A. — 1982
Kassandra — 1992
Leonela — no date known
Llovizna/Drizzle — no date known
Luisana Mia — 1981
Macarena — no date known
Maite — 1981
La Malvada/The Evil Woman — no date known
María Celeste — 1994
María de los Ángeles — 1997
María María — 1989
Marielena — 1981
Marisela — 1983
Marta y Javier — no date known
Mi Adorable Mónica — 1990
Mi Amada Beatriz — no date known
Morena Clara — 1995
Mundo de Fieras/World of Furies — no date known
Natacha — no date known
Niña Bonita — no date known
Pasionaria — no date known
Pecado de Amor/Sin of Love — 1995
Peligrosa/Dangerous — no date known
Pobre Diabla/Poor Devil — no date known

Por Amarte Tanto/Because I Love You So — 1992
Por Estas Calles/In These Streets — 1992
Pura Sangre/Pure Blood — 1996
Que Paso con Jackeline?/What Happened with Jacqueline? — 1982
Quirpa de Tres Mujeres — 1996
Rebeca — 1985
La Revancha/Rematch — no date known
Rosalinda — 1981
Rubí — 1989
La Salvaje/The Wild One — 1984
Selva María/Jungle Maria — no date known
Señora — 1988
La Señorita Perdomo — 1982
Sirena/Siren — 1995
Topacio — 1986
La Traidora/The Traitor — no date known
Volver a Vivir/Begin to Live Again — no date known

In fact, Venevisión has produced so many popular novelas over the last 40 years, it has now spawned a satellite channel dedicated almost entirely to serial drama.

The Telenovela Channel — a joint venture between the United Kingdom's Zone Vision and Venevisión's Vision Europe — premiered to a potential audience of three million viewers in Poland, Hungary and Romania in the spring of 1997.[56] It transmitted its signal on Israel's Amos satellite and within months began to air 15–23 hours of soaps daily to scores of Eastern European fans. Its future plans include Russia, the Czech Republic and some Mediterranean countries as well.[57]

Notes

1. Station/network information taken from *World Radio TV Handbook, 1997 Edition*, ed. Andrew G. Sennitt (New York: Billboard Books, 1997). Television/radio set information and population figures taken from *The World Almanac and Book of Facts 1998* (Mahwah, NJ: K-III Reference Corporation, 1997).

2. This listing is compiled from *WRTH Satellite & TV Handbook*, 4th edition, ed. Andrew G. Sennitt (New York: Billboard Books, 1997). It represents the *available* stations on satellite dishes through a transponder in Region II of the world satellite map. Although it is difficult to tell how many people have access to these channels, it is important to acknowledge the variety of cross-national program content on them.

3. Richard Covington, "Latin America, Television Hotbed," *International Herald Tribune* (May 8, 1996) [database on-line]; available from Lexis-Nexis.

4. These summaries have been created through information in the "archives link" on a comprehensive telenovela Web site created and maintained by Yolette Nicholson <yoletten@site.net)> [database on-line]; available on Netscape. The author is extremely grateful to her for this useful information.

5. Population Services International (PSI) Web site <webmaster@psiwash.org>

[database on-line]; available from Netscape. Prudence is the brand name of a condom PSI promotes.

6. *Ibid.*

7. Correspondence with Valerio Fuenzalida, Televisión Nacional de Chile (September 1996).

8. Telenovela Web site.

9. *Ibid.*

10. di Donato Dinapiera, "Brazil: A Magnet for Talent," *UNESCO Courier* (October 1992), 41 [database on-line]; available from Lexis-Nexis.

11. *Ibid.*

12. "A Brief History," *Variety* (October 7–13, 1996), 64.

13. "Brazilian Soaps—Popular, Racy and High-Budgeted," *Video Age International* (July 1992), 18 [database on-line]; available from Lexis-Nexis.

14. "A Brief History."

15. di Donato Dinapiera, "Brazil: A Magnet for Talent."

16. "A Brief History."

17. Incidentally, this novela was so popular it later became the nation's first major export to over 40 countries, including Western Europe, the USSR, Korea and China.

18. William Schomberg, "Brazil Television Giants Wage Soap Opera Wars," Reuters (May 6, 1996) [database on-line]; available from Lexis-Nexis.

19. "A Brief History."

20. *Ibid.*

21. Rede Globo Web site [database on-line]; available from Netscape.

22. Ian Simpson, "Heads Roll as Brazil's Globo TV Faces Competition," Reuters European Business Report (July 25, 1995) [database on-line]; available from Lexis-Nexis.

23. William Schomberg, "Brazil Television Giants Wage Soap Opera Wars,"

24. "Series/Novelas at Mipcom '95," *Television Business International* (October 1995) [database on-line]; available from Lexis-Nexis.

25. This figure is based on an estimate quoted in "Telenovela Fever Goes Globo," *Television Business International* (February 1995), 64 [database on-line]; available from Lexis-Nexis. The article goes on to give the average export prices of novelas based on the typical number of episodes (130). Each country must pay $300–$15,000 per episode, depending upon the country and the size of its potential audience.

26. Ian Simpson, "Heads Roll as Brazil's Globo TV Faces Competition."

27. "Telenovela Fever Goes Globo."

28. *Ibid.*

29. "SBT Chases Telenovela Top Spot," *Television Business International* (April 1996), 18 [database on-line]; available from Lexis-Nexis.

30. "Brazil: Bartering Novelas into 'Soap' Operas," *Television Business International* (July 1995), 12 [database on-line]; available from Lexis-Nexis.

31. "Brazil: Globo's Top Novelas in Ratings Stumble," *Television Business International* (May 1995), 6 [database on-line]; available from Lexis-Nexis.

32. William Schomberg, "Brazil Television Giants Wage Soap Opera Wars."

33. Quoted in "Brazil: Globo's Top Novelas in Ratings Stumble."

34. Telenovela Web site.

35. *Ibid.*

36. "Telenovela Fever Goes Globo."

37. Eugene Robinson, "Over the Brazilian Rainbow: In This Multi-Hued Society, the Color Line Is a State of Mind," *Washington Post* (December 10, 1995) [database on-line]; available from Lexis-Nexis.

38. *Ibid.*

39. William Schomberg, "Brazil Television Giant Wages Soap Opera Wars."

40. "Brazil: Fiery Star Written Out of Globo Telenovela," *Television Business International* (March 1995), 12 [database on-line]; available from Lexis-Nexis. The incident occurred after Vera Fischer, a former Miss Brazil, and considered at the time to be the nation's leading sex symbol, was fired for being habitually late to the set and fighting with her costars. Viewers especially objected to the firing as well as the way in which she left the novela—by dying in a hastily-written hotel fire.

41. As reported by Laurie Goering, "Brutality Against Gay Men, Lesbians on Rise in Brazil," *Times Picayune* (April 6, 1997) [database on-line]; available on Lexis-Nexis.

42. "Brazilian Actor Accuses His Wife in Soap-Opera Murder Trial," CNN News (January 23, 1997) <http://cnn.news.com> [database on-line].

43. "A Brief History."

44. *Ibid.* According to *The Stuart News/Port St. Lucie News*, Argentina aired three soaps in 1997 with major lesbian characters. Brazil's *Explode Coração/Exploding Hearts* (discussed earlier in the chapter) featured a gay interracial love affair involving soap star Andre Gonçalves, and Mexico's *Nada Personal/Nothing Personal* also suggested a lesbian relationship.

45. "Lesbian Kiss on Colombian Soap Stirs Up Controversy," *The Stuart News/Port St. Lucie News* (June 15, 1997), 15 [database on-line]; available from Lexis-Nexis.

46. Telenovela Web site.

47. *Ibid.*

48. "A Brief History."

49. Telenovela Web site.

50. "A Brief History."

51. "Hard-liners Blamed for Another Transmitter Outage," CNN News (October 20, 1997) [database on-line].

52. Pat Neal, "Bosnian Relief from an Unlikely Source," CNN News (November 11, 1997) [database on-line].

53. *Ibid.*

54. *Ibid.*

55. Telenovela Web site.

56. "From Venezuela with Love," *Television Business International* (January 1997) [database on-line]; available from Lexis-Nexis.

57. *Ibid.*

Europe

Countries included

Albania, Austria, Azores (Portuguese), Belarus, Belgium, Bosnia-Hercegovina, Bulgaria, Croatia, Czech Republic, Denmark, Estonia, Faroe Islands (Danish), Finland, France, Germany (Federal Republic), Gibraltar, Greece, Hungary, Iceland, Ireland, Italy, Latvia, Liechtenstein, Lithuania, Luxembourg, Macedonia, Malta, Moldova, Netherlands, Norway, Poland, Portugal, Romania, Russia, San Marino (Republic of), Slovakia, Slovenia, Spain, Sweden, Switzerland, Ukraine, United Kingdom, Vatican City, Yugoslavia[1]

Stations/Networks

Albania
Population: 3,249,136—293 per sq. mi.
(TV sets—1:13 persons; radios—1:6.1 persons)
Radiotelevisione Shqiptar

Austria
Population: 8,023,244—248 per sq. mi.
(TV sets—1:3 persons; radios—1:1.7 persons)
Osterreichischer Rundfunk (ORF)
Wetter @ Reise Television GmbH

Azores (Portuguese)
Population: n/a (see Portugal)
(TV sets—n/a; radios—n/a)
Radiotelevisão Portuguesa (RTP)

Belarus
Population: 10,415,973—130 per sq. mi.

(TV sets—1:3.7 persons; radios—1:3.3 persons)
Belaruskae Telebachanne
TBN (Television Broadcasting Network)

Belgium
Population: 10,170,241—863 per sq. mi.
(TV sets—1:2.4 persons; radios—1:1.3 persons)
Belgische Radio en Televisie (BRTN)
Belgischer Rundfunk (BRF)
Canal Plus
Radio Télévision Belge de la Communauté Culturelle Française (RTBF)
RTL-TVi

Bosnia-Hercegovina
Population: 2,656,240—135 per sq. mi.
(TV sets—n/a; radios—n/a)

Televizija Sarajevo
TV Bosnia-Hercegovina
TV Tuzla

Bulgaria

Population: 8,612,757—201 per sq. mi.
(TV sets—1:2.7 persons; radios—1:2.2 persons)
Balgarska Televizija
New Television

Croatia

Population: 5,004,112—229 per sq. mi.
(TV sets—1:4.6 persons; radios—1:4.4 persons)
Hrvatska Televizija (HTV)
OTV (Open Television)

Czech Republic

Population: 10,321,120—339 per sq. mi.
(TV sets—1:3.3 persons; radios—1:3.8 persons)
Czech Television
Nova TV
Primiera TV

Denmark

Population: 5,249.632—316 per sq. mi.
(TV sets—1:1.9 persons; radios—1:1 persons)
Danmarks Radio
Telecom A/S
TV2
TV3

Estonia

Population: 1,459,428—84 per sq. mi.
(TV sets—1:2.5 persons; radios—n/a)
EVTV
Kanal Kaks (ch 2)
Reklaamitelevisioon
Tallinn Eesti Televisioon (ETV)

Faroe Islands (Danish)

Population: n/a (see Denmark)
(TV sets—n/a; radios—n/a)
Sjónvarp Foroya

Finland

Population: 5,105,230—39 per sq. mi.
(TV sets—1:2.7 persons; radios—1:1 persons)
MTV OY/MTV3
Yleisradio OY

France

Population: 58,040,230—276 per sq. mi.
(TV sets—1:2 persons; radios—1:1.2 persons)
8 Mont Blanc
ARTE
Canal France Internationale
Canal Plus
France 2
France 3
La Cinquième
M6 (Métropole Télévision)
Télé Bleue
Télé Lyon Metropole
Télé Toulouse
Télévision Française 1 (TF1)

Germany (Federal Republic)

Population: 83,536,115—606 per sq. mi.
(TV sets—1:2.5 persons; radios—1:2.3 persons)
ARD
Bayerischer Rundfunk Fernsehen
Hessischer Rundfunk Fernsehen
MDR Fernsehen
n-tv
NDR Fernsehen
ORB Fernsehen
Pro 7 Television AG
Radio Bremen Fernsehen
RTL-2 Fernsehen GmbH
SDR Fernsehen
SFB Fernsehen
Vox Film und Fernsehen GmbH
WDR Fernsehen
Zweites Deutsches Fernsehen

Gibraltar

Population: n/a (see United Kingdom)
(TV sets—n/a; radios—n/a)
GBC Television

Greece

Population: 10,538,594—207 per sq. mi.
(TV sets—1:4.5 persons; radios—1:2.5 persons)
Antenna TV
Channel 5
Channel 7X
Elliniki Tileorassi (ERT SA)

Hungary

Population: 10,002,541—278 per sq. mi.
(TV sets—1:2.4 persons; radios—1:1.6 persons)
A3 (Pest-Buda TV)
Magyar Televízío (MTV)
Nap TV Kft.
Sió Televísío
TV3 Budapest (BKRT)

Iceland

Population: 270,292—7 per sq. mi.
(TV sets—1:3.5 persons; radios—1:1.4 persons)
Omega Television
Rikisútvarpid-Sjónvarp (RUV)

Ireland

Population: 3,566,833—131 per sq. mi.
(TV sets—1:3.5 persons; radios—1:1.6 persons)
Radio Telefis Eireann (RTE)
BBC

Italy

Population: 57,460,274—494 per sq. mi.
(TV sets—1:3.4 persons; radios—1:1.3 persons)
Italia 1
Italia 7
Radiotelevisione Italiana
Rete 4
TelePiu

Latvia

Population: 2,468,982—99 per sq. mi.
(TV sets—1:2.1 persons; radios—1:1.3 persons)
Latvijas Televizija (LTV)

Liechtenstein

Population: 31,122—502 per sq. mi.
(TV sets—1:2.9 persons; radios—1:2.8 persons)

Lithuania

Population: 3,646,041—145 per sq. mi.
(TV sets—1:2.7 persons; radios—1:2.6 persons)
Aidas
Lietuvos Televizija
LNK (Litpoliinter TV)
5 Kanalas (variation of Tele-3)

Luxembourg

Population: 415,870—416 per sq. mi.
(TV sets—1:2.9 persons; radios—1:1.7 persons)
Télé Luxembourg

Macedonia

Population: 2,104,035—212 per sq. mi.
(TV sets—1:6.1 persons; radios—1:5.6 persons)
Televizija Makedonije

Malta

Population: 375,576—3,078 per sq. mi.
(TV sets—1:2.5 persons; radios—1:4.1 persons)
Malta Broadcasting Authority
Radio Television Malta
Xandir Television

Moldova

Population: 4,463,847—343 per sq. mi.
(TV sets—n/a; radios—n/a)
VTV

Monaco

Population: 31,719—4,292 per sq. mi.
(TV sets—1:1.5 persons; radios—1:1 persons)
Télé Monte Carlo

Netherlands
Population: 15,568,034—971 per sq. mi.
(TV sets—1:2.7 persons; radios—1:1.1 persons)
AVRO
EO
IKON
KRO
NCRV
Nederlandse Omroepprogramma Stichting (NOS)
NOT
Nederlandse Programma Stichting (NPS)
TROS
VARA
VPRO

Norway
Population: 4,383,807—35 per sq. mi.
(TV sets—1:2.2 persons; radios—1:1.3 persons)
Norsk Rikskringkasting
TV-2

Poland
Population: 38,642,565—320 per sq. mi.
(TV sets—1:3.8 persons; radios—1:3.5 persons)
Telewizja Polska S.A.
Telewizja Wisla

Portugal
Population: 9,865,114—277 per sq. mi.
(TV sets—1:5.9 persons; radios—1:4.5 persons)
Radiotelevisão Portuguêsa (RTP)
Sociedade Independente de Comuni-cação (SIC)
Televisão Independente, SA (TVI)

Romania
Population: 21,657,162—236 per sq. mi.

(TV sets—1:5.7 persons; radios—1:5.1 persons)
Radioteleviziunea Romana

Russia
Population: 148,178,487—23 per sq. mi.
(TV sets—1:2.7 persons; radios—1:1.6 persons)
2x2
All Russia Television and Broadcast-ing Company
Channel 5 St. Petersburg
Channel 6 St. Petersburg
MART-International Radio and TV
MIR-International TV
Moscow TV Company (MTV)
NTV
Russian Public TV (ORT)
TV-6 Moscow

San Marino (Republic of)
Population: 24,521—1,022 per sq. mi.
(TV sets—n/a; radios—1:1.9 persons)
San Marino RTV

Slovakia
Population: 5,374,362—284 per sq. mi.
(TV sets—1:1.6 persons; radios—1:0.7 persons)
Slovak Television

Slovenia
Population; 1,951,443—250 per sq. mi.
(TV sets—n/a; radios—n/a)
Pop TV/Pro Plus
Radio Television Slovenija (RTV SLO)

Spain
Population: 39,181,114—201 per sq. mi.
(TV sets—1:2.3 persons; radios—1:3.3 persons)
Antena 3 Television
Canal Sur

Radiotelevisión Española (RTVE)
Televisión de Catalunya (TV-3 and
  Canal 33)
Televisión Murciana
TV Vasce-Euscal Telebista (ETB 1/2)
Televisión de Galicia SA (TVG)
Televisión Valenciana (TVV-Canal 9)

Sweden

Population: 8,900,954—51 per sq.
  mi.
(TV sets—1:2.3 persons; radios—1:1.2
  persons)
Sveriges Television AB (SVT 1/2)
TV4 Nordisk Television Co.
UR-Sveriges Utbildningsradio

Switzerland

Population: 7,207,060—452 per sq.
  mi.
(TV sets—1:2.8 persons; radios—1:1.3
  persons)
Sweiz 4/Suisse 4/Svizzera 4
Sweizerische Radio und Fernsehge-
  sellschaft (SRG)

Ukraine

Population: 50,864,009—218 per sq. mi.
(TV sets—n/a; radios—n/a)
Ukrajinska Telebacennja

United Kingdom

Population: 58,489,975
(TV sets—1:2.9 persons; radios—1:0.9
  persons)
Anglia Television
British Broadcasting Corporation (BBC)
British Sky Broadcasting
Border Television
Carlton Television
Central Independent Television Plc.
Channel Four Television Ltd.

Channel Television
Good Morning Television (GMTV Ltd.)
Grampian Television Plc.
Granada Television Ltd.
HTV Wales
HTV West
Independent Television Commission
  (ITC)
Independent Television News (ITN)
London Weekend Television
Meridian Broadcasting
S4C
Scottish Television
Tyne Tees Television
Ulster Television
Westcountry Television
Yorkshire Television Ltd.

Vatican City

Population: 811
(TV sets—n/a; radios—n/a)

Yugoslavia

Population: 10,614,558—269 per sq. mi.
(TV sets—n/a; radios—1:3.9 persons)
ANTENAC
Channel 23 (K-23)
Channel 33 (K-33)
Galaksija 32
Yugoslav Radio and TV (JRT)
KBN
NTV Studio B
RTS
Televizija Crna Gora (Montenegro)
TV Art Channel
TV Beograd
TV Kanal 27
TV Kraljevo
TV Negotin
TV Novi Sad
TV Politika
TV Pristina

Satellite Channels Available in This Region[2]

3-Sat (Germany)
Abu Dhabi TV (UAE)
Afghanistan TV (Afg.)
AFN-TV (USA)
AFRTS (USA)
AFRTS-SEB (USA)
Al Jazeera Sat. (Qatar)
Al Jazeera Sat. (Algeria)
Albanian TV
Algerian TV
Antena Tres TV (Spain)
ARD-1 (Germany)
ARD/ZDF (Germany)
ART (Saudi Arabia)
ART Europe (UK)
ARTE (Germany)
Asia Business Channel
AsiaNet
ASTRA SPORT (AFS)
ATN (Africa)
ATV (Turkey)
ATV (Poland)
Bahrain TV
Bayerisches Fernsehen (Germany)
BBC Orbit Arabic Service (UK)
BBC Prime (UK)
BBC World (UK)
BHT (Bosnia-Hercegov.)
BOP-TV (Senegal)
Bop TV Mmabatho (Bophuthatswana)
Bop TV-1 (Bophuthatswana)
Bravo (UK)
BSkyB (UK)
C-Span (USA)
Cable Plus Filmovy Kanal (Czech Rep.)
Canal Clásico (Spain)
Canal France Internat. (France)
Canal Horizons (Senegal)
Canal J(eunesse) (France)
Canal Jimmy (France)
Canal On (Spain)
Canal Plus (France)
Canal Sur (Spain)
Cartoon Network (USA)
CCTV4 (China)

CDAT (AFS)
Channel 5 (UK)
Channel Africa (South Africa)
Channel-2 TV Israel
Chinese Channel (UK)
Chinese News Entertainment (China)
Christian Channel Europe (UK)
Ciné Cinéfil (France)
Ciné Cinémas (France)
Cine Classics (Spain)
Cinema (Sweden)
Cinemania (Spain)
Cinemania 2 (Spain)
CMT Europe (USA)
CNBC (UK)
CNN International (USA/UK)
CNN Nordic (USA)
ConAir (USA)
Country Music Europe (USA)
CTC (STS) (CIS)
Deutsche Welle TV (Germany)
Discovery Channel (UK)
Documania (Spain)
DR-2 (Denmark)
DSF Deutsches Sportfernsehen (Germany)
Dubai TV (UAE)
Duna 7 (Hungary)
EDTV (UAE)
Egypt TV
Egyptian Satellite TV (Egypt)
ESPN (USA)
ET-1/2/3 (Greece)
ETV (Ethiopia)
Euro Business News (UK)
Euro D (Turkey)
Euronews (France)
Europe by Satellite
European Business News (EBN) (UK)
Eurosport (France)
Eurosport (Norway)
FilmNet (Poland)
FilmNet 1 Nordic (Norway)
FilmNet 2 (Sweden)
Fox Kids (UK)

France Supervision
France-2 (France)
Future Vision (Saudi Arabia)
Galavision (Mexico)
Granada Good Life (UK)
Granada Plus/Man & Motor (UK)
Granada (Talk TV) (UK)
H.O.T. (Home Order TV)
HBB (Turkey)
Home Shopping Network (UK)
Home TV (India)
HRT Zagreb (Croatia)
HTB (Russia)
IBA Channel 3 (Israel)
InterSTAR (Turkey/Germany)
IRIB-TV 1/2/3 (Iran)
Jordan TV
JRT (Jordan)
JRTV (Jordan)
JSTV (Japan)
Kabel 1 (Germany)
Kanal 5 (Sweden)
Kanal 6 (Turkey)
Kanal 7 (Turkey)
Kanal D (Turkey)
Kanal + (Poland)
Kasachstan 1 (private) (Kasachstan)
Kazakhstan TV
Kuwait Space Channel
Kuwait TV
La Chaîne Info (LCI) (France)
La Cinquième (France)
LBC Lebanon
Libyan TV
M Net South Africa (AFS)
M-2 Morocco
M-6 Métropole 6 (France)
M-Net Int. (South Af.)
MBC (UK)
MCM Afrique (South Africa)
MCM Euromusic (France)
MED-TV (UK)
Middle East Broadcast (MBC) (UK)
Middle East Broad. Centre (UK)
MiniMax (Spain)
Mitteldeutscher Rundfunk (MDR 3)
   (Germany)
Moscow-1 (CIS)
MTV (UK)

MTV (Africa)
MTV Nordic (Denmark)
Muslim TV Ahmadiyya
Muslim-TV MTA+ (UK)
N-3 Nord-3 (Germany)
n-tv (Germany)
NBC Super Channel (UK)
NEPC-TV (India)
NHK Tokyo (Japan)
Nickelodeon (Germany)
Nickelodeon (Sweden)
Nickelodeon (USA)
Nile TV (Egypt)
Nile TV Int. (Egypt)
Nova Shop (Sweden)
NRK 1/2 (Norway)
NTA Ch. 10 (Nigeria)
NTV (Russia)
Oman TV
Onyx TV
Orbit (Morocco)
ORT-1 (CIS)
Ostankino ORT Int. (CIS)
Paramount TV (USA)
Paris Premiere (France)
PIK CYBC (Cyprus)
Planète (France)
Polonia 1 (Poland)
Polsat (Poland)
Premièra TV (Czech Rep.)
Premiere (Germany)
Pro-7 (Germany)
Quantum Channel (UK/USA)
QVC (USA)
QVC Deutschland (Germany)
RAIDUE (Italy)
RAITRE (Italy)
RAIUNO (Italy)
Rendez-Vous (France)
RFO Canal Permanent 2 (France)
RTA-TV (Algeria)
RTL 7 (Poland)
RTL Television (Germany)
RTL-2 (Germany)
RTL-9 (France)
RTM 1 (Morocco)
RTP Internacional (Portugal)
RTS Beograd (RTV Srbjal)
   (Yugoslavia)

RTT-TV-7 (Tunisia)
SABC 1/2/3 (AFS)
SABC-TV (South Africa)
Samanloyu TV (Turkey)
Sara Vision
Sat-1 (Germany)
Saudi Arabia
Saudi Arabia TV 1/2
Saudia (Saudi Arabia)
Sci-Fi Channel (UK)
Sci-Fi Channel Nordic (Denmark)
Sell-a-Vision (Germany)
Sharjah TV (Mauritania)
Sky Movies (UK)
Sky Movies Gold (UK)
Sky News (UK)
Sky One (UK)
Sky Scottish (UK)
Sky Soap (UK)
Sky Sports (UK)
Sky Sports 2/3 (UK)
Sky Sports Gold (UK)
Sky Travel (UK)
Sky-2 (UK)
Sony Entertainment TV (India)
Sudan TV
Super RTL (Germany)
Super Television Channel (USA)
SWF/SDR (S-3) (Germany)
Syrian TV
TCC (The Children's Channel) (UK)
Tel Monte-Carlo (TMC) (Monte-
    Carlo)
Tele-5 (Spain)
Teleclub (Switzerland)
TeleDeporte (Spain)
TelePace/Vatican TV (Italy/Vatican
    State)
Telesat 5 (Spain)
TF-1 (France)
TGRT (Turkey)
The Adult Channel (UK)
The Computer Channel (UK)
The Disney Channel (UK)
The Egyptian Space Channel
The Family Channel (UK)

The History Channel (UK)
The Learning Channel (TLC) (UK)
The Movie Channel (UK)
The Playboy Channel (UK)
The Racing Channel (UK)
The Weather Channel (UK)
TM 3 (Germany)
TM3 (UK)
TNT/Cartoon Network (USA)
TRT Int. (Turkey)
TRT-1/3/4 (Turkey)
TV 1-India
TV 3 de Catalunya (Spain)
TV 3 Denmark
TV 3 Sweden
TV Angola
TV Eurotica (UK)
TV Norge (Norway)
TV Polonia (Poland)
TV Romania Int.
TV Russia 2
TV Sport Eurosport (France)
TV-1000 (Sweden)
TV-2/3 (Norway)
TV-4 (Sweden)
TV-6 Moscow (CIS)
TV3+ (Denmark)
TV5 Internationale/Afrique (France)
TVE Internacional (Spain)
TVX The Fantasy Channel (UK)
UK Gold
UK Living
Vasa TV (Slovakia)
VH-1 (UK/Germany)
VHI Nordic (Sweden)
VIVA (Germany)
Viva 2 (Germany)
VOX (Germany)
WBTV (The Warner Channel) (UK)
WDR (Germany)
What's in store (Netherlands)
WorldNet (USA)
Yemen TV
ZDF (Germany)
Zee TV (UK)
ZTV (Sweden)

Overview of Cultural Patterns and Audience Trends

Although the formation of a European Union has integrated many diverse cultures, economic and technological differences remain—especially between the more developed (and stable) countries in the west and north, and the emerging nations of the former Soviet Bloc. As a result, the ratio of television sets to persons (in countries where TV is even available) ranges from 1:1.5 in Monaco to 1:13 in Albania. Still, even the poorest European country is much better off than some of the richest nations in Africa. As a result, it's safe to say that most Europeans have access to satellite and cable and therefore can receive as many foreign or domestic programs as they desire. Imported shows like *The Bold and the Beautiful, Days of Our Lives, As the World Turns, Another World, Home and Away, Neighbours, Lindenstrasse* and *Shortland Street* abound. In addition, most countries (even those in newly democratized Eastern Europe) have at least one locally produced serial. The United Kingdom, Germany and Sweden are perhaps the leaders of soap opera production, but Russia, Poland and Ireland are not far behind. Popular domestic soaps and telenovelas are also prominent in France, Spain and Greece.

In 1991 reporter Jeremy Coopman noted the surge of soap opera/telenovela programs in Europe, as well as their impact on local culture: "These days, the traditional afternoon siesta is likely to be replaced by a daily dose of 'The Bold and the Beautiful' or 'La Dama de Rosa' ('Lady in Pink'), the torrid Venezuelan sudser. ... And the popularity of serials—from sexy fantasies to gritty domestic fare—is beginning to travel north, where Europeans are cranking out homegrown versions in greater numbers than ever."[3]

Coopman goes on to describe some examples of these "homegrown" serials: from the Netherlands, *Good Times, Bad Times* (an adaptation of Australia's *The Restless Years*, discussed later in this chapter); from Greece, *The Shining*, set in suburban, middle-class Athens; from Denmark, *The Weekly*, involving the lives and loves of a Danish newspaper staff; and from Italy, *Ivy* and *Secrets*, two tales of glitz and glamor amid Italy's ancient splendor.[4] In short, the programming strategy for most countries in Europe is the same—to play to audience taste while preserving a national identity within a "unified" continent. As a result, whereas some European soaps may find their way into other countries (notably *Coronation Street, EastEnders*, and *Lindenstrasse*), many do not "travel" well to other regions. The humor, the customs, the language and other elements of national heritage are uniquely targeted to specific populations within continental Europe.

Some soaps/telenovelas (from Spain, France or Great Britain, for example) may be popular in protectorates like the British West Indies, Martinique or Morocco; but as colonies begin to dwindle or disappear, the need for a sociopolitical identity in the Third World may dissipate. Thus, the "homegrown" soaps are likely to prevail for domestic purposes only, to preserve the cultural landscape of each nation.

Focus: United Kingdom

As discussed in chapter one, the United Kingdom continues to produce and distribute the greatest number of serial dramas in Europe, including *Coronation Street, Crossroads, EastEnders, Eldorado, London's Burning,* and *Emmerdale.* From the first monochromatic images of Ena Sharples on *Coronation Street* to gripping story lines dealing with "racism, abortion, poverty and lesbian love,"[5] the Brits continue to be the reigning monarch of soaps, setting the standard for settings and production values throughout the world. *Little Strawberry* in Russia, for example, has been described as a *Coronation Street*–type drama; programmers in Tanzania and Kazakhstan solicit scripts with *EastEnders* or *Brookside* flavors. The appeal for these shows is primarily of "place," as author Charlotte Brunsdon observes:

> It is not character, in the sense of heroes and heroines, or the promise of action, and enigmas resolved, that is central, but the establishing of the "where"—the place that we know, where life is going on. And it is surely the predictable familiarity of the life represented which pulls us in.... We, too, live in the world of family squabbles, demands for television licence fees and rising unemployment. It is not so much that "life is like that ... but that the generic lack of closure, in combination with the realist premise, offers a homology between soap life and viewer life.[6]

However, because much of the non-European world has cares other than "television licence fees and rising unemployment," it's not surprising that the actual distribution figures for these dramas is quite limited;[7] they air only in Western Europe[8] and in certain parts of North America, Australia and New Zealand. Still, within this seemingly limited sphere, these soaps (especially *Coronation Street, Crossroads, Brookside,* and *EastEnders*) have large numbers of loyal, dedicated and energetic followers as well as a formula for success with mass audiences. Brunsdon notes: "'Coronation Street' has increasingly dealt in comedy and 'Crossroads' has always had strong affiliations with the overdrive of melodrama. 'Brookside' relies mainly on the youth of many of its characters, in combination with fairly regular celebrations and location work."[9]

According to Betsi Curdie, who regularly reviews *Coronation Street* in a publication called "Eye on the Street" (circulated to over 2,000 readers throughout the world), a love affair with British soaps can last nearly a lifetime. Through several ongoing e-mail "chats" with me in April 1997, she described the enduring charisma of *CS,* as well as one of Britain's other popular soaps, *EastEnders.* The following excerpt from one of our "conversations" addresses both international distribution and the possible social effects of Europe's oldest running dramas:

> "Coronation Street" is shown in Canada, six weeks after it has been shown in the UK. Granada, the owners of "Coronation Street" in the UK, require that when the program is aired outside the UK, each episode must be shown at least 30 days later than when it is shown in the UK. As well, the CBC is sent the tape and must convert it to [a] North American format. It is shown 4 times a week in Canada, during the daytime; or you can tune in on the weekend and watch what is called the "omnibus." The omnibus is the collection of the week's episodes. Two hours viewing in total on Sundays.
>
> One of the largest "differences" I have found when comparing UK soaps to American ones, is that they are viewed as two different types of entertainment in their respective countries. In America, "soaps" are generally shown during the day and appeal to a very specific audience. "Coronation Street" and "EastEnders" are both considered prime-time viewing in the UK, and occupy a time slot accordingly. Both are seen after the evening meal in the UK.
>
> The other difference that would come to mind is the distinct lack of "glitz and glamour" which permeates the U.S. evening offerings ("Melrose Place," "Dallas," "Dynasty"). On "Coronation Street" and "EastEnders," people have "just enough." They "exist" in some cases ... on "EastEnders" ... hand to mouth. "Coronation Street" takes place in a fictional northern English town—typical of a burrough outside of Manchester. "EastEnders" takes place in the east end of London, proper.
>
> I am trying to think of one character on either of the programs that would be held to such "star status" as they are in the U.S. and I can think of none. Not one character is "above average" in looks—there was an aggressive effort on behalf of the producers to choose characters that we would see at any time, in any place in Britain. It was the story that held us rapt—and not the clothing or figures.... In the case of "Coronation Street," the producers say, "It's the Street that's the star."
>
> With all of this, the producers could not help but have storylines reflect real life. And it can be quite gritty. "EastEnders" has a different quality to its product. There is a "dangerous edge" to the tone of the program. It is noisy and full of life, sometimes void of colour—keeping greys, browns, deep greens prominent on sets. It also introduces multicultural characters—a direct reflection on the locale. In one case there was a storyline which reflected an East Indian family and an arranged wedding. It was a fascinating look into another culture—thoroughly enjoyable and non-threatening for viewers. A worthy storyline as it glimpsed into another culture that some of us had never seen before. Its impact was a quiet one, but strong.
>
> "EE"'s audience would seem to be young (under 40) and without a class base. "Coronation Street," on the other hand, is lighter, funnier and less "gritty" than "EE." The dynamics of a "Coronation Street" audience is as diverse as any population. Everyone has seen it at least once. Everyone's auntie or cousin or mother is an avid watcher. Everyone seems to know what is going on—regardless of if they watch or not. It is a gentler storyline—one suitable to all aunties and cousins and mothers. It is a more

colourful product. This coupled with the clever use of names, which can reflect the characters before you meet them, make for "must watch" television. Examples include: Mavis and Derrick Wilton, Vera and Jack Duckworth, Sally and Kevin Webster—each name conjurs up an image befitting that character.

Most recently, after a drop in the ratings, "Coronation Street" has hired a new producer to bring the program back to #1 status. It has been an interesting transition. A negligible effort was made to "americanize" the program, offering more radical storylines—one of which was to let a 20-year vet out of his contract. He "died" this week of a heart attack after an encounter with an irate driver on a highway, but only after a great hue and cry from fans. There has [also] been the introduction of a shark-suited mafia type, and other attempts at rattling cages. Remember that these storylines collide with "leaving on the hair colour too long" and "an outing to an up-scale restaurant" for two 60+ year olds. It sometimes works and it sometimes doesn't.

As for the program's effect on its audience—I have never in my life encountered fans of a product like "Coronation Street." They [the viewers] run the gamut from professors in Georgia to swim instructors in Adelaide. They are researchers, secretaries, famous and not-so-famous, gay, hetero, quiet and loud. They defend the program as though it were a child. In Canada, if the program is pre-empted, the CBC switchboard lights up with complaints. It is a wonderful group. I don't know how this transpired—but I myself find myself feeling ill, if I turn on the VCR and see a Toronto Bluejays game instead of "CS."

It is comfortable. And there is a wonderful moment in the credits at the beginning, between the cobbles and the cats, the rain hitting the cars and the rattling of the milk bottles, where you wonder what will happen to your friends this week.[10]

In the early 1990s producers of some British soap operas began to explore the possibilities of co-production or consulting in other countries, notably Russia. (More details on this venture are described later in this chapter.) Prior to this move soap operas from the United Kingdom had limited their distribution (and production expertise) to those countries with English as their first language. Because of their success in this area, other ventures have been made in non-English-speaking television markets. In January 1996, for example, *Coronation Street*, *London's Burning*, and *Emmerdale* expanded their horizons to include Swedish-speaking audiences, running episodes of each at least once a week (sometimes as much as five times every week)[11] on Sveriges Television—Sweden's main TV channel.[12] STV's decision to air the soaps was based in part on its prior success in 1992 with another British soap, *Eldorado*, on BSkyB Satellite Television.[13] Perhaps this "event" will become a trend in other parts of the world, given BSkyB's growing interest in the Pacific Rim (which, to date, reaches more than 350,000 Asian households).[14] If not, however, British soaps are still here to stay, at least in the English-speaking world.

Focus: Ireland

Currently, Irish viewers are able to choose between three national networks—RTE 1, Network 2 and TnaG—for indigenous programming. In addition, most city dwellers subscribe to cable, which affords them greater choices in shows from England, France, Germany, Italy, Spain and the United States. In short, a soap opera fan in Ireland has access to most of the serial drama available in the Western world.

As for domestic soap production, RTE (Radio Telefis Eireann) seems to lead the effort with two dramas: *Glenroe* and *Fair City*. *Glenroe*, set in rural Ireland, airs weekly during primetime, and claims an average audience of 1.3 million. *Fair City*, taking place in Dublin, has a smaller following (about 900,000 each week) but still enjoys a primetime slot and, according to Dermot Horan, RTE head of programme acquisitions, great popularity both at home and abroad.[15] *Glenroe* is now seen in Australia, as well as throughout the United Kingdom; *Fair City* airs in only the United Kingdom at present but may expand its borders in the near future.

For imported soap opera fare, the Irish are most partial to *Home and Away* (Australia), *A County Practice* (Australia), *The Sullivans* (Australia), *Coronation Street* (United Kingdom), *Emmerdale* (United Kingdom) and *Take the High Road* (Scotland)—all aired on RTE. Other channels (on satellite and cable) provide favorites like *The Bold and the Beautiful*, *Santa Barbara*, and *Days of Our Lives* (United States); and *Lindenstrasse* and *Marienhof* (Germany).

Focus: The Netherlands

Like the Irish, Dutch viewers get much of their TV entertainment through cross-border broadcasts from neighboring countries or via satellite/cable. Domestic production budgets in the Netherlands are much smaller than in larger countries, and the ability to export programming is not as great. Thus, it came as quite a surprise in 1990 when *Goede Tijden, Slechte Tijden* (*Good Times, Bad Times*)—the first Dutch-language soap opera—premiered on satellite channel RTL-4. More surprisingly, two years later the serial drama was so popular (capturing a 15 share on average) its time slot was changed to challenge a competitor's top-rated news program.[16] In 1997 the soap continued to broadcast to loyal Dutch viewers.

Goede Tijden, Slechte Tijden exemplifies one of the most notable characteristics of Dutch programming: foreign hits that have been reconstituted for local production. In this case the model for adaptation was the Australian soap *The Restless Years*, produced by Grundy (of *Neighbours* and *Prisoner of Cell Block H* fame). And the conversion between cultures became even more complete when Grundy Worldwide organization agreed to co-produce *Goede Tijden,*

Slechte Tijden with Dutch JE Entertainment. According to *Variety* reporter Chris Fuller, some changes were easier to make than others, and some were not even considered:

> Like "Neighbours" in the UK, the sudser is broadcast twice daily, five days a week, to a fanatical viewership. Over 200 episodes a year are shot at JE's Aalsmeer studios, using a team of Dutch writers. Producer Olga Madsen says she tries to stick as closely as possible to the format of "Restless Years," but there are problems. "Characters popular in the original won't necessarily be popular here," she says. "The Australian milk-bar has been replaced by the traditional Dutch cafe," she adds. "And cliffside scenes have to be changed—the Netherlands is flat!"[17]

After its successful performance record with Dutch audiences, *Goede Tijden, Slechte Tijden* was reconfigured once again, this time for German audiences. Retitled *Gute Zeiten, Schlechte Zeiten*, the soap has paralleled its "sister" soap's popularity on VOX (a European satellite channel), where it consistently draws impressive ratings.

With accomplishments such as *Goede Tijden, Slechte Tijden*, soap operas adapted for audiences in the Netherlands are now commonplace. JE Entertainment leads its peers in this area with Dutch versions of *Coronation Street* and *The Bill*. The Dutch public channel, VARA, has also produced *Het Oude Noorden* (*The Old North*), an adaptation of the BBC's *EastEnders*. And as the European Union continues to bring about social and economic consolidation, the need for a unique cultural identity will no doubt create even more demand for local drama production (either original or adapted from another source). John de Mol production executive Monica Galer explains it best: "You may be able to choose among 20 channels, but those you'll tune into most often will be those in your own language."[18] And, because language is the key factor in constructing a worldview, the cultural landscape of the Netherlands will still be uniquely Dutch if the "natives" have anything to say about it.

Focus: Spain

In Spain telenovelas and game shows are known to be perennial ratings winners. Soccer (especially during the World Cup games) may occasionally take center stage[19] but only if it provides the high drama found in the rest of Spanish television life.

For several decades Spain has produced, distributed and imported hundreds of serial dramas, usually in joint ventureship with stations and production companies in Latin America. Unlike most viewers in other parts of Europe, Spanish audiences are not very impressed with American, British or Australian soaps, preferring instead Spanish-language melodramas like Venezuela's *La Dama de Rosa* and *Cristal*. Although language is clearly the primary reason for this preference, familiarity with similar cultural backgrounds is also a significant factor. In 1997, for example, the most popular novelas aired in Spain included imports from countries sharing Castillian history and heritage: *Abigail* (Venezuela, 1988); *Agujetas de Color de Rosa* (Mexico, 1994); *Café con Aroma de Mujer* (Colombia, 1994); *Kassandra* (Venezuela, no date known), *María Mercedes* (Mexico, 1992); *Milagros* (Argentina, 1993); and *Peligrosa* (Venezuela, no date known).[20] *El Super*, produced in Spain (1996) along with other domestic novelas (e.g., *Dejate Querer, El Desprecio* and *Primer Amor*[21]) has been equally well received on the other side of the Atlantic—truly a shared cultural landscape.

The communal relationship between Spain and its former colonies—through TV drama—makes some logical sense. Ironically, however, although Spanish programming plays well in most former colonies, its shows—including telenovelas—find a much cooler reception in some areas closer to home. In Catalonia, for example, where provincial loyalties have long superseded the national identity, locally produced programming is dedicated to a more separatist agenda. The following three novelas aired on Catalonia's TV 3 in 1996. They show the pride, character and uniqueness of the Catalonian people:

Poblenou—With exteriors of post–Olympics Barcelona, this series was filmed in the city's traditionally working-class neighborhood, Poblenou, and its new, modern, upper-class extension, which grew up around the site for the Olympic city. The series' protagonists, a middle-aged couple with grown children, lead fairly dull, predictable lives until a winning lottery ticket upsets their routine existence sparking a whirlwind of unexpected events.

Secrets de Familia (*Family Secrets*)—After a 25-year absence, Narcis unexpectedly returns to his hometown and family. Why he returns—and why he left—nobody seems to know. But as the web of mystery slowly unravels, buried feelings, secrets and deceit surface, irrevocably changing the lives of all the characters in the series.

Nissaga de Poder (*Dynasty of Power*)—The third generation of the wealthy Montsolis dynasty, producers of the internationally renowned sparkling wine bearing the family name, live in a small town in the heart of Catalonia's wine-producing region. Intrigue, suspicion and cutthroat competition surround the lives of the members of the family and their relationships with others in the town. Beneath all this lies a secret that can't be confessed.

Within each of these story lines lies a cultural history of a people that might otherwise be minimized or, worse, ignored. Certainly, telenovelas are just a part of Catalonia's strategy to maintain its provincial identity, but the constant presence of TV programming of this type certainly complements the goal.

Focus: Sweden

Sweden is a great admirer of serial drama in Europe. Its major television network, Sveriges Television (SVT), produces a number of weekly soaps each year; other stations import foreign soaps (from Australia, Great Britain and the United States) as well. One of SVT's most highly prized serial dramas in the last several years has been *High Seas*, watched by nearly 25 percent of the Swedish population weekly, with more episodes than any other Swedish TV series.[22] *High Seas* has been described by its producers:

> ...rid[ing] the waves of love, business, betrayal, and intrigue. In the midst of it all: the M/S Freja, untiringly plying its Baltic Sea route between Sweden and Finland. Aboard: a colorful crew. Behind the scenes: the Dahlen family of owners. The fierce competition for passengers forces the Dahlens to use both honorable and less-than-honorable methods. This is business at the highest (and lowest) levels; this is deals and love affairs whose motives are not always what they may appear to be.[23]

Based on this description, *High Seas*, although Scandinavian in location, would most likely appeal to almost any soap opera viewer in any part of the world. However, global exports are not of great concern for Swedish televsion producers; cultivating and maintaining national identity is. Ingrid Dahlberg, head of SVT I Drama, voiced the network's (and the nation's) philosophy best when she raised questions (and gave answers) several years ago:

> It's 1995, and Sweden enters the great European community. Here and there, doomsayers issue black prophecies, as always at times of change. What's to become of things Swedish? Can the distinctively Swedish survive? In the world of television, these are familiar strains. The prophets of woe have enjoyed a feeding frenzy in recent years as satellites have filled the skies and audiences confront a growing smorgasbord of domestic and foreign programming. What's to become of things Swedish? Can the distinctively Swedish survive? At SVT I Drama, we know the pessimists are wrong. Of course, programs of Swedish quality and essence can survive the media tsunami washing over Europe. On the contrary, it's programs made to suit everything and everyone that will probably drown.[24]

Fearing cultural imperialism, Sweden (and most of Scandinavia) has long been recognized among the most rigidly homogeneous nations in the world. Until quite recently program importation has been highly monitored, and television has been seen as a contributor to the Swedish national identity, not as one of its detractors. Still, with external influences abounding Sweden has had to accept the ultimate reality of "other-cultural" intrusion but, apparently, not without some rules of its own. In 1996, for example, the United Kingdom announced plans to broadcast episodes of *Coronation Street* to Sweden. This was an historic occasion because it was the first time in *CS*'s history that the dialogue was to be dubbed in a language other than English. Sometimes, if you can't beat them, you must join them. But you can still declare the terms of the union.

Focus: Germany (Federal Republic)

In 1997, although Germany produced only three daily soaps—*Marienhof,
Verbotene Liebe*, and *Lindenstrasse*—its influence on the genre had been
felt strongly throughout Europe for at least ten years. *Lindenstrasse (Linden
Street)*, a joint production between WDR (one of Germany's 11 independent
broadcast stations) and Austria,[25] has aired for over a decade and remains
one of the continent's most popular shows. It's targeted to family audiences
(although WDR executive Dr. Ronald Grabe confesses that certain episodes
can be controversial, with explicit language and some "political incorrect-
ness").[26]

Mirroring the lives of many of its viewers, *Lindenstrasse* takes place in
a middle-class neighborhood in Munich, more specifically the house on 3 Lindenstrasse. Its characters and setting resemble British soaps (*Coronation Street,
Brookside* and *EastEnders*) much more closely than the airbrushed look found
in most American serials, making it particularly attractive to Europeans outside of Germany.

Although *Lindenstrasse* enjoys great popularity around the continent, it
probably will never travel much beyond its borders, unlike *Verbotene Liebe*
(*Forbidden Love*) and *Marienhof*, which reach millions of viewers throughout
Europe via broadcast, cable or satellite. As Dr. Grabe observes, "With soaps,
one can sell the format [as has been done for some of the German daily soaps
based on Australian formats] but hardly the complete series."[27]

Other countries have worked with the Federal Republic of Germany to
create their own domestic serial dramas, most notably Third World nations
in Asia and Africa, addressing serious social issues such as population control, spousal abuse, genital mutilation and the spread of AIDS (see chapters
six and seven). Within Europe Switzerland has teamed up with Germany for
several ventures, broadcasting such recent hits as *Fascht e Familie* (*Not Quite
a Family*), *Die Direktorin* (*The Directoress*) and *Tobias*. Even with a high
interest in serial drama, Josef Burri of SRG Corp. (Schweizerische Rundfunk
Gesellschaft) estimates that 90 percent of the total number of soap operas
aired in Switzerland are still imported—perhaps because of the multilingual
character of the nation. Other European countries have expressed similar
problems with language and dialect diversity as reasons for their limited
numbers of domestically produced soaps.[28]

Focus: Russia

As critic Kate Baldwin suggests in *To Be Continued...*, Russia's foray into
serial drama began as an economic strategy to broadcast inexpensive reruns
(between government proceedings) on its post–cold war stations. The first

program of this type was *Bogaty Tozhe Plachut* (the Russian translation of Mexico's *The Rich Also Cry*):

> In the fall of 1992 the show could be seen three times a week, twice a day—the evening show repeated the following morning.... Each episode was presented in the form of two segments of 20 minutes each, broken by a 5-minute commercial break. The opening 10 minutes of every episode replayed the prior day's closing 10 minutes, so that if you had missed the mounting tension of the last show's closing cuts, you would not be left behind: likewise, if you had been a faithful viewer, as most were, you could relive this accumulative frisson, an experience that made one all the more eager to relieve it.[29]

For the duration of its 249-episode run, *The Rich Also Cry* experienced the highest ratings ever on Russian television. After it ended the country mourned as if it had lost one of its greatest patriots.

Once having tasted the elements of serial drama, Russian viewers—across 11 time zones—demanded a steadier diet of "virtual" love, lust and libido from their television sets. Programmers, in turn, were more than willing to comply. They immediately began to import scores of novelas from Latin America and soaps from the United States, transmitting them either through local TV outlets or via satellite (Ostankino Kanal 1—OK-1, Russia). Some of the more memorable serial ventures, like Mexico's *Simplemente María* and Venezuela's *Dulce Enemiga* and *La Revancha*, encouraged overseas tourism and commercial partnerships.[30]

Because entertainment programming had previously been merely inserted between Russian parliamentary proceedings, broadcasters were not prepared for the conflict between soap operas and political dealings. In August 1993 the inevitable clash occurred, with the introduction of *Parliamentary Hour*, and the pre-emption of viewers' beloved *Santa Barbara*.

In a statement from the chairman of All-Russian State Television and Radio Broadcasting Company (and reported on the BBC World Service), the network took great umbrage at the arbitrary decision-making process:

> It is difficult to say what reasons motivated the people's representatives. It might be that they believe there is nothing more interesting than seeing their inspired faces etched with the worries of state and listening to endless talk about the perfidy and treachery of the executive structures of authority. Or it could be that the people's representatives have simply decided to become as well-loved and popular with the ordinary people as the heroes of the American soap. I do not want to talk about the legal side of this affair, but how does this decision by the parliamentarians correspond to the current law on the media? One other thing is very obvious. The interests of millions of Russians are being trampled upon to satisfy the political ambitions of a few dozen people's deputies.[31]

Although some may think these words brazen (especially coming from a television network executive), the man's opinion was highly supported by President

Boris Yeltsin—himself a huge soap opera/telenovela fan. The parliamentarians had met their match. And they had lost.

The 1993 skirmish abated soon after—with a victory to the viewers—and Russian TV programmers began to flood the airwaves with more soap operas and telenovelas than ever before. This year also marked the introduction of domestic soap opera production—first on radio, later on television.

In January 1993 radio network executives began contemplating the possibilities of producing (or co-producing) their own serial dramas.[32] Their first attempt, *Dom Syem, Podyezd 4*, was similar to a long-running British soap, *The Archers*—but with a distinctly Russian flavor. According to journalist Andrew Culf, "It [*Dom Syem*] is set on a tough city housing estate, and the programme's title, *House 7, Entrance 4*, refers to the bleak tower blocks in Moscow. It features the mafia, drinking of epidemic proportions, and a large dose of violence and bad language. It also has its equivalent of Eddie Grundy, a lovable, drunken plumber whose wife has left him for a handsome businessman.[33] Dom Syem was the result of cooperative efforts made through the BBC Marshall Plan of the Mind Trust, supported by Great Britain's Know How Fund for Russia. The primary goal of this project was to educate post-Soviet Russians about the realities of a market economy, private enterprise and entrepreneurial endeavors through entertainment, and based on the overwhelming response of audiences (almost three million devotees in the first six months), the project was deemed an immediate success.[34] Shortly after its initial release, the *Dom Syem* concept was expanded (and translated) to reach television viewers in the Ukraine, where serious issues in privatized agriculture abound. The major distinction in this type of programming, according to a former BBC World Service managing director, was the lack of "long, didactic speeches," focusing instead on the practical applications of democratization: "The audiences don't just want the success stories; they want to know what to do if things go wrong."[35] Through the venue of serial drama (as proven in other countries with education-entertainment programming), lessons are learned without a sharp, laconic edge. In 1997, for example, *Dom Syem* had an interesting visitor—British prime minister Tony Blair. Blair, while riding in his motorcade to a summit conference, stops to help one of the soap's major characters (Varya), after one of her shopping bags spills onto the street amidst all the confusion. According to Paul Mylrea's report in Reuters, the "chance" meeting is not without its message:

> The unemployed seamstress [Varya] then pours out her heart to him [Blair]—through an interpreter—about her problem. Blair sympathizes, telling her that he is a family man with three children and fully understands. Driving home his Labour party messages that education is the way to improve a country's prospects, Blair [tells] her: "In my country, we have said our priorities are education, education, education." But the seamstress does not recognise the British prime minister until she sees him on television meeting Russian President Boris Yeltsin in the following day's episode.[36]

For Russian TV programming executives, Blair's cameo appearance was good for ratings as well as reinforcing V. I. Lenin's prior educational mandates. For Blair and the British it was a quick means to get viewer recognition for future joint ventures and trade agreements.[37]

Today soap operas and telenovelas continue to top Russia's popularity charts, despite network attempts to provide more exciting news and information programming. In 1995, after returning to the former Soviet Union, for example, Aleksandr Solzhenitsyn was demoralized to learn that his biweekly talk show was watched by only 12 percent of the Russian audience, less than half the rating of *Wild Rose*, a Mexican telenovela.[38] Shortly afterward, it was announced that 220 episodes of *Dynasty* would air on Moscow Television (after MTV had successfully outbid Russian Public Television for the series). *Dallas* would soon follow.[39]

However, in a land with 11 time zones, numerous official languages and seemingly uncountable dialects, imported soap operas and telenovelas were bound to hit a pothole or two on the road to success. Ironically, the American soap *Santa Barbara* has created some interesting political dichotomies in post–cold war Russia. One can best be described in this excerpt from journalist Mary Mycio's special report to the *Los Angeles Times* in October 1995:

> Nina Kuzmichna used to tune out the travails of her real life—an existence on a $20-a-month pension—by tuning into the fantasy troubles of the young, rich and restless in the Russian-dubbed American soap opera "Santa Barbara." But anticipation turned to dismay for the 58-year-old Russian recently when she switched on her television set to find that the Capwell clan and the show's other characters suddenly had Ukrainian voices. "My heart fell," she said. "I didn't understand what was going on."
> ...Russian Television, which broadcasts Russian-dubbed "Santa Barbara" three nights a week from Moscow, was taken off the air in Ukraine in August [1995]; the Ukrainian state network, shedding its Soviet-style provincialism to fill the entertainment vacuum, inaugurated the popular show last month in Ukrainian. But here on Ukraine's Crimean Peninsula, once part of Russia and still dominated by ethnic Russians, local Crimean Television fought back by stealing Russian Television's "Santa Barbara" signal.
> The result is a language war with high ratings. As Kuzmichna and other viewers struggle to follow the saga of Eden, Cain's beautiful hostage, political analysts are viewing it as a new episode in Crimea's troubles with the Ukrainian government in Kiev.
> "What language the show is in will tell you who is making political concessions," said Dominique Saudan, chief of the Organization for Security and Cooperation in Europe's mission to Crimea.
> ...When "Santa Barbara" ... switched to Ukrainian, Crimeans drew the line. Demonstrators marched to Crimea's Parliament building, denouncing what they called linguistic imperialism. "Our phone rang off the hook with complaints when it happened," said Galina Shcherbak, a Crimean Television official. The Parliament's deputy chairman, Vladimir Podkopayev, said Crimea was facing "a state of emergency."

...Lena Glushkova was asked about the beloved California soap's new dubbing as she sipped peach-flavored vodka at the train station in Simferopol, Crimea's capital. "I hate that nationalist language!" she exclaimed. "I hate it!"[40]

But as Boris Yeltsin discovered in 1996, characters on *Santa Barbara* can also be close allies in political elections. As an attempt to thwart the Communist Party candidate in the June 16th presidential election, Yeltsin backers released 10 million copies of a newspaper entitled, "God Forbid!" Its front-page cover model was none other than American actress Stacy Edwards ("Holly" of *Santa Barbara* fame), allegedly saying, "Holly from 'Santa Barbara' is sure that her city would never vote for Communists."[41] Edwards's comments continued on page three of the paper, with an interview that included this plea: "June 20 is my wedding day. Do you know what could be the best present from Russia? [For] your president to be reelected and Communists defeated ... and in a few years Russia will be a happy country."[42] Edwards's manager later declared that the actress neither made those remarks nor supported President Yeltsin. No matter. They served their purpose as part of his successful campaign to retain office.

Another part of Yeltsin's 1996 campaign to remain president was also traced to serial drama—this time, courtesy of ORT (which some claim to be his "personal channel").[43] Allegedly, to influence voters ORT aired a three-part special edition of *Tropicalmiente/Secret of Tropicana*, a popular Brazilian telenovela, hoping to transfer its inevitably happy ending to polling stations later in the day ... or maybe discouraging citizens from voting at all. As odd as it may seem, there is precedent for such a move, as noted by the *Guardian's* Hilary Kingsley:

> Harold Wilson manipulated television schedules to affect the voting process. He persuaded the BBC's chief Sir Hugh Greene to postpone an episode of "Steptoe and Son" on election day 1964 until the polls had closed. He reckoned that the mass audience show would, if screened in its 8 o'clock slot, keep some voters from budging from their armchairs for the rest of the evening. Sir Hugh obliged, Labour won by four seats and Wilson reckoned that the later screening might have been worth 12 seats.... Wilson went on to embrace the stars of popular culture, welcoming The Beatles to No. 10 and giving a sherry party there for the cast of "Coronation Street" to show what a man of the people he was.
> ...Jim Callaghan followed Harold Wilson's example. He stated publicly that "Coronation Street's" Pat Phoenix was the sexiest woman on TV, which may not have been true but which did Jolly Jim no harm at all. Neil Kinnock never won an election: it may be significant that his only pronouncement on soap was about "The Archers." He couldn't stand that Elizabeth Archer and he thought that the show should be re-titled "The Grundys and Their Oppressors."
> ...If history decides that a Brazilian television saga did keep a Communist out of the Russian presidency, Yeltsin may choose to honour the show's stars with medals. Heroes of the Non-Soviet Union, perhaps.[44]

Politics aside, soap operas and telenovelas continue to proliferate within Russia. [45] And in January 1997 the nation's first soap export premiered—a 250-episode comedy, titled *The Little Strawberry*. The drama centers on six main characters who "never leave the bar, terrace or kitchen of a pub named Little Strawberry."[46] Journalist Uli Schmetzer captured the excitement surrounding the historic endeavor:

> The soap opera makers, a private company called Goldvideo, have occupied Moskfilm's Studio Four for several months to make the first 70 installments and have drawn heavily on Moskfilm files. Pasted on pieces of brown carton slabs are 8,000 photos of people eager to be extras. Their personal data is written in ink. All is stored under such labels as "thin men," "tall men," "old women," "young women" or "unforgettable faces." Doctors, academicians, engineers, designers, professors and students are the most numerous applicants for a day job that earns between $10 and $20, depending on whether it is a crowd scene or a small speaking role. "Some do it because they are lonely. Singles come to find company, and others come to take photos of themselves with famous actors to bask in their reflected glory. Most do it for the money," said Tatiana Abrikosova, keeper of Moskfilm's ancient and extensive archives.[47]

Based on the initial audience reaction to *The Little Strawberry*, there can be little doubt that future Russian soaps will follow, perhaps finding programming time—and ratings popularity—in North and South America, Asia, Africa and the Pacific. For now, hundreds of underpaid Moscovite academics and intellectuals are happy merely to supplement their incomes as extras in the Little Strawberry bar—not unlike in 1980s America, in a tiny Boston bar where "everybody knows your name."

Focus: Poland

Like many of their former Soviet satellite neighbors after the end of the cold war, Polish TV programmers were ill equipped to address viewer needs and desires right away. Summarizing their major problems, a 1992 *Los Angeles Times* article offered this analysis:

> Television was a major propaganda tool during the Communist era, and neophyte democrats are finding it hard to relinquish their monopoly control. Low budgets mean lots of locally produced political shows with long interviews and dull commentary. But store-bought and homemade dish antennas are spreading, as are cable systems, enriching the fare with imported entertainment.[48]

Five years later in 1997, Polish television had finally begun to realize its potential. Today Telewizja Polska S.A. is the largest (and only) national public broadcaster in Poland, providing viewers with two channels (TVP1 and TVP2), a satellite network (TV Polonia) and 12 regional affiliates.[49] TV Polonia is especially popular, broadcasting 24 hours a day, seven days a week, and covering Europe, Israel, North Africa, Kazakhstan and North America.

Finding enough material for these outlets has been a major task, and as noted above, some of the final products have not been very successful. However, through perseverence and several deals, like its 1997 agreement with Warner Bros., Telewizja Polska has finally begun to run a healthy and prosperous network. The Warner Bros. contract was one of the largest of its kind, including 1994–1995 feature films, 1997–1998 new TV series and program renewals for more "established" series produced at Warner (like *Suddenly Susan, Murphy Brown*, and *Sisters*). Further, the agreement allowed for broadcast rights to the 1998 Goodwill Games, HBO Boxing events and an epic 24-episode cold war documentary.[50] Telewizja Polska's vice president Janusz Daszcsynski was ecstatic about the contract:

> We are the biggest, the most important public broadcasters in Poland and only the most powerful organizations can sign such an output deal as the one we just concluded with Warner Bros. We are very proud of the long partnership we have had between our companies, and consider Warner Bros. as the provider of the best quality film, series and animation. There is no doubt that this deal is absolutely unique, and the beginning of a new strategic era of TVP S.A.[51]

But Polish TV is not only thriving because of its programming imports. Viewers are becoming much more interested in local shows, including its first indigenous soap opera *Clan*.[52] In 1997 TVP S.A. decided the time was right for serial drama with a Polish emphasis. According to *New York Times* reporter Jane Perlez, the process was by no means simple: "The station ran a contest and invited producers to make three pilot shows. The pilots were then shown to focus groups composed of a cross section of Polish television audiences."[53] The winner, Pawel Karpinski's *Clan*, captured the hearts of the focus groups because of their fascination with how the characters dealt with the new, capitalistic way of life.

Ironically, some of the other soap contenders, which emphasized political corruption and bribery, were not as popular with the viewers. Karpinski surmises that the Poles, tired of stories of government scandal, wanted something new and different: "We speak about love, careers, hate, money, business. But no politics.... In the 1990s, there have been huge opportunities to make money for those who were predisposed to do so. But this created the problems of fraud, bankruptcy. Money can make people crazy."[54] Added to the backdrop of a traditional Polish family—70-year-old Maria and Wladyslia Lubicz, their five children (with spouses) and grandchildren—the serial has captured viewers' imaginations. And why not? With questions such as, "Should Pawel, a surgeon at a public hospital, switch jobs and make money doing plastic surgery at a private clinic?" and "What about the ethics of Jerzy, a shady businessman, who pulled his son out of amateur sports and sold him to a professional soccer team?," audiences clamor to see each episode. Polish producers have learned a great deal within a short period. There is no doubt that *Clan* will have more indigenous competition before very long. And given their state-of-the art satellite technology, Polish serial exports may also loom on the not-too-distant horizon. As Rudolf Huber, a highly respected expert on Eastern European media, observes, "We'll probably see a flood of affordable priced soap operas, novelas and even sitcoms from the CEE region over the next few years. If Mexican soap operas can be a big hit in Poland, why can't Polish soap operas be a big hit in Mexico?"[55]

Notes

1. Station/network information taken from *World Radio TV Handbook, 1997 Edition*, ed. Andrew G. Sennitt (New York: Billboard Books, 1997). Television/radio set information and population figures taken from *The World Almanac and Book of Facts 1997* (Mahwah, NJ: K-III Reference Corporation, 1996).

2. This listing is compiled from *WRTH Satellite & TV Handbook, Fourth Edition*, ed. Andrew G. Sennitt (New York: Billboard Books, 1997). It represents the *available* stations on satellite dishes through a transponder in Region I of the world satellite map. Although it is difficult to tell how many people have access to these channels, it is important to acknowledge the variety of cross-national program content on them.

3. Jeremy Coopman, "High Hopes for Soaps as Europe Lathers Up," *Variety* (July 22, 1991), 1.

4. *Ibid.*, 76.

5. *The People* (November 5, 1995) [database on-line]; available from Lexis-Nexis.

6. Charlotte Brunsdon, *Screen Tastes: Soap Opera to Satellite Dishes* (London: Routledge, 1997), 25.

7. Only recently (1996) has the U.K. considered dubbing its soaps in other languages.

8. The British soaps are aired primarily on satellite or pay-TV channels in Europe, which limits viewership substantially in those countries.

9. Brunsdon, 25.

10. Private e-mail messages from Betsi Curdie, April 1997.

11. Because of its popularity in other countries, *Coronation Street* was contracted to air five days a week.

12. "Swedes Taste the Street," *Daily Mail* (January 4, 1996), 11 [database on-line]; available from Lexis-Nexis.

13. Despite extremely negative reviews in England, *Eldorado* seemed to fare better in overseas markets than at home.

14. Jonathan Miller, "Behind the Screen," *Sunday Times* (August 9, 1992) [database on-line]; available from Lexis-Nexis.

15. Written correspondence with Dermot Horan, Head of Programme Acquisitions, RTE (July 1996).

16. Chris Fuller, "Dutch Carve Soaps for Local Consumption," *Variety* (October 26, 1992), 48.

17. *Ibid.*
18. Quoted in Chris Fuller, "Dutch Carve Soaps for Local Consumption."
19. Michael Williams, "Soccer Match Scores Big for Spanish Pubcaster," *Variety* (June 7, 1992), 41.
20. Telenovela Web site.
21. *Ibid.*
22. Sveriges Television Handbook (Stockholm: 1995). Many thanks to Eva Bergquist, Co-Productions and International Affairs, SVT I, Stockholm, Sweden, for her helpful correspondence and publicity materials.
23. SVT-I Programming Publicity Handout (Stockholm: 1995).
24. *Ibid.*
25. WDR is a part of the greater ARD (Arbeitsgemeinschaft der offentlich-rechtlichen Rundfunkanstalten der Bundesrepublik Deutschland), a group of public broadcasting corporations in the Federal Republic of Germany. The 11 member stations contribute—among other radio and television stations—to the EDF (or First German Programme). This information was provided by Silvia Maric, ARD-Das Erste (written correspondence, July 1996).
26. Written correspondence with Dr. Ronald Grabe, Westdeutscher Rundfunk Koln (WDR) (July 1996).
27. *Ibid.*
28. Written correspondence with Josef Burri, head of series, SRG (Schweizerische Rundfunk Gesellschaft) (August 1996). Another example is Spain, where specific provinces such as Catalonia would prefer their own language and cultural expression. Even countries with shared languages can also reject export programming, however, because of the myopic views from the home culture. For example, one of Spain's biggest soap hits in 1995 was "The Duty Chemist." But although producers negotiated with TV companies in Brazil, Colombia, Venezuela and Miami, stations were reluctant to air the show "because the humour [was] markedly Spanish." (*The People*, op. cit.).
29. Kate Baldwin, "Montezuma's Revenge: Reading *Los Ricos También Lloran* in Russia," in *To Be Continued... Soap Operas Around the World*, ed. Robert C. Allen (London: Routledge, 1995), 285–286.
30. Kim Palchikoff, "Town In a Lather Over Latin Soaps," *Moscow Times* (December 4, 1996) [database on-line]; available from Lexis-Nexis.
31. "Headline Russia: Ministry Attacks Move to Broadcast Parliament Programme at Time of US Soap Opera," BBC Summary of World Broadcasts (August 17, 1993) [database on-line]; available from Lexis-Nexis.
32. "Oh Ahrr, Tovarich," The Press Association Limited (December 4, 1994) [database on-line]; available from Lexis-Nexis.
33. Andew Culf, "Soft Soap Gives Lead to Russia's Everyday Tale of Life with the Moscow Mafia," *Guardian* (May 7, 1994), 10 [database on-line]; available from Lexis-Nexis.
34. Colin Campbell, "Royal Soap Star," *The Times* (October 25, 1994) [database on-line]; available from Lexis-Nexis.
35. Michael Binyon, "BBC's Soap Opera Gets Russia into Free-Market Lather," *Times* (August 4, 1994) [database on-line]; available from Lexis-Nexis.
36. Paul Mylrea, "UK's Blair to Star in Russian Radio Soap," Reuters (October 5, 1997) [database on-line].
37. Gareth Jones, "Education Is What Counts, UK's Blair Tells Russians," Reuters (October 7, 1997) [database on-line].
38. Alessandra Stanley, "A 20th Century Prophet Joins Media Revolution; Exile

Hero Finds New Role Back Home: Solzhenitsyn Shines as Talk Show Host," *International Herald Tribune* (April 15, 1995) [database on-line]; available from Lexis-Nexis. *Wild Rose* received a 26.6 rating.

39. Ellen Barry, "A New Dynasty Begins in Russia," *Moscow Times* (August 11, 1995) [database on-line]; available from Lexis-Nexis.

40. Mary Mycio, "The Great Soap Wars of 1995; Television: Ethnic Russians in Ukraine Protest When Characters on Their Beloved 'Santa Barbara' Begin Speaking Ukrainian," *Los Angeles Times* (October 9, 1995) [database on-line]; available from Lexis-Nexis.

41. David Hoffman, "A Communist Win? 'God Forbid!' in Russia," *Washington Post* (April 30, 1996), A08 [database on-line]; available from Lexis-Nexis.

42. *Ibid.*

43. Hilary Kingsley, "Strange But True; If Boris Yeltsin Wins the Russian Presidential Election, Will History Credit His Victory to the Rescheduling of a Television Soap Opera?" *Guardian* (July 4, 1996), T12 [database on-line]; available from Lexis-Nexis.

44. *Ibid.*

45. According to Yolette Nicholson's Telenovela Web site, the following novelas were aired in Russia in 1997: *Milagros* (Argentina, 1993), *Guadalupe* (USA, Telemundo, 1994), *Abuelo y Yo* (Mexico, 1992), *Dejate Querer* (Spain/Argentina, no date known), *El Árbol Azul* (Argentina, 1991) and *Tu o Nadie* (Mexico, 1985). Ms. Nicholson revised this page July 23, 1997 [database on-line].

46. Uli Schmetzer, "Set of Russian TV Show Is a Soap Opera in Itself," *Chicago Tribune* (December 26, 1996), 24 [database on-line]; available from Lexis-Nexis.

47. *Ibid.*

48. "Tuning in the Global Village: What They'll Be Watching This Week," *Los Angeles Times* (October 22, 1992), 6 [database on-line]; available from Lexis-Nexis.

49. "Warner Bros. International Television Distribution Signs Its Largest Deal Ever in Poland with Telewizja Polska S.A.," Warner Bros. press release (April 24, 1997) [database on-line].

50. *Ibid.*

51. *Ibid.*

52. Some soap opera aficionados would challenge *Clan*'s claim to being the first "homegrown" serial drama. In 1989, for example, the *Los Angeles Times* reported a "first" Polish soap opera, called *Labyrinth*. The story centered on the lives of three families who worked in a laboratory. However, this serial was produced on a much smaller scale, and did not last very long.

53. Jane Perlez, "Normal Soap Opera Formula in U.S. Is Groundbreaking in Poland," a syndicated article in the *Detroit Free Press* (October 21, 1997), 5A and 6A.

54. *Ibid.*, 6.

55. Terry Swartzberg, "Players' Perilous Paradise in Central and Eastern Europe," *Video Age* (March 13, 1996), 46 [database on-line]; available from Lexis-Nexis.

Asia

Countries included:

Bangladesh, British Indian Ocean Territory, Brunei Darussalam, Cambodia, China (People's Republic of), China (Republic of) [Taiwan], Hong Kong, India, Indonesia, Japan, Kazakhstan, Korea (Republic), Korea (Democratic People's Republic of), Kyrgyzstan, Laos (People's Democratic Republic of), Macau, Malaysia (Federation of), Maldives (Republic of), Mongolia, Myanmar (Union of) [Burma], Nepal, Pakistan, Philippines (Republic of the), Singapore, Sri Lanka, Tajikstan, Thailand, Uzbekistan, Vietnam[1]

Stations/Networks:

Bangladesh
Population: 125,340,261—2,200 per sq. mi.
(TV sets—1:172 persons; radios—1:21 persons)
National Broadcasting Authority
Bangladesh Television

British Indian Ocean Territory
Population: n/a (see United Kingdom)
(TV sets—n/a; radios—n/a)
AF Diego Garcia Television (AFRTS)

Brunei Darussalam
Population: 307,616—138 per sq. mi.
(TV sets—1:4.1 persons; radios—1:3.7 persons)
Radio Television Brunei (RTB)

Cambodia
Population: 11,163,861—159 per sq. mi.
(TV sets—1:125 persons; radios—1:9.3 persons)
Cambodian Television
International Broadcasting Corp. Ltd. (IBC)

China (People's Republic of)
Population: 1,210,004,956—327 per sq. mi.
(TV sets—1:5.3 persons; radios—1:5.4 persons)
China Central Television (CCTV)
Oriental TV

China (Republic of) [Taiwan]
Population: 21,655,515—1,550 per sq. mi.
(TV sets—1:3 persons; radios—1:2.5 persons)

119

China Television Company
Chinese TV System
Taiwan Television Enterprise

Georgia

Population: 5,219,810—195 per sq. mi.
(TV sets—n/a; radios—n/a)

Hong Kong

Population: n/a (see People's Rep. of
China)
(TV sets—n/a; radios—n/a)
Radio Television Hong Kong

India

Population: 967,612,804—792 per sq.
mi.
(TV sets—1:25 persons; radios—1:12
persons)
Doordarshan India

Indonesia

Population: 209,774,138—283 per sq.
mi.
(TV sets—1:16 persons; radios—1:6.8
persons)
ANTEVE (PT Cakrawala Andalas
Televisi)
IVM (PT. Indosiar Visual Mandiri)
PT Rajawali Citra Televisi Indonesia
(RCTI)
SCTV (PT Surya Citra Televisi)
Televisi Republik Indonesia (TVRI)
TPI (PT Cipta Televisi Pendidikan
Indonesia)

Japan

Population: 125,716,637—861 per sq. mi.
(TV sets—1:1.5 persons; radios—1:1.1
persons)
Nippon Hosa Kyokay (Japan Broadcasting Corp.)
The National Association of Commercial Broadcasters in Japan

Kazakhstan

Population: 16,898,572—16 per sq. mi.

(TV sets (n/a); radios—1:2.7 persons)
Kazakh Television

Korea (Republic of)

Population: 45,948,811—1,197 per sq.
mi.
(TV sets—1:3.1 persons; radios—1:1
persons)
Education Broadcasting System
Korean Broadcasting System (KBS-TV)
Munhwa Broadcasting Coporation
Seoul Broadcasting Systems
American Forces Korea Network
(Satellite)

Korea (Democratic People's
Republic of)

Population: 24,317,004—513 per sq. mi.
(TV sets—1:23 persons; radios—1:7.9
persons)
Kaesung Television
Mansudae Television
The Radio & Television Broadcasting
Committee of the Democratic Peo-
ples Republic of Korea (KRT)

Kyrgyzstan

Population: 4,540,185—59 per sq. mi.
(TV sets—n/a; radios—n/a)
Kyrgyz Television

Laos (People's Democratic Repu-
blic of)

Population: 5,116,959—55 per sq. mi.
(TV sets—1:119 persons; radios—1:7.9
persons)
Lao National Radio and Television

Macau

Population: n/a (see Portugal)
(TV sets—n/a; radios—n/a)
Teledifusáo de Macau (TDM SARL)

Malaysia (Federation of)

Population: 20,376,235—159 per sq.
mi.

(TV sets—1:6.4 persons; radios—1:2.3 persons)
Radio Television Malaysia

Maldives (Republic of)

Population: 280,391—2,438 per sq. mi.
(TV sets—1:40 persons; radios—1:8.5 persons)
Television Maldives

Mongolia

Population: 2,538,211—4 per sq. mi.
(TV sets—1:24 persons; radios—1:7.4 persons)
Mongol Radio and Television (MRTV)

Myanmar (Union of) [Burma]

Population: 46,821,943—179 per sq. mi.
(TV sets—1:200 persons; radios—1:12 persons)
TV Myanmar

Nepal

Population: 22,641,061—389 per sq. mi.
(TV sets—1:213 persons; radios—1:29 persons)
Nepal Television Corporation (NTV)

Pakistan

Population: 132,185,299—389 per sq. mi.
(TV sets—1:53 persons; radios—1:11 persons)
Pakistan Television Corporation

Philippines (Republic of the)

Population: 76,103,564—656 per sq. mi.
(TV sets—1:2.1 persons; radios—1:6.9 persons)
ABC (Associated Broadcasting Corporation)
ABS/CBN Broadcast Center
IBC (channel 13)
People's Television Network (PTNI)
Radio Philippines (ch 9)
Republic Broadcasting System (ch 7)

Singapore

Population: 3,461,929—13,847 per sq. mi.
(TV sets—1:2.6 persons; radios—1:1.6 persons)
Television Corporation Singapore
Television Twelve (TV-12)
Singapore Cablevision

Sri Lanka

Population: 18,762,075—740 per sq. mi.
(TV sets—1:20 persons; radios—1:5 persons)
Independent Television Network
MTV Channel Ltd.
Sri Lanka Rupavahini (TV) Corporation
Teleshan Network Pvt Ltd. (TNL-TV)

Tajikstan

Population: 6,013,855—108 per sq. mi.
(TV sets—n/a; radios—1:6.7 persons)
Tajik Television

Thailand

Population: 59,450,818—300 per sq. mi.
(TV sets—1:8.5 persons; radios—1:5.3 persons)
Bangkok Entertainment Co. Ltd. (ch 3)
BBTV (Bangkok Broadcasting and Television Company, ch 7)
Mass Communications Organization of Thailand (ch 9)
The Army Television HSA-TV

Uzbekistan

Population: 23,860,452—136 per sq. mi.
(TV sets—1:5.3 persons; radios—1:12 persons)
Uzbek Television

Vietnam

Population: 75,123,880—587 per sq. mi.
(TV sets—1:23 persons; radio—1:9.6 persons)
Television Vietnam

Satellite Channels Available in This Region[2]

ABC Australia
ABC HACBSS (Australia)
ABC-TV HACBSS (Australia)
ABC-TV (interchange) (Australia)
ABS-CBN Philippines
ABS/CBN (AUS/CHN)
AFRTS (USA)
AN-TEVE (Indonesia)
Army TV (ch. 5) (Thailand)
ART (Russia)
Asahi New Star (Japan)
Asia Business News (China/USA)
Asia Business TV (Japan)
Asia TV Network (India)
Asianet (India)
ATVI Australia
Azerbaijan Radio TV
BBC Asia (UK)
BBC Asia (Mandarin) (UK)
BBC World Service TV
(USA/Japan/UK)
BBC WSTV (UK)
BGV Channel (Japan)
Bloomberg Info. TV (Japan)
Business News Network (Japan)
Cable Soft Netw. (Japan)
Cable TV Access Channel (Japan)
Canal France Int.
Car Information TV (Japan)
CBHS Hour (China)
CCTV-4 (China)
CETV Shandong (China)
Channel 3 (Thailand)
Channel 7 (Australia)
Channel 7 (Thailand)
Channel 9 (Australia)
Channel 9 (Thailand)
Channel 11 (Thailand)
Channel KTV (China)
China Central TV 1/2/4
China Educational TV 1/2
China Entertainment TV
Chinese Channel (Hong Kong)
Chinese Channel (Mandarin) (Hong
    Kong)
Chinese Satellite TV (CSTV)

Chinese TV Network (China/USA)
China Central TV 1/2
Cinefil Imagica (Japan)
CNBC Asia (USA)
CNN Int. (USA)
Community TV (India)
Country Music TV (USA)
CSTV Music Channel (China)
CSTV News Channel (China)
Dai Truyen Hinh (Vietnam)
DD Channel 1/2/7/10 (India)
Deutsche Welle TV (Germany)
Diamond Channel (Japan)
Digital Tampa 501/502 (Japan)
Discovery Channel (USA/India)
Doordarshan TV (India)
Dub'I I/II/IV (CIS)
Egyptian Satellite Channel
EM-TV (Papua New Guinea)
Enterprise Channel (Australia)
ESPN/ESPN Internat. (USA)
Family Theatre (Japan)
Feisuo Satellite TV (Japan)
Friendly TV (Japan)
Fuji TV Network (Japan)
Gemini TV (Sri Lanka)
GMA Philippines
Golden West Network (Australia)
Green Channel (Japan)
Guangdong Satellite TV (China)
Guizhou TV Station (Mongolia)
Guizhou TV Station-1 (Hong Kong)
HBO Asia (USA)
Henan Satellite TV
IBC-TV Network (Japan)
Japan Cable Television
Japan Leisure Channel
Japan Religious Channel
Japan Satellite Broadcasting Co.
Japan Sports Channel (Japan)
Karaoke Channel (Japan)
KBP Peoples Network (Philippines)
KBS Satellite TV 1/2 (Korea)
Keirin Channel (Japan)
Kids Station (Japan)
Kikkei Satellite News (Japan)

KN Television
Korea Vision
Kuoshin Satellite TV (Japan)
Lao National TV (Laos)
Life Design Channel (Japan)
M Channel (JMTV) (Japan)
MCM (France)
Meishi Entertainment TV (Taiwan)
Midnight Blue (Japan)
Mondo 21 (Japan)
Money TV (USA)
MTV Asia (UK/India/Hong Kong)
MTV Japan (Music Channel) (UK)
MTV Mandarin (China)
Music Asia (India)
Muslim TV Ahmadiyya Int. (India)
Myanmar TV (Burma)
NBC Asia (USA)
NEPC-TV (India)
Network 10 Australia
NHK Int. TV (Japan)
NHK Tokyo (Japan)
NHK-TV-Japan
Nihon Cable TV Netw. (Japan)
Nihon TV Network (Japan)
Nikkei Satellite News (Japan)
Nine Netw. (Australia)
NTV (CIS)
Orbita I/II (CIS)
P-Sat (Japan)
Pakistan TV
PHTV-Information Channel (China)
PHTV-Sanlih Channel (China)
Pioneer Music Satellite (Japan)
Playboy Channel (Japan)
Prefec Mulch (Japan)
Prefec Today (Japan)
Prime International (USA)
Prime Sports (Hong Kong)
Prime Sports (Mandarin) (Hong Kong)
Queensland Television (Australia)
Radio TV Brunei
Rainbow Channel (Japan)
Rajawari Citra Televisi Indonesia (RCTI)
Ray TV (Sri Lanka)
RCTS (Imparja) (Australia)
RFO Tahiti (France)
RTE Int. (Spain)

RTP International (Portugal)
Satellite ABC (Japan)
Satellite Culture (Japan)
Satellite News (Japan)
Satellite Theatre (Japan)
Shandong TV Station 1 (China)
Shopping Channel (Japan)
Sichuan TV Station (China)
Singapore Int. TV
Sky News (Japan)
Sky TV (Australia)
Sony Entertainment Network (USA)
Sony Entertainment TV(Japan)
Sound with Radio (Japan)
Space Shower TV (Japan)
Space Vision Network (Japan)
Star Channel (Japan)
Star Movies (China)
Star Plus (Hong Kong)
Star Plus (Japan)
Star TV (China/Burma/Australia)
Star TV Chinese (Hong Kong)
Star TV Plus (Hong Kong)
Sun Music TV (Tamil Svc.) (Sri Lanka)
Super Channel (USA)
Taiwan Satellite TV
Televisi Pendidikan Indonesia (TPI)
Theatre Television (Japan)
TNT/Cartoon Network (USA)
Travel Channel (Japan)
TV 4 Channel (China)
TV 5 (France)
TV 6 Mockba (CIS)
TV Asahi (Japan)
TV Mongol (Mongolia)
TV New Zealand
TV Oceania (Japan)
TV Shopping Network (China)
TV-1 (Malaysia)
TV-3 (Malysia)
TVBS (China)
TVI (India)
TVRI (Indonesia)
Unique Business Channel (China)
Vi Jay TV (Sri Lanka)
Viva Channel (Japan)
Voice of the Earth (Japan)
VTV-4 (Vietnam)

Walt Disney TV (USA)
Weather Channel (USA)
World Entertainment (Japan)
World Net (India)
Worldnet (USA/Mongolia)
WorldNet/C-Span/Deutsche Welle TV
  (USA)

Xinjiang TV Station-1 (China)
Xizang TV Station 1 (China)
Yunnan TV Station-1 (Hong Kong)
Zee TV (English) (Hong Kong)
Zee TV (Mandarin) (Hong Kong)
Zhejiang TV Station (China)

Overview of Cultural Patterns and Audience Trends

The vast geographical diversity among countries in Asia parallels the enormous array of TV programming strategies used here. In some areas television is little more than a reality; it is seen primarily as a governmental tool for information dissemination. In other places, notably India, Japan, Thailand and China, programming is much more sophisticated, blending entertainment with cultural identity and political ideology. Again, approaches vary widely here (as seen from the following country profiles)—from subtle "hints" to overt novela story lines. Despite the presentational style, however, the cultural "identification" is clear, which explains the enormous popularity of Asian soaps within the region, as well as their apparent failure to "translate" the Western world.

One exception to this generalization occurs, ironically, in less-developed nations, like Bangladesh, Cambodia or Pakistan. Here many serial dramas are created as a part of a "social marketing" directive, sponsored by such world organizations as Population Services International (PSI), a nonprofit corporation funded by various health and social service organizations around the world, including the United States, Great Britain, the Netherlands, Japan and Germany. PSI describes its projects as

> ...control[ling] both the supply of a product that enables behavior change and the messages that motivate demand for those products. PSI projects use mass media, community events, and interpersonal communications to bring consumers face-to-face with high quality, affordable products such as condoms, contraceptives, iodized salt, ORS, and bed nets that PSI supplies.... Some of the numerous ... communications activities used by PSI projects include point-of-sale material; radio call-in shows, [radio] soap operas, documentaries, profiles and other programs; television soap operas, documentaries, debates, and other informational programs; musical songs and videos; cinema ads and trailers; theater troupe presentations and puppetry; mobile film and video units; product demonstrations and information distribution at work places, community meeting places and special events; print materials, posters, brochures, cartoons and inserts; informational kiosks and peer education activities at special and sporting events, and in high traffic areas throughout communities; and providing information to and training target populations such as journalists, pharmacists, women's groups, retailers, and clergy.[3]

Some of PSI's more innovative uses of serial drama in Asia include the promotion of iodized salt in Bangladesh, Cambodia, India and Pakistan (in response to IDD—iodine deficiency disorder—a severe dehydration problem caused by diarrheal diseases) and increased use of mosquito bed nets in Cambodia and Myanmar.[4] Birth control and AIDS information have been disseminated via education-entertainment programs in Bangladesh, Pakistan and Cambodia (where a radio soap opera, set in a beauty salon, features women sharing advice on dealing with sexual issues).

PSI also finds audiences for its products and persuasive campaigns in other underdeveloped nations (for specific references, see chapters four and seven—South America and Africa). Although privately funded, these projects often complement the host government's public sector help programs and, hence, are given informal government approval.[5]

Focus: Kazakhstan

In 1996 the British Foreign Office formed a joint creative venture with Kazakhstan, where soap opera production seemed virtually unthinkable. The final result became *Crossroads*, an "open" serial reflecting the daily life of post-Communist Kazakhs. Within several months this modest soap opera became the third most popular show in the nation. But the success of *Crossroads* was neither "overnight" nor unplanned. The government of Great Britain (through its Know How Fund) donated $1.6 million to conceptualize the show, and about $800,000 came from sponsor contributions (including Wrigley Co., British American Tobacco and Austrian Airlines). BBC consultants supervised the first 27 episodes before returning to the U.K.[6] The cost—$12,000 per episode—has been well worth the price: over 20 percent of the population have become regular viewers.

Crossroads is based on the British working-class serial drama tradition, but it also provides viewers with information about free-market economies. Media reviewer Adam Dawtrey, for example, described one of the characters as "an 87 year-old grandmother who set an example to the whole nation when the scriptwriters sent her off to open her first-ever bank account."[7]

This type of soap—intended (in the Mexican novela tradition) to educate and motivate behavior—stood in great contrast to other soaps like *The Rich Also Cry* and *Santa Barbara*, which are also in the country. But it has equaled, if not exceeded the popularity of its competitors because of its ability to create viewer identification. After a year's worth of shows, the series was purchased in 1997 by Moscow's NTV, which beams it throughout the Commonwealth of Independent States (CIS); and preliminary plans have already been made for a second Kazakh soap.

Focus: Japan

Telenovelas have been an extremely popular television genre in Japan for several decades. They have also served as an important cultural export to most Asian countries, and some Western nations as well, although, according to NTV (Nippon Television Corporation) executive Ray Sorimachi, "far less so in Western countries, suggesting that the extent of variation in cultural norms could possibly be roughly measured by the relative ability of TV program[s] to cross cultures."[8]

Until 1993 most Japanese soaps mirrored traditional beliefs, attitudes and values, especially as they pertained to women viewers. The heroine usually gave up an exciting professional future to marry her handsome boyfriend, later to be terrorized by her mother-in-law. And husbands were the only ones who engaged in extramarital affairs.

But producers soon discovered (through declining ratings) that younger audiences were not buying this premise. As a result, a new era of Japanese novelas has emerged, featuring strong women characters with high professional goals and hearty sexual appetites. Ratings have risen sharply because of the new story lines, and "the new woman" is now in vogue. Some examples of Japan's more recent soaps include the following:

The Good Wife—features a 24-year-old female medical student who battles for recognition in a male world while also trying to maintain a stable marriage with her handsome businessman husband.

Hirari—recounts the story of a young Tokyo woman who drops out of accounting school to enter the profession of sumo wrestling (a centuries-old, "men only" sport).

The Last Friend—tells of a 36-year-old magazine editor who becomes pregnant from an affair she initiated with her boss (who is also her best friend's husband).

Salon de Kinshiro Tokoyama—follows the dilemmas of a man who must give up his barber shop and home to four feuding sisters.

According to Motoyasu Ishi, editor of the Japanese edition of *TV Guide*, "These story lines play well because women can watch them in the afternooon while their husbands are out. It's escapism, and it helps women relax."[9] Koji Kanazawa, executive producer of *Hirari*, adds, "Our goal is to give people encouragement. We want them to watch us at 8 A.M. and believe they can get through the day."[10]

Not all networks program soap operas in Japan. TV Asahi Broadcasting Corporation (ANB) and Tokyo Broadcasting System, Inc. (TBS), for example, are not deeply involved in soap opera production. Both Fuji TV and Nippon Television Corporation (NTV) produce hundreds of primetime dramatic series (for both domestic and export distribution), but NTV (with the exception of its affiliate Tokai Television[11]) does not originate any daytime drama. Despite this disparity, the market for soaps both at home and abroad has been a financial bonanza for those who have made the investment, including WOWOW (satellite) and the aforementioned Fuji TV and NTV.

WOWOW began in 1984 as part of Japan Satellite Broadcasting, Inc. The company moniker (pronounced "wau wau") was decided upon for two reasons: it "is a double 'Wow!'"[12] and the "w's" also symbolize "World-Wide-Watching," which expresses WOWOW's "commitment to bringing our viewers fresh events and wonders from all over the world."[13] In 1997 WOWOW teamed with American-owned DirecTV,[14] a privately owned digital satellite broadcast system supported by advertising as well as subscription fees. This merger may explain the emphasis on American programming now found on the channel (including *The Bold and the Beautiful* and *Santa Barbara*). It may also explain WOWOW's clear commitment to air entertainment from all over the world, especially drama, variety programming and films.

Fuji TV is the flagship of Japan's largest media corporation, Fujisankei Communications Group.[15] Within Japan 28 affiliated stations target young viewers (especially women) through variety and drama series. This demographic is particularly attractive to advertisers, as shown by Fuji's domination of Japan's ad revenues in 1996 ($2.69 billion).

But life had not always been this rewarding for the Fujisankei Group. As *Variety* journalist Jon Herskovitz reports,

> In the early 1980s, Fuji TV revamped its image and programming strategy as it began to court younger and increasingly affluent audiences. [Prior to this time, drama series targeted older Japanese women.] ... In 1988 it launched its first "Trendy Drama" series, nightly serials aimed at young female viewers.... The trendy dramas caught on and established Fuji TV as the ratings leader in Japan. The network held the top slot for 12 consecutive years before being bumped to the No. 2 position by Nippon Television in 1996.... Its core programming for younger audiences has been turned into an export product in other Asian countries, and trendy dramas have also become staples in the Japanese video rental market.[16]

In 1997 Fuji TV teamed up with Rupert Murdoch's News Corps., Sony and a Japanese software company to form JSkyB, the first Japanese network to use a digital signal via satellite. This clearly established Fuji as a leader in Asian television, which, in turn, will gain target audiences beyond Japan and into the Pacific Rim, including (especially) Taiwan and Hong Kong. This move to appeal to China is an especially brave one, considering the rather uneasy relationship these countries have endured since World War II. However, as Jon Herskovitz reports: "Asia was too large a market to ignore, and networks discovered that their Japanese programming dubbed into the local language was well received by younger viewers in Asian countries."[17]

In addition to China, Fuji also plans to move into the Indonesian, Filipino, Singaporean and Malaysian markets in the near future. The reason? Herskovitz goes on to quote a London-based marketing corporation (Baskerville

Communications Corp.), which estimated 400 million homes with television in 1997 and predicts at least 460 million by 2005.[18] And as reporter Robert Neff and Larry Holyoke observe:

> In Asia, Japan's neighbors are throbbing to its cultural beat as never before—from the TV soap opera "Tokyo Love Story" to the pop group Southern All-Stars. The wave is linking young people "from Tokyo to Singapore," says Shiro Honda, a program officer at the Toyota Foundation.... This is not the heady world of Hollywood, where Japanese and countless other investors have all gotten burned. But from the looks of it, Japan's affair with global entertainment has barely begun.[19]

One of the first program exports by Fuji was *Tokyo Love Story* (mentioned above), a contemporary story about maintaining romantic relationships amid the pressures of urban life. Viewers were attracted to the slick technical quality in addition to the glamor of Tokyo.[20] Another popular serial both at home and abroad was *Fujisankei Drama*, featuring Hideshi, a 35-year-old man in the midst of a midlife crisis. While enjoying his marriage with Akemi (also 35), Hideshi is also carrying on with one of the secretaries at his office. After his lover becomes pregnant (and decides to keep the baby), Hideshi tries to keep both relationships in balance, but Akemi begins to suspect him and has an affair herself with an old classmate from the Fine Arts University.[21]

Other successful exports have included *101st Proposal, Under One Roof, Long Vacation, Just the Way You Are*, and *Tokyo Cinderella Story*, all featuring trendy food, fashion and general "flash," along with high production values.[22]

NTV (Nippon Television Network Corporation) is also one of the leading producers of export programming in Japan. Established in 1952, NTV has news bureaus in the United States, Great Britain, Russia, France, Germany, Thailand, China, the Philippines, South Korea, Brazil and Egypt. It airs in local languages in over 40 countries, earning much of its reputation through its "oshin" serial dramas.

"Oshin" dramas usually run 25–30 minutes and last for six months. The consistent theme in these serials is the power of a woman's indomitable spirit. Every heroine strives on her own in traditional Japanese industries, which are known for their male chauvinism. The hard and challenging way of life these women endure brings viewers to tears ... and to another episode.

A specific example of "oshin" drama is *Pearl Flower* (25 minutes, 129 episodes), described by NTV publicists in this way:

> Noriko's family used to grow pearls, but she starts working at a pearl dealing house in Kobe after her father's death and her family's bankruptcy. Other female workers there give her a hard time in a very mean way. She finally gets engaged to the owner's son and feels very close to happiness until he is lost in a foreign country he has been visiting on business. When his younger brother, who has been loving her enough to hurt other people, marries her, her missing fiance comes back home. He accuses her for

not having waited for him. She is forced to choose between them. Meanwhile, their dealing house goes broke. The brothers go separate ways. Can she be happy some day?[23]

Similar story lines take place in other Japanese industries such as textiles, kimonos and Japanese paper.

Other NTV serials (the non-oshin type), like *Le Jeu Interdit* (12 episodes), *Night Embrace* (10 episodes), *Only My Beeper Knows* (12 episodes), *Pole Position* (11 episodes), *The Public Prosecutor* (12 episodes), *Salon de Kinshiro Tokoyama* (11 episodes), *Second Chance for Love* (10 episodes), *Cheat Me Sweetly* (11 episodes) and *I Prefer to Be Single* (11 episodes), last only a few weeks but are an hour long each time.[24] They are as popular as the "oshin" dramas with audiences.

Focus: Hong Kong

On July 1, 1997, Hong Kong was officially returned to mainland China. Although much is still to be determined in this new relationship, Hong Kong's media influence will most likely continue in much the same way it has for the last several decades, based on a recent interpretation of the Hong Kong Special Administrative Region (HKSAR). In anticipation of questions about Hong Kong's ability to maintain and develop relations with foreign countries, the Xinhua News Agency issued the following statement on May 27, 1997:

> Hong Kong will become a special administrative region of China when the Chinese Government resumes its exercise of sovereignty over the region. Hong Kong, therefore, will not be permitted to maintain and develop diplomatic relations with foreign countries and regions on its own.
>
> This in no way means that the HKSAR cannot have relations and exchanges with foreign countries. It means rather that the HKSAR should maintain and develop relations with foreign countries under specified conditions and circumstances under the principle of safeguarding national sovereignty.
>
> For example, the HKSAR may, using the name, "Hong Kong, China," maintain and develop relations, and conclude and implement agreements, with foreign states and regions and relevant international organizations in economic, trade, banking, shipping, telecommunications, tourism, cultural, sports and other appropriate fields.[25]

Based on this interpretation of the "Basic Law," it seems logical to assume that Hong Kong will continue its ventures in co-production and satellite/cable distribution for at least the next several years.

In 1997 Hong Kong's Star TV was already established as the major satellite/cable force in the Pacific. Whether it be in Nanjing, Shanghai, X'ian or Beijing, Star TV reaches millions of people each day with program offerings from the United States, Great Britain, Japan, Singapore, India, Australia, France, Spain, Italy, Germany, Malaysia, Thailand and Indonesia, as well as Hong Kong and mainland China.[26] Many of these channels also carry soap operas or telenovelas from different countries, subtitled or dubbed in Mandarin. In a three-week period during May 1997, for example, viewers with Star TV in Beijing were treated to *Santa Barbara* (from the mid–1980s); *The Bold and the Beautiful* (from 1992); several Latin American telenovelas; two or three Japanese telenovelas; Singaporean, Thai, Indian, Indonesian and Malay soaps; at least seven or eight Chinese-produced (or co-produced) serials; and twice as many from Hong Kong. Some were romantic novelettes; some were political history lessons; some were stories of "making it" in different worlds; and some were merely sensual fantasies. The choices were vast and intercultural, and each drama created a cultural landscape (either fictional or nonfictional) that was easy to understand and tempting to follow. Generally, the format for each program (regardless of country) was the same: (1) a brief summary of the past episode(s), (2) the dramatic action for the day, (3) a preview of the next episodes, and (4) a summary of the day's action with production credits superimposed over the visuals. Commercial breaks occurred on most stations, but the format differed here. Some were interspersed between scenes; others were shown before and after the complete episode; still others showed noncommercial material (such as nature videos) during show breaks to fill in time.

Focus: China

With a ratio of one TV set per 5.3 people, the popularity of television has risen dramatically as a primary influence on Chinese society (especially its youth) within the past several years. In fact, most younger people in today's China would much rather discuss the hottest singer from Hong Kong or the newest flick with Gong Li than the traditional folktales found in Chinese opera, calligraphic stones or scrolls. Accordingly, one of the most popular program genres at this time is the TV serial drama; it demands little formal education, is easy to follow and shows people and things to which many Chinese have never been exposed. A college-educated Chinese man interviewed by journalist Sheryl Wudunn characterized their popularity succinctly, saying, "Chinese has this thirst for watching daily life. They like gossiping, and *Aspirations* [China's first post–Tiananmen Square soap] is like a peep into one of their neighbor's lives."[27] Serial drama also shows great potential to be extremely persuasive in its message content—which makes it particularly attractive to present and future Chinese leaders.

All channels in China are owned and run by the government, whose understanding of the value of mass entertainment has been well documented. The government also recognizes the importance of education—and propaganda in—a developing nation, and constantly seeks ways of imparting both. Because of its accessibility and popular attraction, televised serial drama has developed quickly in mainland China, and most of it is filled with political and social messages within the dramatic content—not unlike serials in other developing nations.

Most media scholars would probably agree that the first real Chinese serial drama (or "inside drama," as the Chinese refer to it[28]) was *Red Mansion Dream*, which aired in spring 1987 on China's central television station (the most influential TV station in the country at that time). It comprised 36 episodes, each lasting about 60 minutes, and was broadcast twice each week during Chinese primetime (8:00–9:00 P.M.).

Red Mansion Dream was to serve as a template for many subsequent Chinese serials produced by the government, grounded (according to several Chinese viewers surveyed) in "traditional classic Chinese novels, which are of great literary value, famous for several hundred years, and highly appreciated."[29] This serial, as well as others produced in the years to follow (including *The Journey West* and *The Evolving of Three Countries*) not only entertained and educated millions of Chinese viewers but was also exported to Japan, Korea and other countries in Southeast Asia as a cultural icon. China had now entered into a different phase of propaganda.

Unfortunately, however, China's dramatic entry into TV exportation was temporarily shelved only months after it had begun, due to a lack of dramatic material. Shortly after the 1989 Tiananmen Square crisis, many of the country's leading writers constructed a wall of silence, releasing very little literature or media scripts—all this happening at a time when television in China was growing by leaps and bounds.

By the end of the 1980s, more than 700 million Chinese (60 percent of the total population) had become regular viewers of television. Over 140 million TV sets were scattered throughout the country, with 19,500 ground-relay satellite stations for remote provinces and autonomous regions. CTV (China's first cable TV system) could be found in more than 10 million houses, and more than 500 TV stations (12 times the 1980 total) were in business, accounting for almost one-quarter of the country's total advertising revenue. Thus, the lack of programming material after the Tiananmen Square crisis posed a serious threat at a time when China most needed to show the world a sense of unity and calm.

In 1991 the wheels of production once again began to turn but not in quite the same way they had before. This was "today's China"—a far different country from its previous incarnation. The new Chinese drama that emerged was a welcome change, according to *Washington Post* journalist Lena H. Sun:

> There are no overt political messages. At a time when the prestige and popularity of the Chinese government has sunk to perhaps its lowest level in four decades of Communist rule, "Expectations"—much to the envy of party

leaders—has captured the attention and loyalty of an ordinarily disaffected audience.... This show was an outlet for many of their emotions.[30]

Expectations (also known as *Aspirations* or *Yearning*, depending on the country of export) followed a family's evolution from the Cultural Revolution to present day China. The "inside drama" included over 50 episodes, in which workers were portrayed as heroes, and intellectuals were vilified. According to the *New York Times*, the heroine, Liu Huifang, was

> a saintly figure, selfless enough to break up her marriage for the sake of a young waif whom she takes in as her own child. The child, who becomes disabled in an accident, turns out to be the lost daughter of the sister of her husband, Wang Husheng, and the sister's boyfriend. In the end, she returns the daughter after she has nursed and comforted the child after an operation that cures the handicap.[31]

People's Daily commented that the show "had a significant morally educative effect," although word on the street was much more negative. Academics saw through the government's smokescreen to promote class struggle. Women wanting careers saw the portrayal of the submissive wife as social propaganda.[32] One writer observed: "It is a spiritual opium for the people. There is currently a moral collapse in society, so everyone has a nostalgia for the past."[33]

Since *Expectations*, hundreds of soap operas sharing some definite characteristics have been produced in mainland China. First of all, Chinese serial drama is clearly more similar to the telenovela than the American soap in format. Each story comprises a specific number of episodes and usually airs 20–30 hours, but some run between 4 and 5 hours and others over 80 hours). In addition, although romance and family relationships are popular themes, they usually occur within a specific historical period or amidst a certain political backdrop. Not surprisingly, the heroes and heroines of each drama represent the government's stance on the issue at hand.

A good example of this programming approach is *The Story of Lao Geng*, a drama about a middle-aged peasant who has spent most of his adult life in the countryside. His wife died several years earlier, leaving him to raise their two children—a son and a daughter. Now an adult, the son has chosen to marry and remain in the countryside with his father; the daughter has decided to move to the city. The serial follows Lao Geng as he tries to understand city life (while visiting his daughter) and to adjust to China after the Cultural Revolution.

At times, the story lines are very funny. Viewers see Lao Geng try to find another wife in the city, bargain for apples (and get cheated in the process) or disco at a popular nightspot with one of his old friends from the countryside. Also, because Lao is a very warm and likable character, the audience sympathizes with him, feeling his discomfort as he tries to move from one world to another and ultimately realizing (with him) that the new, Westernized life is complicated and sometimes treacherous. Life was much happier back in the countryside. But he is forever changed after his city experience and continues to walk between these two lifestyles.

Chinese serials with similar approaches to *The Story of Lao Geng* (but with more descriptive titles) include *Farewell to Moscow* (13 episodes); *Single-Parent Family* (23 episodes); *Sisters from Outside Make a Living in Beijing* (20 episodes); *The Romance of Three Kingdoms* (84 episodes); and *Hong Kong in Troubled Times* (46 episodes). Each novela provides "persuasive" entertainment for the politically charged 1990s—with dramatic action as direct as the titles. Other, more subtle titles—but with equally strong persuasive presentations—are listed below, along with brief plot summaries (provided by the entertainment sections of *China Daily*):

Heroes Have No Regret (38 episodes)—Situ Yuandong, director of the Board of Hong Kong Far East Company, wants to invest in Nanbing, a small city in southern China. But his nephew, Situ Wenbing, tries to foil Yuandong's investment. Kidnappings and murders occur one after another in Nanbing. A battle of justice and sins begins.[34]

Sun Wu, the Great Strategist (20 episodes)—tells the story of Sun Wu, a famous military strategy designer during the Autumn and Spring Period (770–476 B.C.). The story of Sun is interwoven with the fighting and diplomatic exchanges between the numerous kingdoms of that time. A glimpse of Sun's life is a review of the history of the period.[35]

Sino-British Street (30 episodes)—the narrow and winding Zhongying Street has separated Hong Kong from the Chinese mainland since the late 1890s in the wake of Britain's signing an agreement with Qing Dynasty leaders renting Hong Kong until 1997. Disputes have occurred between the two sides about the street in the past 50 years. The serial depicts life and people on this street, featuring romance as well as social upheavals in Hong Kong.[36]

Given the political atmosphere for the next few years, as the island of Macau is handed over to China in 1999, and the persuasive campaign continues for Taiwan's return "to the motherland," the tenor of Chinese dramas is likely to remain the same.

Focus: India

To quote a 1997 CNN report,

[India] is a country where four out of five people barely eke a living from the often unforgiving soil. Yet, India has also produced the world's second-largest contingent of scientists and engineers. This is a land where tens of millions of citizens do not have access to running water or electricity. But India is also the source of the best advanced software for computer companies in the United States. Life in the villages appears at first glance to be much the same as it was hundreds of years ago. But look again: the communal television set is beaming the American soap opera "The Bold and the Beautiful"—dubbed into Hindi.[37]

India is indeed a nation of "yin" and "yang." Visitors often liken their experiences in this country to a visit on the moon, where nothing seems to make logical sense. Just around the corner from the beautiful wealth of the Taj Mahal, one sees unimaginable squalor amid the untouchables; Mother Teresa, beloved by the rest of the world, was often considered a political enemy here. Yet despite these contradictions, Indians seem united in at least one way—their love for television.

As the nation celebrated its fiftieth year of independence on August 15, 1997, media observers saw television emerging as a powerful force, much like a growing middle class. Although less than half of its 950 million inhabitants could read, and telephones and television sets were still relatively scarce among the lower social echelons, the future of a media-rich India seemed bright:

> Years of monopoly by the state-run Doordarshan channel, with its staid emphasis on "educational" programs and pro-government news bulletins, have been replaced by an era of multi-channel entertainment. Thanks to the satellite dish, a ubiquitous feature on the roofs of soaring skyscrapers and humble hovels alike, the Indian TV viewer is exposed to international news channels such as the BBC and CNN. Indian producers have jumped on the cable bandwagon, spinning steamy soap operas and shows that expose a lot of skin.[38]

But as media channels continue to grow, the single-mindedness of Indian television seems to be diminishing. An example of this phenomenon can be found in the decline of traditional, "fable-like" novelas, popular for several decades in India and still seen in many other Asian nations today.

In fact, India in the 1990s is rebelling against its traditional "education-entertainment" drama, opting instead for the less-political lure of glamor and glitz. To some, this direction hardly bodes well for a still-developing nation.

The "serial with social conscience" was originated in the 1970s by the Indian government (as well as by private agencies like Population Communications International—PCI). It was heavily influenced by Mexico's example of the "motivational telenovela"—entertainment that reflects both educational reform and social consciousness (see chapter three). As in Mexico, many of India's early soaps combined high drama with such issues as birth control, the HIV virus, preventive health measures, literacy, substance abuse, political immorality and women's rights.[39] And it worked.

Hum Log, for example, was one of the first and most highly acclaimed "educational" telenovelas. The story focused on the problems caused by the centuries-old Indian tradition of sending young adolescent girls into early marriage, relegating them to second-class citizenship for the rest of their lives. Through the main character, viewers learned about women's rights, birth control alternatives, and the value of planned pregnancies.[40] *Humraahi*, another popular "early" soap, featured a 14-year-old girl named Angoori, who was forced to live her life within the class limitations of her family. She yearned for an education and a life of independence but was coerced into an arranged marriage. Against her better judgment, she then became pregnant and ultimately died in childbirth.

Both shows were extremely well received—*Hum Log* was estimated to have been seen in 78 percent of India's TV households—because the heroines touched many hearts. This reaction was exactly what producers were hoping for, according to journalist Fred Hift:

> Telenovelas mirror life as it is experienced by millions of people, and their dramatic nature maximises people's natural tendency to identify with on-screen characters and adopt them as role models. Positive and negative are clearly defined in both telenovela and soap operas. The good is good, the bad is bad. And because telenovelas have the time to meander, and to become part of the viewer's daily life, they are effective message bearers capable of affecting and changing popular attitudes.[41]

Religion and history are also parts of cultural identity; as such, they were also incorporated into early "motivational" serial dramas. One of the most popular shows of this genre variation was *Mahabharat*. But according to critic Shekhar Deshpande's review of scholar Ananda Mitra's book on Indian popular culture, *Mahabharat* was "more than [just] a 'religious soap opera'"[42]:

> It is a multifaceted narrative that defines these terms and therefore defeats the simple and pure notions of good and evil or just and unjust.... There is little doubt ... that the excessive emphasis on these religious dramas about Hinduism (proper, so to speak), have helped fuel passions about the newly synthesized "Hindu" identity in Indian social life. The opportunists on the fanatical Right needed some ladders with which to climb the mountain of religious hatred and no doubt they used the re-awakening of consciousness caused by televised Hinduism to fortify the house of religious rage.[43]

With the introduction of cable television in 1991, traditional Indian novela form began to lose much of its previous identity. Today serial dramas on the Star TV, Zee TV and UTV satellites compete formidably with the national network Doordarshan (which previously monopolized all programming). The material on the private networks is quite different, however. Serials on Star and Zee are often imported from other countries—*The Bold and the Beautiful*, for example, is among Star TV's "most watched" programs. The same is true for another Murdoch entity, United Television (UTV). But the shows are all dubbed in Hindi, to "Indianize" them more.[44]

In addition to serving its highly diversified domestic population, Zee TV (a satellite station covering Europe, India, Mauritius, China and most of Southeast Asia) concentrates on providing serial drama (as well as news, sports and other entertainment programming) for Hindi-language audiences around the world. Some of Zee TV's Indian products include the following:

Andaz—promoted as "The hottest soap opera to hit Indian television! Power, love, and greed drive weekly episodes featuring a star-packed cast."[45]

Parampara—features a wealthy Indian clan and its bitter in-fighting over the family fortune.[46]

Tara—filmed on a very high budget (by Indian standards), with top TV stars, lavish costumes and beautifully shot scenes, the "plot centers around the lives of four women, their love affairs and scheming ambitions. The main character is the beautiful Tara and the show, spoken in Hindi, spans three generations of her family's life."[47]

Not to be topped, however, the state-run Doordarshan network has also added more "steam" to its soaps, maintaining its competitive edge. Take *Swabhimaan (Self Esteem)*, a 524-episode version of (what one writer called) "The Bold and the Beautiful Meet Dynasty in Baywatch for All Eternity."[48] As *Time* reporter Emily Mitchell describes it:

> "Self-Esteem" follows the fortunes of the fabulously wealthy and scheming Malhotra family. The head of the clan dies, leaving behind a mistress named Svetlana, an alcoholic wife, a handsome son and an embittererd younger brother to fight over the family business. Son Rishab hates Svetlana and freezes her bank accounts; the wife tries to destroy her rival through black magic; Rishab's cousin is seduced ... but why continue? The complicated plot entwines more than 100 characters and spans two generations. Its producers are betting that viewers, most of them female, will be entranced by the glamorous life depicted, with the exotica of Scotch-drinking women who say things like, "The only joys of living abroad are English underwear and French perfume."[49]

With characters and dialogue like that, is there any doubt that the series has been viewed by millions and is dubbed in three languages?

Focus: Thailand

The kingdom of Thailand is about four-fifths the size of Texas and borders Malaysia, Myanmar, Laos and Cambodia. Over eight million people live in Bangkok, but most of the nation's population of 55 million live in rural areas, where television signals can be sporadic and undependable.[50] In addition, heavy governmental control over the media has stifled the development of a diversified entertainment industry.

In recent years, however, things have changed. Thai citizens are now able to choose from a variety of cable and satellite services, in addition to their traditional broadcast channels. In 1997 viewers had three pay-TV options: 1) IBC (airing CNN International as well as Thai Channels 5, 7, 9, 11 and ITV), sending its signal via converter to the UHF channels of standard TV sets; 2) Thai Sky (providing CNN International, Turner Network Television, the Cartoon Network, Thai

Channels 5, 7, 9, 11 and ITV); and 3) UTV (also providing CNN International, Turner Network Television, the Cartoon Network, Thai Channels 5, 7, 9, 11 and ITV), which introduced a new fiber optic component, offering the opportunity for interactive TV in the Bangkok and Khon Kaen metropolitan areas.[51]

With these new TV options available, viewers can now choose from Japanese, Chinese, Indian and Malaysian shows, in addition to their own cultural fare. Thai folk stories (a variation on the Latin American telenovela) are particularly popular these days because they require little formal education to understand and are reminiscent of superstitions and fables told to all Thai children. (An example of one of the more popular Thai novelas with this theme was *Absent-Minded Cupid*, the story of a little girl who is given the soul of a woman killed in an accident.) Asian variations of classic Western plays (like *Romeo and Juliet* or *Camelot*) are also prevalent.

Combined with sophisticated production techniques (which are often provided by those videographers who have been educated in Western TV technology), the appeal of these programs is unmatched. Thus, Thai production companies have little trouble finding financial backing for such projects.[52] Grammy Entertainment, for example, was begun in 1983; within ten years, it led the country in soap opera, game show and music production. In 1994 Grammy became another leader—as the first entertainment company to be listed on the Thai Stock Exchange. Ever mindful of globalization, Paiboon Damrongchaitham, founder and chairman of Grammy, decided on this move for obvious reasons, according to *Financial Times* reporter Victor Mallet: "...to invest in its retail network for the marketing of its Thai music catalogue; to participate in a satellite television channel and other joint ventures; to pay for new studios and equipment; and to convert Thai songs into Chinese for big markets in China, Hong Kong and Taiwan."[53]

Although Grammy is clearly a leader in this area, it is by no means sole proprietor. Production and distribution of Thai programs continue to rise, and the business is no longer restricted to a domestic audience. In fact, some Thai soaps can now be found in cyberspace, thanks to a recent pilot project conducted by Exact Productions—the "Darayan" Web site.

Created by KSC Comnet in March 1996, the "Darayan" site provided daily updates on the popular 21-episode TV drama about a ghost (Darayan) who refuses reincarnation in order to wait for the rebirth of her lover and their enemies. Exact managing director Takolkiat Viravan described the venture to the *Bangkok Post* as a "first" for the company. PR executive Saranput Homsuwan added that an entertainment Web site held great potential for elevating Thailand's international image, as well as advancing Internet use among the Thai people: "The Internet will become the sixth necessity for Bangkokians after food, water, medicine, clothes and cars."[54] Although this prediction may have been a bit overstated, it nevertheless affirms that Thai serial drama has matured greatly in a relatively short time.

Focus: Philippines

Many diverse populations exist in the Philippines, as indicated by the viewing options available to its people. Seventy-five TV channels (including six national networks and two international networks) provide the nation's 66 million people with news and entertainment from Japan, India, the United States, Australia, the United Kingdom, China, Hong Kong and Latin America. On these channels Filipinos have access to almost any soap opera or telenovela they desire. To be sure, *The Bold and the Beautiful* and *Santa Barbara* are big hits here. But most of the time Filipino viewers actually prefer the "closed serial" format of telenovelas, much like their compatriots in Latin America and Asia. Many of the customs, social hierarchies and familial backgrounds of these two geographic regions are deeply ingrained in the history of the Philippines, so it is not surprising that Filipino popular culture is equally influenced. In addition, joint ventures and trade agreements in recent years have also made an impact on viewer choice.

To fully appreciate the depth of viewer commitment to serial drama, one need only look at the fallout from airing a novela (featuring popular Latino actress Thalia Ariadna Sodi Miranda) in 1996. According to a published report by Lydia Martin:

> Things got so out of control ... that the time slot of her novela had to be changed by presidential decree because wives had stopped tending to their husbands at dinner time. Lawmakers in a town north of Manila even went so far as to order the local power company not to schedule power outages during her daily broadcast. "Very seldom do we see our people in Guimba preoccupied and mesmerized with such a soap opera," a city councilman told reporters. "And to deprive them of such enjoyment would be to act like a killjoy."[55]

In 1996 a new UHF station, channel 23, entered the Filipino market. The station's primary programming strategy was to bring even more imported drama to its VHF counterpart, ABS-CBN.[56] The reason for this decision was simple: Foreign programming is much less expensive to obtain, and the risk is relatively low because its performance is chronicled in other countries.

Some of the telenovelas (along with their country of origin) airing in the Philippines during the 1997 TV season included the following[57]:

Lazos de Amor (Mexico)
Luz Clarita (Mexico)
María la del Barrio (Mexico)
Los Parientes Pobres (Mexico)
Simplemente María (Mexico)
La Traidora (Venezuela)

Based on the current economic and political standing of this nation, as well as its future direction, TV producers in the Philippines will not likely concentrate on indigenous soap opera production. Rather, their strategy to import serial drama (and thus spend less to serve larger, more diverse audiences) seems to make great sense. Cultural imperialism is not as great a threat to most Filipinos as to citizens in other countries—after all, they've lived with it for decades.

Notes

1. Station/network information taken from *World Radio TV Handbook, 1997 Edition*, ed. Andrew G. Sennitt (New York: Billboard Books, 1997). Television/radio set information and population figures taken from *The World Almanac and Book of Facts 1998* (Mahwah, NJ: K-III Reference Corporation, 1997).

2. This listing is compiled from *WRTH Satellite & TV Handbook*, 4th edition, ed. Andrew G. Sennitt (New York: Billboard Books, 1997). It represents the *available* stations on satellite dishes through a transponder in Region III of the world satellite map. Although it is difficult to tell how many people have access to these channels, it is important to acknowledge the variety of cross-national program content on them.

3. *PSI: Communications to Motivate Healthy Behavior* (Population Services International, Inc., 1996) [database on-line]; available from (webmaster@psiwash.org).

4. *Ibid*. According to PSI's Internet literature, the organization has been marketing iodized salt since 1986, when it started its pilot program in Bangladesh: "In 1995 alone, almost 35 million packets were distributed, representing an estimated 75% of all ORS (oral rehydration salts) through commercial channels." The program has since been expanded to include India and a total population of about 400 million.

5. *Ibid*.

6. Adam Dawtrey, "U.K.-bred Soaper Is Socko in Kazakh," *Variety* (December 16–22, 1996), 66.

7. *Ibid*.

8. Written correspondence from Ray Sorimachi, International Operations & Business Development, Nippon Television Network Corporation [NTV] (July 31, 1996)

9. Quoted by David J. Morrow in "Ratings Climb as TV Soaps Show Savvy Career Women," *Detroit Free Press* (May 12, 1993), 7A. Descriptions of *The Good Wife, Hirari*, and *The Last Friend* are also taken from this source.

10. David Morrow, "Sumos and Soaps Provide Relief," *Detroit Free Press* (March 29, 1993), 3A.

11. According to written correspondence from Ken Mishima, director, International Department, Fuji Television Network, Inc. (August 9, 1996), Tokai Television Broadcasting Co., Ltd., produces telenovela-like soaps that typically run for three months.

12. WOWOW Japan Satellite Broadcasting, Inc. Web site <http://www.wowow.co.jp> [database on-line].

13. *Ibid*.

14. "Newsbytes Pacifica Headlines," Newsbytes Pacifica Home Page (November 1, 1996) [database on-line].

15. Jon Herskovitz, "New Digs, Deals Mark New Era," *Variety* (September 15–21, 1997), 43.

16. *Ibid*., 44.

17. Jon Herskovitz, "Pumping Hot Dramas, Variety Shows in the Asian Pipeline," *Variety* (September 15–21, 1997), 56.

18. *Ibid.*

19. Robert Neff and Larry Holyoke, "Show Biz: Don't Count Japan Out," *Business Week* (April 24, 1995), 126.

20. Herskovitz, "Pumping Hot Dramas."

21. International Channel Home Page (icinfo@i-channel.com) [database on-line].

22. Herskovitz, "Pumping Hot Dramas."

23. NTV Web site (http://www.ntv.co.jp) [database on-line].

24. *Ibid.*

25. "No Independent Diplomatic Ties for HK," *China Daily* (May 29, 1997), 4.

26. This listing is based on the 1997 hotel offerings in each of the Chinese cities mentioned. Not all of these channels are available everywhere, but they are available in some places on Star TV.

27. Sheryl Wudunn, "Beijing Journal; Why So Many Chinese Are Teary: The Soap Opera Epoch Has Dawned," *New York Times* (February 1, 1991) [database on-line]; available from Lexis-Nexis.

28. The Chinese refer to soaps as "inside dramas" because many of the earlier ones were shot inside the studio only. Later, location footage was included, but the name stuck anyway.

29. Much of my survey research was gathered by a very talented graduate student, Wu Xuhe, at Southeast University, Nanjing (May–August 1997). I am deeply grateful for his dedication and scholarship.

30. *Ibid.*

31. Wudunn, "Beijing Journal."

32. Catherine Sampson, "Television Tear-Jerker Enraptures China," *Times* (January 30, 1991) [database on-line]; available from Lexis-Nexis.

33. *Ibid.*

34. "TV Highlights," *China Daily* (May 31, 1997), 6.

35. *Ibid.*

36. "TV Highlights," *China Daily* (May 17, 1997), 5.

37. "The Great Divide" (August 4, 1997) [database on-line]; located on the CNN Interactive Page <htttp://www.cnn.com>.

38. "Beyond 50: The Challenges Ahead of India" (August 4, 1997) [database on-line].

39. Fred Hift, "Seeing the Issue in Black and White: Telenovelas Created for Audiences from Rio to Bombay are Prompting Big Changes," *Worldpaper* (January 1994), 10.

40. *Ibid.*

41. *Ibid.*

42. Shekhar Deshpande, "Religion, Art and Politics," *Ethnic News Watch* (July 31, 1994), 64.

43. *Ibid.*

44. Uma Da Cunha, "India's Cablers Join Forces," *Variety* (December 2–8, 1996), 50.

45. International Channel Web site <icinfo@i-channel.com> [database on-line].

46. *Ibid.*

47. *The People* (November 5, 1995) [database on-line]; available from Lexis-Nexis.

48. Emily Mitchell, Victoria Foote-Greenwell and Meenakshi Ganguly, "International Edition; Europe; Sightings," *Time* (May 1, 1995), 69.

49. *Ibid.*

50. "Cable TV Comes to Thailand—Telcom Report International (1995) [database on-line].

51. Thailand Television Channels Web site [database on-line].

52. Much of the information for this section was provided for the author through some of her former students—visiting Thai international students—who have returned to their homeland and now occupy positions at production companies there.

53. Victor Mallet, "Thai Media Group Plans Flotation," *Financial Times* (October 21, 1994), 24.

54. "Thailand: Thai Soap Opera on the Net," *Bangkok Post* (March 27, 1996) as reported on the Reuter Textline [database on-line]; available from Lexis-Nexis.

55. Lydia Martin, "Queen of the Novelas: Thalia Has Conquered the Soap Opera World and Now Sets Sights on Hollywood," *Fort Worth Star-Telegram* (March 19, 1997), 9 [database on-line]; available from Lexis-Nexis.

56. Carol Espiritu, "Philippines Eager to Buy Foreign Fare," *Variety* (December 2–8, 1996), 46.

57. Telenovela Web site, Yolette Nicholson <yoletten@site.net> [database on-line].

Africa

Countries included:

Algeria, Angola, Benin, Botswana, Burkina Faso, Burundi (Republic of), Cameroon, Canary Islands, Cape Verde, Central African Republic, Chad, Congo (Democratic Republic of), Congo (Republic of), Côte d'Ivoire, Djibouti (Republic of), Egypt, Equatorial Guinea, Ethiopia, Gabon, Gambia, Ghana, Guinea (Republic of), Kenya, Lesotho, Liberia, Libya, Madagascar, Madeira, Mali, Mauritania (Islamic Republic of), Mauritius, Mayotte, Morocco, Mozambique, Namibia, Niger, Nigeria, Réunion, Rwanda, São Tomé and Príncipe, Senegal, Seychelles, Sierra Leone, Somalia (Republic of), South Africa, Sudan, Swaziland, Tanzania, Togo, Tunisia, Uganda, Zambia, Zimbabwe[1]

Stations/Networks:

Algeria
Population: 29,803,370—32 per sq. mi.
(TV sets—1:13 persons; radios—1:4.2 persons)
Enterprise Nationale de Television (ENTV)
Orbit Satellite Radio and Television Network

Angola
Population: 10,623,994—22 per sq. mi.
(TV sets—1:152 persons; radios—1:33 persons)
Televisão Popular de Angola

Benin
Population: 5,902,178—136 per sq. mi.
(TV sets—1:182 persons; radios—1:11 persons)
Office de Radiodiffusion et TV de Benin (ORTB)

Botswana
Population: 1,500,765—7 per sq. mi.
(TV sets—1:59 persons; radios—1:8 persons)
Gaborone Television Corp.

Burkina Faso
Population: 10,891,159—103 per sq. mi.

143

(TV sets—1:182 persons; radios—1:36 persons)
Télévision Nationale Burkina

Burundi (Rep.)
Population: 6,052,614—564 per sq. mi.
(TV sets—1:667 persons; radios—1:16 persons)
Télévision Nationale du Burundi

Cameroon
Population: 14,677,510—80 per sq. mi.
(TV sets—1:42 persons; radios—1:6.8 persons)
Cameroon Radio Television (CRTV)

Canary Islands
Population: n/a (see Spain)
(TV sets—n/a; radios—n/a)
Antena 3 Television (Canal 36 Cumbre)
Canal Buenas Nuevas
Canaryvisión
Libertad Televisión (Ch 50 Escaleritas)
Onda Televisión Maspalomas (OMT6)
Tele Gran Canaria (Ch 40)
Televisión Española en Canarias
TVE-TVEC

Cape Verde
Population: 393,843—253 per sq. mi.
(TV sets—1:313 persons; radios—1:6.8 persons)

Central African Republic
Population: 3,342,051—14 per sq. mi.
(TV sets—1:204 persons; radios—1:14 persons)
Radiodiffusion Télévision Centrafrique

Chad
Population: 7,166,023—14 per sq. mi.
(TV sets—1:714 persons; radios—1:4.1 persons)
Teletchad
Orbit Satellite Radio and Television Network

Congo (Democratic Republic of)[2]
Population: 47,440,362—52 per sq. mi.
(TV sets—1:687 persons; radios—1:10 persons)
Antenna A
Canal Z
OZRT

Congo (Republic of)
Population: 2,583,198—20 per sq. mi.
(TV sets—1:143 persons; radios—1:8.7 persons)
Radiodiffusion Télévision Congolaise

Côte d'Ivoire
Population: 14,986,218—120 per sq. mi.
(TV sets—1:17 persons; radios—1:7 persons)
Télévision Ivorienne

Djibouti (Republic of)
Population: 434,116—49 per sq. mi.
(TV sets—1:23 persons; radios—1:12 persons)
Radio Television Djibouti
Orbit Satellite Radio and Television Network

Egypt
Population: 64,791,891—168 per sq. mi.
(TV sets—1:9.2 persons; radios—1:3.3 persons)
Egyptian Radio and TV Union
Orbit Satellite Radio and Television Network

Equatorial Guinea
Population: 442,516—41 per sq. mi.
(TV sets—1:104 persons; radios—1:2.4 persons)
Télévision Nacional

Ethiopia
Population: 58,732,577—134 per sq. mi.

(TV sets—1:233 persons; radios—
1:5.1 persons)
Ethiopian Television

Gabon

Population: 1,190,159—12 per sq. mi.
(TV sets—1:26 persons; radios—1:6.8
persons)
Radio Télévision Gabonaise

Gambia

Population: 1,204,984—292 per sq.
mi.
(TV sets—n/a; radios—1:7.7 persons)
Information & Broadcasting Service

Ghana

Population: 18,100,703—197 per sq.
mi.
(TV sets—1:11 persons; radios—1:4.4
persons)
Ghana Broadcasting Corporation

Guinea (Republic of)

Population: 7,405,375—78 per sq. mi.
(TV sets—1:130 persons; radios—1:23
persons)
Radiodiffusion Télévision Guinéen

Kenya

Population: 28,803,065—128 per sq.
mi.
(TV sets—1:91 persons; radios—1:11
persons)
Kenya Broadcasting Corporation
Kenya Television Network (KTN-TV)

Lesotho

Population: 2,007,814—171 per sq. mi.
(TV sets—1:100 persons; radios—1:30
persons)
Lesotho National Broadcasting Service

Liberia

Population: 2,602,068—68 per sq.
mi.

(TV sets—1:53 persons; radios—1:4.4
persons)
Liberian Broadcasting Corporation

Libya

Population: 5,648,359—8 per sq.
mi.
(TV sets—1:10 persons; radios—1:4.4
persons)
Peoples Revolution Broadcasting TV

Madagascar

Population: 14,061,627—62 per sq.
mi.
(TV sets—1:50 persons; radios—1:5.2
persons)
Radio Télévision Malagasy

Madeira

Population: n/a (see Portugal)
(TV sets—n/a; radios—n/a)
Radio Televisão Portuguesa, E.P.

Mali

Population: 9,945,383—20 per sq.
mi.
(TV sets—1:769 persons; radios—
1:23 persons)
Radiodiffusion Télévision du Mali

Mauritania (Islamic Republic of)

Population: 2,411,317—6 per sq.
mi.
(TV sets—1:40 persons; radios—1:6.8
persons)
Télévision Nationale de Mauritanie
(TVM)
Orbit Satellite Radio and Television
Network

Mauritius

Population: 1,154,272—1,464 per sq.
mi.
(TV sets—1:4.5 persons; radios—
1:2.7 persons)
Mauritius Broadcasting Corporation

Mayotte
Population: n/a (see France)
(TV sets—n/a; radios—n/a)
R.F.O. Mayotte

Morocco
Population: 30,391,423—171 per sq. mi.
(TV sets—1:13 persons; radios 1:4.6
persons)
M2 (2emme Chaîne TV Marocaine)
Radiodiffusion Télévision Marocaine
Orbit Satellite Radio and Television
  Network

Mozambique
Population: 18,165,476—57 per sq. mi.
(TV sets—1:286 persons; radios—1:27
persons)
Televisão de Moçambique (TVM)

Namibia
Population: 1,727,183—5 per sq. mi.
(TV sets—1:43 persons; radios—1:7.2
persons)
Namibia Broadcasting Corporation

Niger
Population: 9,388,859—18 per sq. mi.
(TV sets—1:204 persons; radios—1:16
persons)
Télé-Sahel

Nigeria
Population: 107,129,469—300 per sq.
mi.
(TV sets—1:26 persons; radios—1:5.1
persons)
Nigerian Television Authority

Réunion
Population: n/a (see France)
(TV sets—n/a; radios—n/a)
Antenne Réunion
Canal Réunion
Société Nationale de Radio-Télévi-
  ion d'Outre-Mer (RFO)

TV Sud
TV-4

Rwanda
Population: 7,737,537—760 per sq.
mi.
(TV sets—n/a; radios—1:15 persons)

São Tomé and Príncipe
Population: 147,865—383 per sq. mi.
(TV sets—1:6.2 persons; radios—1:3.7
persons)
Televisão de São Tomé e Príncipe

Senegal
Population: 9,403,546—123 per sq. mi.
(TV sets—1:27 persons; radios 1:8.5
persons)
Canal Horizons Sénégal
Radiodiffusion Télévision Sénégalaise

Seychelles
Population: 78,142—443 per sq. mi.
(TV sets—1:11 persons; radios—1:2
persons)
Seychelles Broadcasting Corporation

Sierra Leone
Population: 4,891,546—176 per sq. mi.
(TV sets—1:91 persons; radios—1:4.3
persons)
Sierra Leone Broadcasting Service

Somalia (Republic of)
Population: 9,940,232—40 per sq.
mi.
(TV sets—n/a; radios—1:24 persons)
Ministry of Information
Orbit Satellite Radio and Television
  Network

South Africa
Population: 42,327,458—89 per sq. mi.
(TV sets—1:9.9 persons; radios—1:3.2
persons)
Bop-TV (Bophuthatswana Television)

CCV-TV (Contemporary Community Value TV)
M-Net Television (Electronic Media Network Ltd.)
South African Broadcasting Corporation Transkei TV
Trinity Broadcasting Network Transkei

Sudan

Population: 32,594,128—33 per sq. mi. (TV sets—1:13 persons; radios—1:3.9 persons)
Sudan Television

Swaziland

Population: 1,031,600—153 per sq. mi. (TV sets—1:50 persons; radios—1:6.1 persons)
Swaziland Television Authority

Tanzania

Population: 29,460,753—80 per sq.mi. (TV sets—1:476 persons; radios—1:38 persons)
Dar es Salaam (DTV)
Television Zanzibar (TVZ)
Independent Television (ITV)

Togo

Population: 4,735,610—215 per sq. mi.
(TV sets—1:133 persons; radios—1:4.7 persons)
Télévision Togolaise

Tunisia

Population: 9,183,097—144 per sq. mi. (TV sets—1:12 persons; radios—1:5 persons)
Radiodiffusion Télévision Tunisienne
Orbit Satellite Radio and Television Network

Uganda

Population: 20,604,874—221 per sq. mi. (TV sets—1:91 persons; radios—1:9.3 persons)
Uganda Television

Zambia

Population: 9,349,975—32 per sq. mi. (TV sets—1:37 persons; radios—1:12 persons)
Zambia National Broadcasting Corporation

Zimbabwe

Population: 11,423,175—75 per sq. mi. (TV sets—1:37 persons; radios—1:12 persons)
Zimbabwe Broadcasting Corp.

Satellite Channels Available in This Region[3]

3-Sat (Germany)
Abu Dhabi TV (UAE)
Afghanistan TV (Afg.)
AFN-TV (USA)
AFRTS (USA)
AFRTS-SEB (USA)
Al Jazeera Sat. (Qatar)
Al Jazeera Sat. (Algeria)
Albanian TV
Algerian TV

Antena Tres TV (Spain)
ARD-1 (Germany)
ARD/ZDF (Germany)
ART (Saudi Arabia)
ART Europe (UK)
ARTE (Germany)
Asia Business Channel
AsiaNet
ASTRA SPORT (AFS)
ATN (Africa)

ATV (Turkey)
ATV (Poland)
Bahrain TV
Bayerisches Fernsehen (Germany)
BBC Orbit Arabic Service (UK)
BBC Prime (UK)
BBC World (UK)
BHT (Bosnia Hercegov.)
BOP-TV (Senegal)
Bop TV Mmabatho (Bophuthatswana)
Bop TV-1 (Bophuthatswana)
Bravo (UK)
BSkyB (UK)
C-Span (USA)
Cable Plus Filmovy Kanal (Czech
    Rep.)
Canal Clásico (Spain)
Canal France Internat. (France)
Canal Horizons (Senegal)
Canal J(eunesse) (France)
Canal Jimmy (France)
Canal On (Spain)
Canal Plus (France)
Canal Sur (Spain)
Cartoon Network (USA)
CCTV4 (China)
CDAT (AFS)
Channel 5 (UK)
Channel Africa (South Africa)
Channel-2 TV Israel
Chinese Channel (UK)
Chinese News Entertainment (China)
Christian Channel Europe (UK)
Ciné Cinéfil (France)
Ciné Cinémas (France)
Cine Classics (Spain)
Cinema (Sweden)
Cinemania (Spain)
Cinemania 2 (Spain)
CMT Europe (USA)
CNBC (UK)
CNN International (USA/UK)
CNN Nordic (USA)
ConAir (USA)
Country Music Europe (USA)
CTC (STS) (CIS)
Deutsche Welle TV (Germany)
Discovery Channel (UK)
Documania (Spain)

DR-2 (Denmark)
DSF Deutsches Sportfernsehen (Ger-
    many)
Dubai TV (UAE)
Duna 7 (Hungary)
EDTV (UAE)
Egypt TV
Egyptian Satellite TV (Egypt)
ESPN (USA)
ET-1/2/3 (Greece)
ETV (Ethiopia)
Euro Business News (UK)
Euro D (Turkey)
Euronews (France)
Europe by Satellite
European Business News (EBN) (UK)
Eurosport (France)
Eurosport (Norway)
FilmNet (Poland)
FilmNet 1 Nordic (Norway)
FilmNet 2 (Sweden)
Fox Kids (UK)
France Supervision
France-2 (France)
Future Vision (Saudi Arabia)
Galavision (Mexico)
Granada Good Life (UK)
Granada Plus/Man & Motor (UK)
Granada (Talk TV) (UK)
H.O.T. (Home Order TV)
HBB (Turkey)
Home Shopping Network (UK)
Home TV (India)
HRT Zagreb (Croatia)
HTB (Russia)
IBA Channel 3 (Israel)
InterSTAR (Turkey/Germany)
IRIB-TV 1/2/3 (Iran)
Jordan TV
JRT (Jordan)
JRTV (Jordan)
JSTV (Japan)
Kabel 1 (Germany)
Kanal 5 (Sweden)
Kanal 6 (Turkey)
Kanal 7 (Turkey)
Kanal D (Turkey)
Kanal + (Poland)
Kasachstan 1 (private) (Kasachstan)

Kazakhstan TV
Kuwait Space Channel
Kuwait TV
La Chaîne Info (LCI) (France)
La Cinquième (France)
LBC Lebanon
Libyan TV
M Net South Africa (AFS)
M-2 Morocco
M-6 Métropole 6 (France)
M-Net Int. (South Af.)
MBC (UK)
MCM Afrique (South Africa)
MCM Euromusic (France)
MED-TV (UK)
Middle East Broadcast (MBC) (UK)
Middle East Broad.
Centre (UK)
MiniMax (Spain)
Mitteldeutscher Rundfunk (MDR 3)
 (Germany)
Moscow-1 (CIS)
MTV (UK)
MTV (Africa)
MTV Nordic (Denmark)
Muslim TV Ahmadiyya
Muslim-TV MTA+(UK)
N-3 Nord-3 (Germany)
n-tv (Germany)
NBC Super Channel (UK)
NEPC-TV (India)
NHK Tokyo (Japan)
Nickelodeon (Germany)
Nickelodeon (Sweden)
Nickelodeon (USA)
Nile TV (Egypt)
Nile TV Int. (Egypt)
Nova Shop (Sweden)
NRK 1/2 (Norway)
NTA Ch. 10 (Nigeria)
NTV (Russia)
Oman TV
Onyx TV
Orbit (Morocco)
ORT-1 (CIS)
Ostankino ORT Int. (CIS)
Paramount TV (USA)
Paris Première (France)
PIK CYBC (Cyprus)

Planète (France)
Polonia 1 (Poland)
Polsat (Poland)
Premièra TV (Czech Rep.)
Premiere (Germany)
Pro-7 (Germany)
Quantum Channel (UK/USA)
QVC (USA)
QVC Deutschland (Germany)
RAIDUE (Italy)
RAITRE (Italy)
RAIUNO (Italy)
Rendez-Vous (France)
RFO Canal Permanent 2 (France)
RTA-TV (Algeria)
RTL 7 (Poland)
RTL Television (Germany)
RTL-2 (Germany)
RTL-9 (France)
RTM 1 (Morocco)
RTP Internacional (Portugal)
RTS Beograd (RTV Srbjal, Yugo-
 slavia)
RTT-TV-7 (Tunisia)
SABC 1/2/3 (AFS)
SABC-TV (South Africa)
Samanloyu TV (Turkey)
Sara Vision
Sat-1 (Germany)
Saudi Arabia
Saudi Arabia TV 1/2
Saudia (Saudi Arabia)
Sci-Fi Channel (UK)
Sci-Fi Channel Nordic (Denmark)
Sell-a-Vision (Germany)
Sharjah TV (Mauritania)
Sky Movies (UK)
Sky Movies Gold (UK)
Sky News (UK)
Sky One (UK)
Sky Scottish (UK)
Sky Soap (UK)
Sky Sports (UK)
Sky Sports 2/3 (UK)
Sky Sports Gold (UK)
Sky Travel (UK)
Sky-2 (UK)
Sony Entertainment TV (India)
Sudan TV

Super RTL (Germany)
Super Television Channel (USA)
SWF/SDR (S-3) (Germany)
Syrian TV
TCC (The Children's Channel) (UK)
Tel Monte-Carlo (TMC) (Monte-
	Carlo)
Tele-5 (Spain)
Teleclub (Switzerland)
TeleDeporte (Spain)
TelePace/Vatican TV (Italy/Vatican
	State)
Telesat 5 (Spain)
TF-1 (France)
TGRT (Turkey)
The Adult Channel (UK)
The Computer Channel (UK)
The Disney Channel (UK)
The Egyptian Space Channel
The Family Channel (UK)
The History Channel (UK)
The Learning Channel (TLC) (UK)
The Movie Channel (UK)
The Playboy Channel (UK)
The Racing Channel (UK)
The Weather Channel (UK)
TM 3 (Germany)
TM3 (UK)
TNT/Cartoon Network (USA)
TRT Int. (Turkey)
TRT-1/3/4 (Turkey)
TV 1-India
TV 3 de Catalunya (Spain)

TV 3 Denmark
TV 3 Sweden
TV Angola
TV Eurotica (UK)
TV Norge (Norway)
TV Polonia (Poland)
TV Romania Int.
TV Russia 2
TV Sport Eurosport (France)
TV-1000 (Sweden)
TV-2/3 (Norway)
TV-4 (Sweden)
TV-6 Moscow (CIS)
TV3+ (Denmark)
TV5 Internationale/Afrique (France)
TVE Internacional (Spain)
TVX The Fantasy Channel (UK)
UK Gold
UK Living
Vasa TV (Slovakia)
VH-1 (UK/Germany)
VHI Nordic (Sweden)
VIVA (Germany)
Viva 2 (Germany)
VOX (Germany)
WBTV (The Warner Channel) (UK)
WDR (Germany)
What's in store (Netherlands)
WorldNet (USA)
Yemen TV
ZDF (Germany)
Zee TV (UK)
ZTV (Sweden)

Overview of Cultural Patterns and Audience Trends

Compared to other global regions, many African nations were delayed in their technological development due to economic and political instability. In addition, geographic terrain and social conditions vary widely. As a result, the ratio of television sets to persons (although rising dramatically within the last two years) still ranges from 1:4.5 in Mauritius to 1:769 in Mali—and in some areas TV sets are not a viable option at all. Radio, on the other hand, seems accessible to most Africans regardless of race, religion, habitat, education or economic status. Thus, whereas most countries in the rest of the world dropped radio serials from their program schedules by 1962, much of Africa's audio drama remains an important part of its media culture. Several countries, notably South Africa and Kenya, have made significant inroads in television, and in August 1997 M-Net (a successful satellite network) introduced its own "Soap Channel," featuring eight British, American and Australian soaps in a six-hour time block.[4] Still, radio is the primary form of mass communication in this part of the world.

Whether through radio or television, however, African programmers seem to share common strategies in serial drama production: (1) subjects for entertainment-education (inspired by students of Mexico's Miguel Sabido); (2) BBC-like soaps (a carryover from colonial days); (3) historical novels (similar to the Latin American telenovela); (4) ideological persuasion (e.g., nationalistic pride, dedication to a specific cause); and (5) folklore (mythic tales).

Because of Africa's colonial past (and sometimes present) as well as its identity as an underdeveloped continent, African media producers frequently import entertainment programming from other countries (such as American, British and Australian soaps and Latin American telenovelas). Often, they also co-produce programs with other countries or share responsibilities for "social marketing" with private organizations like Population Services International (PSI). Primary target audiences for PSI include Bolivia, some areas of the former Soviet Union, and most developing nations in Africa and Asia. (For a description of PSI's background, see chapter six). Their major areas of research and social action are "condoms for AIDS prevention, a wide range of contraceptives for family planning, and a number of other health products, like oral rehydration salts, antibiotics, iodized salt, fuel-efficient wood-burning stoves, mosquito nets, and other products to prevent death and morbidity from disease, affecting children and women in particular."[5] Examples of social marketing through serial drama (among other strategies) include: (1) the introduction of oral rehydration salt (ORS) therapy with the cooperation of the governments of Morocco, Cameroon and Benin (with plans to expand the program to Mozambique); (2) suggested ways to treat malaria (a disease that affects more than 500 million people) through educational programs in the Central African Republic, Malawi, Tanzania and Zambia; (3) contraceptive instruction and advice in Nigeria, Guinea, Rwanda, Tanzania, Malawi and Lesotho; and (4) AIDS prevention in Burkina Faso, Côte d'Ivoire, Cameroon, Togo, South Africa and Tanzania.[6]

But why serial drama? According to scholar Vibert C. Cambridge, the soap opera format is popular in Africa for several reasons: "The program genre is low cost and can reach large audiences. A well produced radio serial can address many issues. This makes it eminently suitable for addressing issues that impact on self-efficacy. History driven and culture oriented pieces can be used to provide insights into the myriad aspects of global Africa heritage. A heritage that is shareable with all peoples."[7] Within these general parameters, however, are the specific programming goals of each country. To see these differences one need only look at the variations of serial drama in several African nations, specifically South Africa, Kenya, Côte d'Ivoire, Niger, Mauritius and Tanzania.

Focus: South Africa

As noted earlier in this chapter, South Africa has been a leader in television technology, developing cable and satellite channels years before some of its poorer neighbors on the continent. Unfortunately, this pioneering effort was often overshadowed by the nation's strict apartheid policies. Programming was often limited to the desires and needs of the white minority. Other races and ethnic groups were ignored in the world of television (as well as in other areas of socioeconomic life). In 1991, shortly after the coalition government had been elected, the South African Broadcasting Corporation (SABC) announced plans for a new entertainment channel to better serve the "new [nonracist] South Africa."[8] Scheduled to begin broadcasts in 1992, "Contemporary Values Television" (CCV-TV) was described in *Variety* as a fusion of SABC's (then) existing entertainment channel, TV-4 (most popular with black viewers), with its two ethnic channels, TV-2 (Zulu/Xhosa) and TV-3 (Sotha/Tswana). The programming strategy was based on political exigency, with a healthy dose of marketplace competition:

> By offering more entertainment in the form of soap operas, comedies, documentaries and a greater choice of movies, CCV aims to increase its viewership among blacks and will also try to lure white viewers from TV-4's stablemate, TV-1, and from rival networks M-Net (a popular pay-tv channel) and Bop-TV, beaming to Johannesburg from the Bophuthatswana tribal homeland. CCV will broadcast in English, Afrikaans, Hindi, Northern Sotho, Southern Sotho, Tamil, Tswana, Xhosa and Zulu from 6 p.m. to midnight.[9]

South African broadcasters had learned—like their colleagues in other countries—that in addition to providing a social service to the country, the inclusion of a culturally diverse audience would attract advertisers as well. And in 1992, when economic forecasters predicted that advertising revenues would top $811 million—with TV capturing over a third of the "pie"—this appeal was significant.

Economics aside, South African programmers have also been politically responsible by assuming a very proactive stance in social marketing, particularly on health care. One of the most effective soap operas produced on this topic was *Soul City*, developed in 1994. Journalist Sue Armstrong, in *New Scientist*, describes the story premise and objectives: "The drama centres on a health clinic that serves a poor community. It has all the ingredients of a traditional 'soap': romance, tragedy, humour and suspense. But the story addresses a range of serious issues, such as antenatal care for pregnant women, the advantages of breastfeeding, childhood diarrhea, immunisation, household accidents and child abuse."[10] Initially, *Soul City* targeted audiences in South Africa's cities (where even residents without electricity could hook their TV sets to car batteries). Within a few months plans were devised to expand the nation's Rural Television Network—a plan to place TV sets in rural trading stores to provide television access in more rustic environments—to give the serial more exposure. Because people living in remote areas had already proven their loyalty to a similar radio soap, *Healing Hearts* (broadcast twice a day on three stations—Radio Zulu, Radio Xhosa and Radio Sotho), South African programmers felt confident they could expand their potential audience by about 15.5 million.[11] They were ultimately proven correct.

Focus: Kenya

Kenya began radio serial production in the 1960s for both entertainment and educational purposes. Their programming strategy developed in part from the success of Australian soap operas, several of which had provided social action themes as well as dramatic story lines. The other reason was quite clear. As United Press International correspondent Philip Williams observed in 1987, "Kenya's 20 million population is a runaway problem. That total will almost double on present trends before the year 2000, reach 50 million before 2010 and peak at 100 million in 2025. The average Kenyan family raises eight children, 25 percent of all families are polygamous and the average population growth rate is 4.1 percent—higher in western Kenya, which probably has the highest growth rate in the world."[12] As a result, in 1987 the Kenyan government (with the help of outside funding) embarked on the creation and production of two dramatic serials—one on radio, one on television—to address the serious problem of population management. The public responded immediately; both soaps were extremely successful and enjoyed great audience support throughout their broadcast runs (218 episodes and 198 episodes respectively).

Kenya's radio serial, *Ushiwapo Shikimana*, highlighted the challenges and rewards of family life, including cultural obstacles and difficulties in balancing a career with children. The basic message—family planning—was apparently well received by Voice of Kenya's listeners, who wrote regularly about the soap's impact on their personal lives.[13]

Kenya's TV serial, *Tushauriane*, became a smash hit shortly after its premiere in May 1987. The first 30-minute episode featured several "hot button" topics: family feuds over land, intertribal marriage, school absenteeism, and a 16-year-old girl impregnated by a man old enough to be her grandfather.[14] The controversial themes were quite new to *Tushauriane*'s viewers, who watched the broadcast in Swahili rather than English (for a broader audience). The program's dramatic content was strong enough to sustain its popularity, while conveying a message that spoke to a more "modern, non-traditional approach to marriage, children and the home."[15]

Since the first bold entry into social serial drama, Kenya has continued its strategy of providing education within entertainment programming. In 1995 a twice-weekly radio soap, *Ndinga Nacio* (*Go On Then, Tell Me*) achieved a sort of "cult following" after having failed first as an agricultural magazine show.[16] Not losing sight of national goals and objectives in his first attempt in 1994, David Campbell of the Agriculture Information Centre in Nairobi, went back to his drawing board, this time studying the approach of a time-honored British soap, *The Archers*.

> We wanted to get people involved on a continual basis. 'Way back, "The Archers was 30 per cent propaganda, 15 per cent technical information, and the rest was story. Now "The Archers" has very little information and propaganda, but in Kenya 82 per cent of the population are on the land and farming. Most of them depend for their livelihoods on agriculture.
> We needed to try to reach the women who actually do most of the farming. They are terribly busy during the day and don't get time to sit and listen, so we had to create a story which people would really want to make time for.[17]

Campbell, teaming with the Overseas Development Administration (ODA), went on a research mission to find out what Nairobi women wanted and needed to know. The result was tremendously successful, but as most programmers know, a show's success can also breed more problems. In this case the ODA wanted to expand the program nationwide—a complication to be reckoned with. Campbell explains that, in addition to language and dialect problems, "Politically, it is a bit tricky. We have to devise a story-line where different tribes come into the story. And if we get too political, we could get taken off the air. Even the signature tune is an issue. We don't want to identify it with any one kind of tribal music, so we might have to go outside Kenya and get a tune from Zaire."[18]

Given a 1995 order from Kenya's minister of information to restrict broadcasts of "culturally devastating" programs, Campbell's concerns are quite valid.[19] However, the benefits would most likely overshadow the risks in such ventures. So far, the show has continued to succeed, and more like it are in the planning stages.

Focus: Côte d'Ivoire

Côte d'Ivoire, like some of its African neighbors, has made serious attempts to produce "motivational" soap operas, often with the help of Population Services International or PSI (described earlier in this chapter). One of its biggest hits in recent years was *Sida dans la Cité*, the first French-language television serial addressing the AIDS epidemic in that country. The 1995 drama, airing Tuesday nights during primetime, was the culmination of a partnership between PSI and the National AIDS Committee of Côte d'Ivoire. To "hook" viewers, program promoters asked these questions:

What would you do if you discovered you carried the AIDS virus? Might you tell your wife that you haven't been faithful? Would you use condoms to prevent the spread of the disease? If your husband announces that he is seropositive, how would you react? Your doctor advises you to take the AIDS test, but your best friend tells you not to. Would you do it?[20]

The show was an instant hit with its audience, earning a 75-share average during its series run. The drama also captured first prize for "Best Fiction Film—TV/Video Category" in the 1995 FESPACO Film Festival in Burkina Faso.

In a nation where more than 640,000 people of its total population of 14,986,218 are identified as carriers of the AIDS virus, the success of *Sida* was monumental and certainly not accidental, according to producer Rob Eiger: "We decided to use the popular art form of the television soap opera not only to educate the public about the dangers of AIDS, but to encourage the active participation of the viewers."[21] As in many successful indigenous soaps, *Sida*'s plotlines combined local color and characterization with interesting, reality-based dialogue. In addition, several nationally-known celebrities donated their time and talents to the effort.

Research with focus groups reaffirmed "Sida's" ratings' success, proving that educational-entertainment serials, if produced well, can be a real asset to a developing nation's objectives. According to PSI, the only serious viewer complaint was that the episodes lasted only 15 minutes—a comment rarely voiced with most television programming.

Since winning the prestigious FESPACO Film Festival award, *Sida dans la Cite* has aired in other nations, like Tanzania, Guinea and Burkina Faso, especially in those areas with large numbers of refugee migration. Thus, quite unintentionally, Côte d'Ivoire is now an emerging soap opera export nation—perhaps a sign of more quality "motivational" serial dramas to come from this rather unlikely source.

Focus: Niger[22]

Télé-Sahel, the only television network in Niger, broadcasts each day to a potential audience of 6,400,000 people (80 percent of Niger's total population). For its serial programming, Télé-Sahel uses a strategy found in many other small African nations—a "folk novela" format, combining elements of popular folktales, general entertainment and education. Unlike the Latin American novelas, the number of episodes in a folk novela is small (resembling an American miniseries more than a long-running drama). The abbreviated length is due to several factors: (1) cost (about $45,000 for each novela); (2) audience interest (over 90 percent of Télé-Sahel's dramatic programming runs no more than two episodes); and (3) diversity in language (over 97 percent of Télé-Sahel's programming is interpreted in French, Hawsa and Zarma).

A total of 97 percent of Niger's folk novelas are produced domestically. The remaining 3 percent are imported from Côte d'Ivoire, Togo, Guinea and Mali. Niger does not export any of its dramatic productions and seems to have no plans to do so.

Some of the 1996 folk novelas in Niger included the ten shows listed and described below. The summaries were generously provided by Télé-Sahel and O.R.T.N.[23]:

Shiga Ukku (Getting in Trouble)—Unbeknownst to her husband (or so she thinks), Abdu plans a rendezvous with Fati in a cabin. Her husband, aware of what is going on, surprises her first in the cabin. When he arrives, Abdu mistakenly believes it is Fati, and gives him her baby for a while. Once the baby is in his hands, the husband runs away and Abdu runs after him. Fati then asks for the baby, and total pandemonium occurs.

Dan Kagane (For Your Comprehension)—Dan Kagane explains a citizen's rights and duties. It also shows how to vote.

Hagoy da Waiboro (Be Careful with Women)—A wife wants to get rid of her husband she no longer loves. To do so, she decides to put poison in the porridge the husband is supposed to drink. When he is on the brink of drinking the poisonous porridge, a thief from under the bed gets out and orders him not to drink.

Uwar Miji (Mother-in-Law)—The tribulations of a mother-in-law. When she thinks the way her two daughters-in-law behave is not best, she plays her son's role and puts them out. She divorces them with her son.

Irkoy Beri (Good God)—In this drama, God punishes a woman. She has left her husband because he has no means to buy the sheep they must sacrifice on sacrifice day. Finally, the husband buys the sheep on credit. But when sacrifice day arrives, God refuses to accept the sacrificial animals that cannot be slaughtered (because the couple doesn't actually own them).

Kowa Ya Taka Doka (Law Is Law)—A policeman, accustomed to penaliz[ing] people because of no respect for the law, is judged himself. He has committed adultery and as law is law, he must be in prison.

El-hadji Ka Django (El-hadji Becomes Django)—A story of El-hadji, an old rich man who falls in love with a very young girl. A dancing party is organized and El-hadji is invited to honor it. His beloved accepts[,] too, but only when he changes his traditional clothes into western ones—to get dressed as Django (a cinema actor).

Bakauye Bakauye Ne (A Countryside Folk Is a Countryside Folk)—A country man comes to town with his donkey loaded with firewood to sell. He is overtaken by thieves.

Ramen Mugunta (A Pit)—A dibia arrives in a village when another dibia welcomes him. But the latter, feeling that the former has more power than he, decides to eliminate him. He sends poisonous food to his host. As he is away, the food is sent back and unfortunately, without knowing, he eats it and dies.

Laabu Si Tari (Land Never Dies)—A story of a country man. He comes to town, thinking he can easily find a job and thereby get money. His hopes disappointed, he returns to his village and decides to till the land instead. He meets his challenge.

Representatives from Télé-Sahel indicated that they receive no satellite or cable programming. However, they mentioned that two organizations, ACCT and URTNA, collect and distribute videocassettes throughout Africa free of charge. They utilize this service, as do many other African nations.

Focus: Mauritius

Marie Josee Baudot, a representative from the head office at Mauritius Broadcasting Corporation, reports that Mauritius (pop. 1.15 million) has three public TV channels.[24] The total number of TV households within the country number 166,000, with a potential viewership of 500,000. The official language is English, but because Mauritius is multiracial and an ancient French colony, French and Creole are understood by the entire population. In addition to these three languages, MBC also broadcasts in twelve Asian languages and dialects. Although Mauritius does not produce its own serial dramas, telenovelas (imported from other countries) are extremely popular with the viewers. A 1996 program schedule featured four telenovelas—*Le Droit d'Aimer*, *Helena*, *Femmes de Sablé* and *Rosa*—all on the air at one time. Given the tiny nation's rather meager resources, this schedule reveals a commitment to serial programming that will most likely expand in the future.

Focus: Tanzania

In Tanzania radio continues to dominate in rural homes, but television is clearly beginning to take hold in the cities. One of the major visionaries in this regard has been Franco Tramontano, managing director for Dar es Salaam Television (DTV). According to Tramontano, TV reaches about 30 percent of the urban households. And although the cost of a set may be prohibitive to the average citizen, viewing figures continue to grow.[25] DTV was established in 1994 to meet present and future needs, importing 100 percent of its programming, dubbed in Swahili. DTV is a privately funded station, unlike ITV, which is backed by the government and broadcasts all-African programs. It carries some advertising (although minimal) but is primarily underwritten by various grants from the United Nations, some social interest groups in the United States and other world organizations.

Soap operas (or "life plays" or "dramas" as they are often called) in Tanzania usually run 30 minutes, air once each week (at night) and last for approximately four weeks. Some are locally produced under great hardship;[26] others are imported from other countries like Kenya. Most "life play" themes cover topics of social consciousness like AIDS, FGM (female genital mutilation) and marital infidelity. The focus, as Franco Tramontano emphasizes, is almost always on "social responsibility" in programming.[27] One such drama, *House*

Girl (or *Ugumba*) was particularly popular in 1997. The plot involved an errant husband having an affair with a servant girl, and (based on viewer feedback) the program successfully presented a lifelike scenario of a serious problem found in Tanzanian society. When asked about the general efficacy of serial drama as an instrument of social change in Tanzania, Tom Mwerka, PASA assistant coordinator for the USIS (U.S. Information Service), echoed Franco Tramontano's idealism about its direction and potential: "Some are good. Some are educative. They try to make statements about real life. They address issues that are important. They can also provide models [of behavior] to avoid. They [can] make people feel guilty of their bad behavior."[28] He went on to note that "life plays" are extremely popular with a broad audience, including all age groups and both men and women. The possibilities for creating a dramatic forum for social problem solving are seemingly endless, but the future will show if and when they can be realized.

Notes

1. Station/network information taken from *World Radio TV Handbook, 1997 Edition*, ed. Andrew G. Sennitt (New York: Billboard Books, 1997). Television/radio set information and population figures taken from *The World Almanac and Book of Facts 1998* (Mahwah, NJ: K-III Reference Corporation, 1997).
2. The Democratic Republic of the Congo was formerly known as Zaire.
3. This listing is compiled from *WRTH Satellite & TV Handbook*, 4th edition, ed. Andrew G. Sennitt (New York: Billboard Books, 1997). It represents the *available* stations on satellite dishes through a transponder in Region I of the world satellite map. Although it is difficult to tell how many people have access to these channels, it is important to acknowledge the variety of cross-national program content on them.
4. "And Now ... a Soap Channel!" *TV Magazine Africa* (August 1997), 13. The soap operas featured on this channel include *Coronation Street*, *Neighbours*, *As the World Turns*, *Peyton Place*, *Guiding Light*, *Search for Tomorrow*, *Edge of Night* and *Another World*. The six-hour time block will be repeated every 24 hours in South Africa and every 12 hours on the rest of the continent.
5. *PSI: Communications to Motivate Healthy Behavior* (Population Services International, Inc., 1996) <webmaster@psiwash.org> [database on-line].
6. *Ibid.*
7. Vibert C. Cambridge, "Radio Soap Operas in Global Africa: Origins, Applications, and Implications," in *Staying Tuned: Contemporary Soap Opera Criticism*, ed. Suzanne Frentz (Bowling Green, OH: Bowling Green State University Popular Press, 1992), 124.
8. "International Update," *Variety* (December 9, 1991), 44.
9. *Ibid.*
10. Sue Armstrong, "South African Soap Aids the Health of the Nation," *New Scientist* (August 27, 1994), 5.
11. *Ibid.*
12. Philip Williams, "Kenya Uses a Soap Opera to Preach Population Control," U.P.I. (May 23, 1987) [database on-line]; available from Lexis-Nexis.
13. Cambridge, 122.

14. Williams (May 23, 1987).

15. *Ibid.*

16. Charlotte Eagar, "African Archers Target Tribal Folk," *Observer* (August 27, 1995) [database on-line]; available from Lexis-Nexis.

17. *Ibid.*

18. *Ibid.*

19. "Kenya to Show 'Culturally Devastating' Films Late," Reuters North American Wire (August 29, 1995) [database on-line]; available from Lexis-Nexis.

20. *PSI: Communications to Motivate Healthy Behavior* (Population Services International, Inc., 1996).

21. *Ibid.*

22. This information, in its entirety, was provided by O.R.T.N. (Direction de la Télévision Nationale—Niger) (July 1996).

23. Each of these descriptions is quoted directly from the O.R.T.N. programming summary.

24. Response to author's request for information, received from Mauritius Broadcasting Corporation (July 1996).

25. The figures and opinions quoted throughout this section come from an interview with Franco Tramontano, managing director of Dar es Salaam Television (August 1997). I am deeply indebted to both Mr. Tramontano and to Professor Michael Keith (Boston College), who gathered materials and conducted this interview while traveling on a State Department trip to Tanzania.

26. According to Mr. Tramontano, it is very difficult to do local production due to high costs and a paucity of experienced actors and actresses.

27. Interview, Tramontano (August 1997).

28. Interview with Tom Mwerka, PASA Assistant Coordinator, USIS (August 1997). Once again, I am deeply indebted to both Mr. Tramontano and to Professor Michael Keith.

Near and Middle East

Countries included:

Afghanistan, Armenia, Azerbaijan, Bahrain, Cyprus, Iran, Iraq, Israel, Jordan, Kuwait, Lebanon, Oman (Sultanate of), Qatar, Saudi Arabia, Syrian Arab Rep., Turkey, Turkmenistan, United Arab Emirates, Yemen (Republic of)[1]

Stations/Networks:

Afghanistan
Population: 23,738,085—90 per sq. mi.
(TV sets—1:102 persons; radios—1:8.5 persons)

Armenia
Population: 3,465,611—301 per sq. mi.
(TV sets—1:4.4 persons; radios—1:5.6 persons)

Azerbaijan
Population: 7,735,918—232 per sq. mi.
(TV sets—n/a; radios—n/a)

Bahrain
Population: 603,318—2,251 per sq. mi.
(TV sets—1:2.3 persons; radios—1:1.8 persons)
Bahrain Television
Orbit Satellite Television and Radio Network

Cyprus
Population: 752,808—211 per sq. mi.
(TV sets—1:3.1 persons; radios—1:3.3 persons)
Cyprus Broadcasting Corporation
Lumiere Television
Radio-TV Channel O Logos

Iran
Population: 67,540,002—107 per sq. mi.
(TV sets—1:16 persons; radios—1:4.2 persons)
I.R.I.B. (Islamic Republic of Iran Broadcasting)

Iraq
Population: 21,219,289—132 per sq. mi.
(TV sets—1:13 persons; radios—1:4.6 persons)
Iraqi Broadcasting and Television Establishment (IBTE)

Israel

Population: 5,534,672—702 per sq. mi.
(TV sets—1:3.6 persons; radios—1:2.1 persons)
Channel Two Television
Israel Educational Television
Israel Television
Palestinian Broadcasting Corp. TV

Jordan

Population: 4,324,638—125 per sq. mi.
(TV sets—1:13 persons; radios—1:4.1 persons)
Jordan Radio & Television Corp. (JRTV)
Orbit Satellite Television and Radio Network

Kuwait

Population: 2,076,805—301 per sq. mi.
(TV sets—1:2.6 persons; radios—1:2.2 persons)
Kuwait Television
Orbit Satellite Television and Radio Network

Lebanon

Population: 3,858,736—976 per sq. mi.
(TV sets—1:2.8 persons; radios—1:1.1 persons)
Lebanese Broadcasting Corp. Int.
TéléLiban

Oman (Sultanate of)

Population: 2,264,590—19 per sq. mi.
(TV sets—1:1.5 persons; radios—1:1.7 persons)
Oman TV
Orbit Satellite Television and Radio Network

Qatar

Population: 665,485—150 per sq. mi.
(TV sets—1:2.5 persons; radios—1:2.3 persons)
Qatar Television Service (QTV)
Orbit Satellite Television and Radio Network

Saudi Arabia

Population: 20,067,965—23 per sq. mi.
(TV sets—1:3.9 persons; radios—1:3.4 persons)
Channel 3 TV
Saudi Arabian Television
Orbit Satellite Television and Radio Network

Syrian Arab Republic

Population: 16,137,899—225 per sq. mi.
(TV sets—1:16 persons; radios—1:3.9 persons)
Syrian Arab Television
Orbit Satellite Television and Radio Network

Turkey

Population: 63,528,225—211 per sq. mi.
(TV sets—1:5.5 persons; radios—1:6.2 persons)
Turkish Radio & Television Corporation (TRT)
Turkmen Television

United Arab Emirates

Population: 2,262,309—70 per sq. mi.
(TV sets—1:9.3 persons; radios—1:3.2 persons)
UAE Television Service
UAE-TV-Abu Dhabi
Orbit Satellite Television and Radio Network

Yemen (Republic of)

Population: 13,972,477—67 per sq. mi.
(TV sets—1:36 persons; radios—1:31 persons)
Public Corporation of Radio and TV
Orbit Satellite Television and Radio Network

Satellite Channels Available in This Region[2]

3-Sat (Germany)
Abu Dhabi TV (UAE)
Afghanistan TV (Afg.)
AFN-TV (USA)
AFRTS (USA)
AFRTS-SEB (USA)
Al Jazeera Sat. (Qatar)
Al Jazeera Sat. (Algeria)
Albanian TV
Algerian TV
Antena Tres TV (Spain)
ARD-1 (Germany)
ARD/ZDF (Germany)
ART (Saudi Arabia)
ART Europe (UK)
ARTE (Germany)
Asia Business Channel
AsiaNet
ASTRA SPORT (AFS)
ATN (Africa)
ATV (Turkey)
ATV (Poland)
Bahrain TV
Bayerisches Fernsehen (Germany)
BBC Orbit Arabic Service (UK)
BBC Prime (UK)
BBC World (UK)
BHT (Bosnia Hercegov.)
BOP-TV (Senegal)
Bop TV Mmabatho (Bophuthatswana)
Bop TV-1 (Bophuthatswana)
Bravo (UK)
BSkyB (UK)
C-Span (USA)
Cable Plus Filmovy Kanal (Czech Rep.)
Canal Clásico (Spain)
Canal France Internat. (France)
Canal Horizons (Senegal)
Canal J(eunesse) (France)
Canal Jimmy (France)
Canal On (Spain)
Canal Plus (France)
Canal Sur (Spain)
Cartoon Network (USA)
CCTV4 (China)
CDAT (AFS)

Channel 5 (UK)
Channel Africa (South Africa)
Channel-2 TV (Israel)
Chinese Channel (UK)
Chinese News Entertainment (China)
Christian Channel Europe (UK)
Ciné Cinéfil (France)
Ciné Cinémas (France)
Cine Classics (Spain)
Cinema (Sweden)
Cinemania (Spain)
Cinemania 2 (Spain)
CMT Europe (USA)
CNBC (UK)
CNN International (USA/UK)
CNN Nordic (USA)
ConAir (USA)
Country Music Europe (USA)
CTC (STS) (CIS)
Deutsche Welle TV (Germany)
Discovery Channel (UK)
Documania (Spain)
DR-2 (Denmark)
DSF Deutsches Sportfernsehen (Germany)
Dubai TV (UAE)
Duna 7 (Hungary)
EDTV (UAE)
Egypt TV
Egyptian Satellite TV (Egypt)
ESPN (USA)
ET-1/2/3 (Greece)
ETV (Ethiopia)
Euro Business News (UK)
Euro D (Turkey)
Euronews (France)
Europe by Satellite
European Business News (EBN) (UK)
Eurosport (France)
Eurosport (Norway)
FilmNet (Poland)
FilmNet 1 Nordic (Norway)
FilmNet 2 (Sweden)
Fox Kids (UK)
France Supervision
France-2 (France)
Future Vision (Saudi Arabia)

Galavisión (Mexico)
Granada Good Life (UK)
Granada Plus/Man & Motor (UK)
Granada (Talk TV) (UK)
H.O.T. (Home Order TV)
HBB (Turkey)
Home Shopping Network (UK)
Home TV (India)
HRT Zagreb (Croatia)
HTB (Russia)
IBA Channel 3 (Israel)
InterSTAR (Turkey/Germany)
IRIB-TV 1/2/3 (Iran)
Jordan TV
JRT (Jordan)
JRTV (Jordan)
JSTV (Japan)
Kabel 1 (Germany
Kanal 5 (Sweden)
Kanal 6 (Turkey)
Kanal 7 (Turkey)
Kanal D (Turkey)
Kanal + (Poland)
Kasachstan 1 (private) (Kasachstan)
Kazakstan TV
Kuwait Space Channel
Kuwait TV
La Chaîne Info (LCI) (France)
La Cinquième (France)
LBC Lebanon
Libyan TV
M Net South Africa (AFS)
M-2 Morocco
M-6 Métropole 6 (France)
M-Net Int. (South Af.)
MBC (UK)
MCM Afrique (South Africa)
MCM Euromusic (France)
MED-TV (UK)
Middle East Broadcast (MBC)
  (UK)
Middle East Broad. Centre (UK)
MiniMax (Spain)
Mitteldeutscher Rundfunk (MDR 3)
  (Germany)
Moscow-1 (CIS)
MTV (UK)
MTV (Africa)
MTV Nordic (Denmark)

Muslim TV Ahmadiyya
Muslim-TV MTA+(UK)
N-3 Nord-3 (Germany)
n-tv (Germany)
NBC Super Channel (UK)
NEPC-TV (India)
NHK Tokyo (Japan)
Nickelodeon (Germany)
Nickelodeon (Sweden)
Nickelodeon (USA)
Nile TV (Egypt)
Nile TV Int. (Egypt)
Nova Shop (Sweden)
NRK 1/2 (Norway)
NTA Ch. 10 (Nigeria)
NTV (Russia)
Oman TV
Onyx TV
Orbit (Morocco)
ORT-1 (CIS)
Ostankino ORT Int. (CIS)
Paramount TV (USA)
Paris Première (France)
PIK CYBC (Cyprus)
Planète (France)
Polonia 1 (Poland)
Polsat (Poland)
Premièra TV (Czech Rep.)
Premiere (Germany)
Pro-7 (Germany)
Quantum Channel (UK/USA)
QVC (USA)
QVC Deutschland (Germany)
RAIDUE (Italy)
RAITRE (Italy)
RAIUNO (Italy)
Rendez-Vous (France)
RFO Canal Permanent 2 (France)
RTA-TV (Algeria)
RTL 7 (Poland)
RTL Television (Germany)
RTL-2 (Germany)
RTL-9 (France)
RTM 1 (Morocco)
RTP Internacional (Portugal)
RTS Beograd (RTV Srbjal, Yugo-
  slavia)
RTT-TV-7 (Tunisia)
SABC 1/2/3 (AFS)

SABC-TV (South Africa)
Samanloyu TV (Turkey)
Sara Vision
Sat-1 (Germany)
Saudi Arabia
Saudi Arabia TV 1/2
Saudia (Saudi Arabia)
Sci-Fi Channel (UK)
Sci-Fi Channel Nordic (Denmark)
Sell-a-Vision (Germany)
Sharjah TV (Mauritania)
Sky Movies (UK)
Sky Movies Gold (UK)
Sky News (UK)
Sky One (UK)
Sky Scottish (UK)
Sky Soap (UK)
Sky Sports (UK)
Sky Sports 2/3 (UK)
Sky Sports Gold (UK)
Sky Travel (UK)
Sky-2 (UK)
Sony Entertainment TV (India)
Sudan TV
Super RTL (Germany)
Super Television Channel (USA)
SWF/SDR (S-3) (Germany)
Syrian TV
TCC (The Children's Channel) (UK)
Tel Monte-Carlo (TMC) (Monte-
  Carlo)
Tele-5 (Spain)
Teleclub (Switzerland)
TeleDeporte (Spain)
TelePace/Vatican TV (Italy/Vatican
  State)
Telesat 5 (Spain)
TF-1 (France)
TGRT (Turkey)
The Adult Channel (UK)
The Computer Channel (UK)
The Disney Channel (UK)
The Egyptian Space Channel
The Family Channel (UK)
The History Channel (UK)
The Learning Channel (TLC) (UK)

The Movie Channel (UK)
The Playboy Channe (UK)
The Racing Channel (UK)
The Sci-Fi Channel (UK)
The Weather Channel (UK)
TM 3 (Germany)
TM3 (UK)
TNT/Cartoon Network (USA)
TRT Int. (Turkey)
TRT-1/3/4 (Turkey)
TV 1-India
TV 3 de Catalunya (Spain)
TV 3 Denmark
TV 3 Sweden
TV Angola
TV Eurotica (UK)
TV Norge (Norway)
TV Polonia (Poland)
TV Romania Int.
TV Russia 2
TV Sport Eurosport (France)
TV-1000 (Sweden)
TV-2/3 (Norway)
TV-4 (Sweden)
TV-6 Moscow (CIS)
TV3+ (Denmark)
TV5 Internationale/Afrique (France)
TVE Internacional (Spain)
TVX The Fantasy Channel (UK)
UK Gold
UK Living
Vasa TV (Slovakia)
VH-1 (UK/Germany)
VHI Nordic (Sweden)
VIVA (Germany)
Viva 2 (Germany)
VOX (Germany)
WBTV (The Warner Channel) (UK)
WDR (Germany)
What's in store (Netherlands)
WorldNet (USA)
Yemen TV
ZDF (Germany)
Zee TV (UK)
ZTV (Sweden)

Overview of Cultural Patterns and Audience Trends

More than any other area of the world, this region's TV networks are highly censored and tightly controlled either by conservative governments, dictatorial regimes or religious proscription. As a result, most of the indigenous programming is news oriented, with (according to the *Los Angeles Times)* "bland, stodgy, politically correct fare."[3] The only exception to highly restricted television broadcast services in the Near and Middle East appears to be Israel, which offers public networks (government owned but editorially independent), as well as several private stations.

For those who can afford satellite or cable, the variety of available shows is practically endless. In United Arab Emirates, for example, viewers have free and uncensored access to the BBC World Service, Rupert Murdoch's Star TV and Star Plus, as well as India's Zee TV.[4] Lebanese audiences can choose from 25 networks airing everything from Lebanese music videos to British documentaries, along with American, Syrian, Egyptian, Indian and Latin American soap operas/telenovelas.[5] However, for nonsatellite/cable households most program choices are limited to thematic variations of news, religion, education, politics and culture. Among those nations enjoying more broadcast freedom, Cyprus and Israel provide the best examples.

Focus: Cyprus

Most Cyprians seem to enjoy their soap operas or telenovelas from other countries, since funding for local drama production is somewhat limited. Soaps from the United States, Mexico, Greece and Australia are very popular here — *The Bold and the Beautiful* is a special crowd-pleaser.

In 1996 (according to Cyprus Broadcasting Corporation's Marios Skordis), Cyprians found another dramatic alternative — a new, indigenous serial, *Me, Lito Domestica.* Unlike the soap imports mentioned above, this was a period piece set in Cyprus during the 1930s and '40s. And, although it received only a tepid (8 percent) response from viewers, it nevertheless provided its target audience (families) with some historical background they may not have gotten otherwise.[6]

Other social dramas (in the entertainment-education tradition of Mexico's Miguel Sabido) are likely to follow *Me, Lito Domestica,* but at present it seems that the target for these "soaps" is domestic viewers only. No plans have been made for program export, for Cyprian nationalism and cultural identity have a higher priority.

Focus: Israel

Much of Israel's television history has been grounded in news, politics and informational programming for obvious reasons. Begun in 1967, the Israeli Broadcasting Authority defined its television stations in the following way:

> The Israel Broadcasting Authority shall broadcast radio and television programs as a public service. The Authority shall broadcast educational and entertainment programs, as well as information in the areas of social, economic, monetary, cultural, scientific and arts policy.
> ...Israel TV's first channel consists of two divisions:
> The News Division directs news, current affairs magazines, sports and special local and overseas broadcasts. News in English, aimed at local English speakers, tourists, diplomats and viewers in the neighboring countries, is broadcast once a day.
> The Program Division, which administers Israeli original TV productions, comprises five departments:
> 1. The Documentary Department produces original films, series and special broadcasts.
> 2. The Entertainment Department is responsible for weekend recreational programs, Israeli and Middle Eastern musical productions, games shows [sic] and special broadcasts for the Jewish festivals.
> 3. The Drama Department is in charge of original plays and dramatic series, with its most recent success including the prestigious "Kastner."
> 4. The Children's and Youth Department produces some three hours of programming a day for the younger age groups.
> 5. The Israel Heritage Department schedules programs for the Jewish and national holidays, with emphasis on the Hebrew language, Jewish music and productions about Jewish communities abroad. The programs Division cooperates with the film purchasing department to present selections of cinema movies and TV series.
> ISRAEL TELEVISION IN ARABIC
> Arabic TV broadcasts 20 hours a week to an audience of Arabic speakers in Israel and the neighboring countries. Its news and current affairs broadcasts included two daily news shows, discussions of topical interest, weekly news and sports magazines and direct broadcasts of sporting events.
> The Programs Division produces magazines on the arts, literature, agriculture, medicine and family related matters, as well as guest shows and specials for the Christian, Moslem and Druze festivals....[7]

In the early 1990s Israeli viewers seemed to tire of this fare, opting instead for imported entertainment shows (including soap operas and telenovelas) found on cable and satellite. As a result, domestic audience shares plummeted.

To some, the wise counterprogramming strategy would seem obvious—to buy soaps, novelas, game shows, talk shows and primetime drama from other countries. However, given Israeli communications law (which requires at least 60 percent of a station's programming to be locally produced), the call was not an easy one. Thus, by 1994 local programmers decided to do something more daring—to produce as much non-news programming as possible themselves.[8] Today Israelis have a wide selection of serial dramas to choose from. Indigenous soaps, such as *Fool's Gold*, *Deadly Fortune* and *Mediterranean Affairs*, have captured large domestic audiences, as well as interest abroad. The secret for success in Israeli soaps is not found in production values or high budgets. Rather, viewers can identify more closely with the language, the characters and the culture. According to the *Asia Times*, for example, the 1996 production of *Mossad* kept "hundreds of thousands of Israeli television viewers glued to their screens"—much to the chagrin of the real Mossad, Israel's secret service.[9] Soap director Dudi Mor explains: "I can assure you that the Mossad people don't like what they see. They are used to being behind the screen and pulling the strings, but now we reveal their dark secrets. What we want to tell people is that the staff at the Mossad are just people like you and me and not some sort of James Bond super heroes. The soap opera is based on real events, though we have not included any real-life story in its totality."[10] Incidentally, *Mossad* has also found great popularity in Argentina and other Latin American nations, where many Jews reside and where stories of secret police are equally widespread.

In addition to the relatively new industry of indigenous soap production, Israeli viewers have access to almost any soap opera or telenovela they want to see via "Amos," the Israeli satellite. Amos began commercial operation in 1996, beaming in two directions—one over the Middle East and one over Europe (especially Hungary, Poland and the Czech Republic).[11] Amos provides its viewers with most American, British and Australian soaps and in 1997 participated in a joint venture to beam a channel entirely devoted to Latin American telenovelas to Central and Eastern Europe (see chapter four).

Notes

1. Station/network information taken from *World Radio TV Handbook, 1997 Edition*, ed. Andrew G. Sennitt (New York: Billboard Books, 1997). Television/radio set information and population figures taken from *The World Almanac and Book of Facts 1998* (Mahwah, NJ: K-III Reference Corporation, 1997).
2. This listing is compiled from *WRTH Satellite & TV Handbook*, 4th edition, ed. Andrew G. Sennitt (New York: Billboard Books, 1997). It represents the *available* stations on satellite dishes through a transponder in Region I of the world satellite map. Although it is difficult to tell how many people have access to these channels, it is important to acknowledge the variety of cross-national program content on them.
3. "Tuning in the Global Village: What They'll Be Watching This Week," *Los Angeles Times* (October 20, 1992), 6.
4. United Arab Emirates Television Home Page, on the Ultimate TV Web site [database on-line].
5. Lebanon Television Home Page, on the Ultimate TV Web site [database on-line].
6. Written correspondence with Marios Skordis, Cyprus Broadcasting Corporation (July 1996).

7. Selected portions of the Israel Broadcasting Authority Law, Israel Broadcasting Authority, Jerusalem, Israel [database on-line].

8. Barry Chamish, "Israel Awash in Soap Suds," *Hollywood Reporter* (November 8, 1994) [database on-line]; available from Lexis-Nexis.

9. Yaroslav Trofimov, "Israeli Soap Reveals Mossad's Dark Side," *Asia Times* (November 6, 1996), 7 [database on-line]; available from Lexis-Nexis.

10. *Ibid.*

11. Daniela Ferguson, "Israeli Satellite Amos Begins Operations," R. R. Computers & Communication, Beer-Sheva, Israel <http://mandy.com/rrc001.html> [database on-line].

Pacific

Countries included:

Australia, Cook Islands, Easter Island, Fiji, Galapagos Islands, Guam (U.S. Territory), Kiribati, Marshall Islands, Micronesia (Federated States of), New Caledonia, New Zealand, Norfolk Island, N. Mariana Islands (U.S. Commonwealth), Palau (Republic of), Papua New Guinea, Polynesia (French), Samoa (American), Samoa (Western), Tonga, Wallis and Futuna[1]

Stations/Networks:

Australia
Population: 18,438,824—6 per sq. mi.
(TV sets—1:2 persons; radios—1:0.8 persons)
ABC-TV (Australian Broadcasting Corp.)
Federation of Australian Commercial Television Stations
Imparja Television
Network 10 Australia
SBS (Special Broadcasting Service)
The Nine Network
The Seven Network

Cook Islands
Population: n/a (see New Zealand)
(TV sets—n/a; radios—n/a)
Cook Islands Television

Easter Island
Population: n/a
(TV sets—n/a; radios—n/a)

Fiji
Population: 792,441—112 per sq. mi.
(TV sets—1:59 persons; radios—1:1.6 persons)
Fiji Broadcasting Comm.

Galapagos Islands
Population: n/a (see Ecuador)
(TV sets—n/a; radios—n/a)
Telegalapagos

Guam (U.S. Territory)
Population: n/a (see United States)
(TV sets—n/a; radios—n/a)
KGTF Television
Kuam Television

Kiribati
Population: 82,449—263 per sq. mi.
(TV sets—n/a; radios—1:4.8 persons)
Television Kiribati

Marshall Islands

Population: 60,652—866 per sq. mi.
(TV sets—n/a; radios—n/a)
AFRTS Television

Micronesia (Federated States of)

Population: 127,616—470 per sq. mi.
(TV sets—1:15 persons; radios—1:1.5 persons)
TV Station Pohnpei
TV Station Truk
TV Station Yap

New Caledonia

Population: n/a (see France)
(TV sets—n/a; radios—n/a)
RFO-TV
Canal Calédonie

New Zealand

Population: 3,587,275—34 per sq. mi.
(TV sets—1:2 persons; radios—1:1 persons)
Action TV
Canterbury Television
Television New Zealand Ltd.
TV 3

Norfolk Island

Population: n/a (see Australia)
(TV sets—n/a; radios—n/a)
Norfolk Islands Television

N. Mariana Islands

Population: n/a (see United States)
(TV sets—n/a; radios—n/a)
Micronesia Broadcasting Corporation

Palau (Republic of)

Population: 17,240—91 per sq. mi.
(TV sets—n/a; radios—1:1.8 persons)
STV-TV Koror

Papua New Guinea

Population: 4,496,221—25 per sq. mi.
(TV sets—1:345 persons; radios—1:13 persons)
EMTV

Polynesia (French)

Population: n/a (see France)
(TV sets—n/a; radios—n/a)
Canal Polynesie
Société Nationale de Radio Télévision d'Outre Mer (RFO)

Samoa (American)

Population: n/a (see United States)
(TV sets—n/a; radios—n/a)
KYZK-TV

Samoa (Western)

Population: 219,509—200 per sq. mi.
(TV sets—1:26 persons; radios—1:2.2 persons)
Television Samoa

Tonga

Population: 107,335—370 per sq. mi.
(TV sets—1:63 persons; radios—1:1.8 persons)
ASTL-TV-3

Wallis and Futuna

Population: n/a (see France)
(TV sets—n/a; radios—n/a)
Radiodiffusion Française d'Outre-Mer (RFO)

Satellite Channels Available in This Region[2]

ABC Australia
ABC HACBSS (Australia)
ABC-TV HACBSS (Australia)
ABC-TV (interchange) (Australia)

ABS-CBN Philippines
ABS/CBN (AUS/CHN)
AFRTS (USA)
AN-TEVE (Indonesia)

Army TV (ch. 5) (Thailand)
ART (Russia)
Asahi New Star (Japan)
Asia Business News (China/USA)
Asia Business TV (Japan)
Asia TV Network (India)
Asianet (India)
ATVI Australia
Azerbaijan Radio TV
BBC Asia (UK)
BBC Asia (Mandarin) (UK)
BBC World Service TV (USA/Japan/ UK)
BBC WSTV (UK)
BGV Channel (Japan)
Bloomberg Info. TV (Japan)
Business News Network (Japan)
Cable Soft Netw. (Japan)
Cable TV Access Channel (Japan)
Canal France Int.
Car Information TV (Japan)
CBHS Hour (China)
CCTV-4 (China)
CETV Shandong (China)
Channel 9 (Thailand)
Channel 11 (Thailand)
Channel 3 (Thailand)
Channel 7 (Australia)
Channel 7 (Thailand)
Channel 9 (Australia)
Channel KTV (China)
China Central TV 1/2/4
China Educational TV 1/2
China Entertainment TV
Chinese Channel (Hong Kong)
Chinese Channel (Mandarin) (Hong Kong)
Chinese Satellite TV (CSTV)
Chinese TV Network (China/USA)
China Central TV 1/2
Cinefil Imagica (Japan)
CNBC Asia (USA)
CNN Int. (USA)
Community TV (India)
Country Music TV (USA)
CSTV Music Channel (China)
CSTV News Channel (China)
Dai Truyen Hinh (Vietnam)
DD Channel 1/2/7/10 (India)

Deutsche Welle TV (Germany)
Diamond Channel (Japan)
Digital Tampa 501/502 (Japan)
Discovery Channel (USA/India)
Doordarshan TV (India)
Dub'I I/II/IV (CIS)
Egyptian Satellite Channel
EM-TV (Papua New Guinea)
Enterprise Channel (Australia)
ESPN/ESPN Internat. (USA)
Family Theatre (Japan)
Feisuo Satellite TV (Japan)
Friendly TV (Japan)
Fuji TV Network (Japan)
Gemini TV (Sri Lanka)
GMA Philippines
Golden West Network (Australia)
Green Channel (Japan)
Guangdong Satellite TV (China)
Guizhou TV Station (Mongolia)
Guizhou TV Station-1 (Hong Kong)
HBO Asia (USA)
Henan Satellite TV
IBC-TV Network (Japan)
Japan Cable Television
Japan Leisure Channel
Japan Religious Channel
Japan Satellite Broadcasting Co.
Japan Sports Channel
Karaoke Channel (Japan)
KBP Peoples Network (Philippines)
KBS Satellite TV 1/2 (Korea)
Keirin Channel (Japan)
Kids Station (Japan)
Kikkei Satellite News (Japan)
KN Television
Korea Vision
Kuoshin Satellite TV (Japan)
Lao National TV (Laos)
Life Design Channel (Japan)
M Channel (JMTV) (Japan)
MCM (France)
Meishi Entertainment TV (Taiwan)
Midnight Blue (Japan)
Mondo 21 (Japan)
Money TV (USA)
MTV Asia (UK/India/Hong Kong)
MTV Japan (Music Channel) (UK)
MTV Mandarin (China)

Music Asia (India)
Muslim TV Ahmadiyya Int. (India)
Myanmar TV (Burma)
NBC Asia (USA)
NEPC-TV (India)
Network 10 Australia
NHK Int. TV (Japan)
NHK Tokyo (Japan)
NHK-TV-Japan
Nihon Cable TV Netw. (Japan)
Nihon TV Network (Japan)
Nikkei Satellite News (Japan)
Nine Netw. Australia
NTV (CIS)
Orbita I/II (CIS)
P-Sat (Japan)
Pakistan TV
PHTV-Information Channel (China)
PHTV-Sanlih Channel (China)
Pioneer Music Satellite (Japan)
Playboy Channel (Japan)
Prefec Mulch (Japan)
Prefec Today (Japan)
Prime International (USA)
Prime Sports (Hong Kong)
Prime Sports (Mandarin) (Hong
   Kong)
Queensland Television (Australia)
Radio TV Brunei
Rainbow Channel(Japan)
Rajawari Citra Televisi Indonesia
   (RCTI)
Ray TV (Sri Lanka)
RCTS (Imparja) (Australia)
RFO Tahiti (France)
RTE Int. (Spain)
RTP International (Portugal)
Satellite ABC (Japan)
Satellite Culture (Japan)
Satellite News (Japan)
Satellite Theatre (Japan)
Shandong TV Station 1 (China)
Shopping Channel (Japan)
Sichuan TV Station (China)
Singapore Int. TV
Sky News (Japan)
Sky TV (Australia)
Sony Entertainment Network (USA)
Sony Entertainment TV (Japan)

Sound with Radio (Japan)
Space Shower TV (Japan)
Space Vision Network (Japan)
Star Channel (Japan)
Star Movies (China)
Star Plus (Hong Kong)
Star Plus (Japan)
Star TV (China/Burma/ Australia)
Star TV Chinese (Hong Kong)
Star TV Plus (Hong Kong)
Sun Music TV (Tamil Svc.) (Sri
   Lanka)
Super Channel (USA)
Taiwan Satellite TV
Televisi Pendidikan Indonesia (TPI)
Theatre Television (Japan)
TNT/Cartoon Network (USA)
Travel Channel (Japan)
TV 4 Channel (China)
TV 5 (France)
TV 6 Mockba (CIS)
TV Asahi (Japan)
TV Mongol (Mongolia)
TV New Zealand
TV Oceania (Japan)
TV Shopping Network (China)
TV-1 (Malaysia)
TV-3 (Malysia)
TVBS (China)
TVI (India)
TVRI (Indonesia)
Unique Business Channel (China)
Vi Jay TV (Sri Lanka)
Viva Channel (Japan)
Voice of the Earth (Japan)
VTV-4 (Vietnam)
Walt Disney TV (USA)
Weather Channel (USA)
World Entertainment (Japan)
World Net (India)
Worldnet (USA/Mongolia)
WorldNet/C-Span/Deutsche Welle TV
   (USA)
Xinjiang TV Station-1 (China)
Xizang TV Station 1 (China)
Yunnan TV Station-1 (Hong Kong)
Zee TV (English) (Hong Kong)
Zee TV (Mandarin) (Hong Kong)
Zhejiang TV Station (China)

Overview of Cultural Patterns and Audience Trends

Unlike most other regions of the world, the Pacific is best characterized by relatively small land masses sprinkled within a large body of water. Thus, the dependency on satellite technology in this area is immense—broadcast signals cannot travel far, and oftentimes cable is too expensive to be cost effective. Further, some areas are either too poor or uninhabited to have television stations of their own—either radio is a more preferred medium, or mass media is hardly used at all. Norfolk Island's Broadcasting Service, VL2NI, typifies the existing situation among many of the smaller land masses in this region. And a letter from one of the station representatives, Connie Telfer-Smith, expresses some of the frustration that goes with it:

> I would love to inundate you with pages of facts and figures but, in fact, there is nothing to offer you. Norfolk Island does not operate a television service from the government umbrella and our little radio station runs on faith and paper clips. Television is comparatively new to the island, the first transmission was on Monday, 7 August 1987, from the Australian Broadcasting Commission, followed two years later by SBS, the Australian multicultural-lingual station. This, plus video tapes, provides the square eyed with entertainment here. There is a fair amount of soap opera programming but that would obviously be part of your Australian profile. As a drama major, I'd also love to tell you that serial dramas originate in Norfolk Island, but so far I haven't even been successful in getting local radio drama into being, let alone being in a position to export![3]

In fact, in the late 1990s only two countries—Australia and New Zealand—have emerged as major producers/distributors of dramatic programming in this part of the world—and Australia certainly leads by a wide margin. For other nations or territories (like Papua New Guinea or American Samoa), cultural importation is much more common. Still, most would agree that serial drama from the Pacific affects most of the Western Hemisphere, as evidenced by the popularity of programs such as *Neighbours*, *Shortland Street* and *Pacific Drive*, as well as the booming business of travel and tourism to this corner of the world.

Focus: Australia

Perhaps the most interesting aspect of Australian serial drama is that it is more popular among global audiences than within its own borders. According to Sue Turnbull, a media scholar at La Trobe University,[4] Australian viewers prefer other programming (including serial imports like *Days of Our Lives*, *Young and the Restless*, *The Bold and the Beautiful* and *Santa Barbara*) to domestic soaps.[5] This may explain, at least in part, the "down under" nation's recent forays into satellite communication and distribution.

In 1993 the Australian Broadcasting Corporation (ABC) launched its first expedition into satellite communication, sending English-language programs to eighteen countries in Asia.[6] This was certainly an ambitious, if not financially secure, venture. No specific funding was alloted for the initiative; instead, the ABC international channel was supported by monies intended for the network's domestic service.

To make matters worse, audience numbers in the "hinterlands" were difficult if not impossible to predict, given the geographic terrain and remote locations targeted. In addition, without ratings projections, private funding was not a serious option. To invest, advertisers needed more reason than the hope of high viewership. The popularity potential for programs featuring Australian culture was not established, and there was little basis to expect high commercial interest.

In 1996, despite prior financial constraints, ABC surprised everyone by extending its satellite reach to encompass even more areas in South Asia and other Pacific Island nations. Journalist Liz Fell, through interviews with Australian Television's chief executive, Michael Mann, analyzed the rationale for renewed financial support in this way: "Mann sees benefits in promoting Australian goods and services across the region. Australian Television has in three years built a profile of Australia which is worth hundreds of millions of dollars in publicity for our companies and for tourism."[7]

As a result, over $14.3 million were earmarked for global broadcasting by the government, specifically in the international distribution of Australian drama and sports. The satellite technology was to provide 15 hours of Australian TV throughout the day and 9 hours of CNBC programming overnight. This programming would then be retranslated at facilities in Singapore, the Philippines, Taiwan and Papua New Guinea for local distribution at a very low cost to the cable/satellite operator.[8]

Today those who download the feed can choose either specific programs or the entire ABC schedule. However, they must air whatever programs they select in their entirety—not unlike other transnational distributors, who forbid complete editorial privileges to their affiliates.[9]

Mann explained the government's strategy: "We're not in the business to make money. We're just trying to make ends meet so that any relief we can get by reducing our costs or by getting revenue is beneficial to everybody, including importantly the Australian taxpayer."[10] And, if recent audience surveys are to be believed, the strategy of presenting Australia to non-Australians seems to work quite well. Liz Fell reports:

> Laos takes the Australian Television regional news; GZTV in Guangdong [China] prefers sport, documentaries and music; and Vietnam TV has found viewers tune into the science features.... Short news updates, with

English subtitles are also produced in Bahasa Indonesian, Thai, Vietnamese, Cantonese and Mandarin by news staff at Radio Australia....
[ABC executive Michael] Mann says he agrees with those who suggest Australian Television should show Chinese soap operas to attract more viewers. The point is that we're not broadcasting to get a bigger audience for Chinese soap operas. We're here to showcase Australia.[11]

Among the Australian soap operas most renowned throughout the world are:

The Sullivans—Premiering in 1976, with more than 1,100 episodes, this drama focuses on a family during World War II, who share joys, tragedies, love and laughter.

Paradise Beach—Produced in 1994, the soap features three teenagers who leave the drabness of the suburbs in search of sun, sand and surf and find it on Paradise Beach. Relationships blossom as the trio makes its journey.[12]

Home and Away—Premiering in 1988, the story focuses on Tom and Pippa Fletcher and their five foster children, who moved to Summer Bay after Tom lost his job in the city. One or more of the children is constantly in love or in trouble, as they grow up in the beach community.[13]

Pacific Drive—Set in a vibrant city on Australia's Gold Coast, the serial features young professionals who divide their time between sandy beaches and hot boardrooms. Already shown in many areas of the world (including the U.S.), this soap is now being targeted for the Pacific Rim as well.[14]

Probably the best-known success story in Australian TV history has been *Neighbours*, the consistently top-rated serial drama produced by the Grundy Organisation. *Neighbours* premiered in 1985; since then, it has been translated into many languages and is aired in more than 60 countries.[15] Recently some of *Neighbours*'s biggest fans have been found in Russia, where the soap seems to be winning a popularity contest over the more established Latin American telenovelas. According to Angst executive Nick Lazaredes (the Australian film and television company that distributes the soap), "One of the reasons 'Neighbours' is so successful is that people can relate to it…. There is a certain reality to it— it's not the kind of glitzy, romance-driven soap opera. 'Neighbours' has its share of sex, intrigue and murder, but it is done in a more wholesome way."[16]

Ironically, although Australia has imported many soaps from other countries over the years, it was rather slow to adopt one of the most respected dramas from its mother country, Great Britain—*Coronation Street. Coronation Street* is regularly viewed in Canada, New Zealand and Ireland, but it was slow to capture the imagination of most Aussies. It first aired on Swan TV in 1970, where it soon descended into a dismal failure. In 1983 Grundy tried once again, through local syndication on five stations; once again, it was a ratings disappointment. Finally, in 1994 another attempt was made on channel 9 (through Granada LWT International). Although not a blockbuster hit, *Coronation Street* has at last managed to remain on the programming schedule.

The reasons underlying this reluctance to accept a British soap may be political in nature, but the more accepted explanation is environmental, according to the *Daily Mail*: "Imports such as Neighbours and Home and Away have ... scenes of sunshine, surf-kissed beaches and hunky stars ... have attracted armies of British fans."[17] On the other hand, the murky setting of a working-class neighborhood under the gray skies of England has not proven as seductive to Australians. Still, with the Aussies' love for serial drama, well-written story lines seem to be overcoming the climatic handicap.

Incidentally, Australians are not the only viewers who seem to favor bright skies and airbrushed bodies. Such fare is the major reason for the country's soap opera success abroad. After building their serial drama reputation with such hits as *A Country Practice*, *Prisoner of Cell Block H*, *The Sullivans* and *E-Street*, as well as *Neighbours*, the new trend is to follow the paths of *Home and Away*, *Echo Point* and *Paradise Beach*, with "sun, sand and all things tanned," and to create more shows like them (e.g., *Pacific Drive*) according to reporter Belinda Goldsmith.[18] Goldsmith quotes the Australian Bureau of Statistics' claims that over $47 million were earned in the 1993–1994 season from Australian TV exports, most of which were soaps. In that year the biggest fans of Aussie television were British ($21 million), but the United States, New Zealand and Japan were also enthusiastic followers.

In addition to the golden beaches featured in Australian dramas, British surveys have revealed that audiences find "the outdoor lifestyle of Australian soaps ... more healthy than America's gin-soaked 'Dallas,' anorexic 'Models, Inc.,' or Britain's beer-guzzling 'EastEnders.'"[19] Thus, with large amounts of sun, surf, fun and a healthy diet besides, Australian soaps seem destined for ongoing success—if not within its borders, then certainly outside of them.

Focus: New Zealand

Although New Zealand produces fewer soap operas than its neighbor, Australia, it is still perceived as a "player" in the world of serial drama. Probably its greatest claim to television fame (for both domestic viewers and international audiences) has been *Shortland Street*, originating in 1992 and once described as "Neighbours meets Casualty"[20]: "Set in a hospital emergency ward, it follows the lives and loves of doctors, nurses and patients. The first episode showed hunky Dr. Chris Warner caught with his pants down with a sexy gym instructor."[21] From there Dr. Warner and his quirky receptionist, Kirsty Knight, have delighted audiences from Malta to Sri Lanka with their various escapades.

Aside from *Shortland Street*, New Zealanders can choose from a diversity of imported English/Australian/American fare such as *Brookside* (Orange), *Coronation Street* (different episodes on the TV1 and Orange channels), *East-Enders* (TV1), *Emmerdale* (TV1), *Home and Away* (TV2), *Neighbours* (TV1),

The City (Orange), *General Hospital* (TV3*), The Young and the Restless* (TV2), *Days of Our Lives* (TV2) and *The Bold and the Beautiful* (TV2).[22] In short, New Zealand is possibly one of the greatest soap-saturated nations per square mile.

Focus: Papua New Guinea

Unlike Australia and New Zealand, Papua New Guinea is in its television infancy—still learning about the medium's value as a cultural tool and still questioning which programming is best for the indigenous population. John Taylor, chief executive for EMTV, describes the current video "landscape," and his concerns for the future:

> At this time (August 1996), Papua New Guinea [PNG] has no "soaps." The TV service is a new thing, having been in existence for less than 10 years. There is only one terrestrial service [EMTV] but the country has been bombarded with many satellite services from Australia, Asia, USA and Europe making it very difficult to get local production up and going. There are also language problems, too, of the world's 2,700 different languages, 862 of them are in PNG [not dialects, different languages]. English of course is spoken and Motu, a language of the southern coastal people, but the "lingua franca" is Neo Melenesian Pigin or tok pisin. All the other languages are called tok ples languages. Literacy is also a problem, with existing low levels of read/write skills that are still falling.
> So you can see that getting people to write local soapy drama is difficult. Which culture do you place the soap in? Which language do you write it in? Where do you produce it? [EMTV hasn't the production skills or the facilities to produce that type of TV production, or the revenue to pay someone else to do it either.] The total population of PNG is only just over 4 million, with most of them living in the bush with no power. About 8 to 9 hundred thousand people have the capacity to see EMTV, mainly in the urban areas, even though we distribute our signal via the Russian Gorizont 142.5 E satellite so everybody has the potential to see us.[23]

EMTV's dilemma reflects the major problem faced by other tiny, underdeveloped countries: To provide the technological means for education and information, it may be necessary to sacrifice the identity and cultural life of its inhabitants. And what are the actual costs? American Samoa—with a bit more experience in television effects—has some answers.

Focus: American Samoa

In response to a request for information, Tom Norman, chief engineer for KVZK-TV, was gracious enough to provide some insight into the television system of American Samoa, as well as some social inquiry of his own:

You inquired about "daytime drama," or soap operas as carried by KVZK-TV. At present, there are none.

KVZK-TV is actually three television channels (2, 4, and 5), all operating with the same call sign. Channel 2 is a PBS affiliate, and is operated as a Public Television Station, with the same kinds of guidelines regarding commercial content as govern a stateside Public Television Station. The programming day consists of CNN news delivered via satellite from the Armed Forces Radio and Television Service (therefore stripped of commercial content), PBC programs, and locally produced programs. Channel 4 carries programming recorded in Honolulu from the three major network affiliate stations, with the tapes shipped to Samoa via air and played here a week following the original air date in Honolulu. Channel 5 has been dark since Hurricane Val in December of 1991, but is expected to return to service later this year.

When Channel 5 returns to the air, I anticipate that there will be programming hours available to allow insertion of possibly one daytime drama. Which one it will be, I cannot say. We occasionally hear requests for them, from people who are enthusiastic about such things.

If I may, I would like to step onto my soapbox and observe a thing or two for your consideration, relating to your issue. First, my wife is an attorney. When she was in private practice stateside, she used to be visited once a week on average by a woman who was convinced her husband was cheating on her. Cherie would lead the conversation into what soap operas the woman was watching, and what was happening in the plot lines at the moment. She would, in almost every case, discover that the cheating was going on inside the woman's mind, as a direct result of exposure to the soap opera's plot line. She would advise the woman to go home and shut off the soap operas. At the end of two or three weeks, if she was still convinced her husband was cheating, she told her to come back. In ten years of private practice, Cherie saved hundreds of marriages by this means.

It appears to me that if vicarious living extends from soap operas to the living rooms of American women, that vicarious violence and other social ills very likely do, too. It seems to me that if this can be said of American society, it is probably true of other societies as well. Are you on to something whose impact could shatter the existing norms for media social responsibility? Are you about to explain to the world why it is that there is a fundamental difference between print and electronic media, because of how they are assimilated?[24]

These are provocative and unanswered questions from a very insightful man.

Notes

1. Station/network information taken from *World Radio TV Handbook, 1997 Edition*, ed. Andrew G. Sennitt (New York: Billboard Books, 1997). Television/radio set information and population figures taken from *The World Almanac and Book of Facts 1998* (Mahwah, NJ: K-III Reference Corporation, 1997).

2. This listing is compiled from *WRTH Satellite & TV Handbook*, 4th edition, ed. Andrew G. Sennitt (New York: Billboard Books, 1997). It represents the *available* stations on satellite dishes through a transponder in Region III of the world satellite map. Although it is difficult to tell how many people have access to these channels, it is important to acknowledge the variety of cross-national program content on them.

3. Correspondence with Connie Telfer-Smith, Radio VL2NI, Norfolk Island Broadcasting Service (August 1996).

4. As quoted by Belinda Goldsmith, "Australians Mold Soap Operas for Overseas Markets," *Reuters North American Wire* (September 11, 1995) [database on-line]; available from Lexis-Nexis.

5. Mike Harris et al., "Euros Awash in Sexy Soap Operas," *Variety* (July 22, 1991), 76.

6. Liz Fell, "Ambassador Class," *Cable and Satellite Asia* (March 1996), 38 [database on-line]; available from Lexis-Nexis.

7. *Ibid.*

8. *Ibid.*

9. Interviews with other transnational programmers, like Voice of America, Vatican Radio and Radio Free Europe/Radio Liberty have revealed a similar policy.

10. Quoted in Fell, "Ambassador Class."

11. *Ibid.*

12. These descriptions were built from the contributions of Sarah Wiltshire, Programming Department, Nine Network Australia. Written correspondence (May 1996).

13. Information obtained from the "Home and Away" Web site, featuring episode summaries <http://www.ozemail.com.au> [database on-line].

14. This description was formed from information provided by Sarah Wiltshire, Programming Department, Nine Network Australia and Mark Woods's article, "Oz Outlets Exploding," *Variety* (January 6–12, 1997), N10.

15. "Urgent Hit TV Soap Producer Admits Child Sex Charges," *Agence France Presse* (December 18, 1996) [database on-line]; available from Lexis-Nexis.

16. As interviewed by Genine Babakian, in "'Neighbours' Hoping to Send 'Maria' Packing," *Moscow Times* (February 11, 1995) [database on-line]; available from Lexis-Nexis.

17. "Forget Neighbours, the Poms Are Giving Us Cobber Nation Street," *Daily Mail* (October 7, 1994), 12.

18. Goldsmith, "Australians Mold Soap Operas."

19. *Ibid.*

20. *The People* (November 5, 1995) [database on-line]; available from Lexis-Nexis.

21. *Ibid.*

22. Taken from program summaries in *TV Guide* (June 21, 1996), 73.

23. Correspondence with John Taylor, EMTV, Papua New Guinea (August 1996).

24. Correspondence with Tom Norman, KVZK-TV, American Samoa (October 1996).

The Future—Soap Operas, Satellites and the Internet

During my many months of "surfing" the Internet in search of soap opera data, this e-mail came across my screen.

Figure 10.1
Language and Transnational Ad Campaigns

Date: Fri, 14 Nov 1997 09:25:43 -0500
Subject: Ad Campaigns Gone Wrong
Mime-Version: 1.0

Coors put its slogan, "Turn it loose," into Spanish, where it was read as "Suffer from diarrhea."

Clairol introduced the "Mist Stick," a curling iron, into German only to find out that "mist" is slang for manure. Not too many people had use for the "manure stick."

Scandinavian vacuum manufacturer Electrolux used the following in an American campaign: Nothing sucks like an Electrolux.

The American slogan for Salem cigarettes, "Salem-Feeling Free," was translated into the Japanese market as "When smoking Salem, you will feel so refreshed that your mind seems to be free and empty."

When Gerber started selling baby food in Africa, they used the same packaging as in the US, with the beautiful baby on the label. Later they learned that in Africa, companies routinely put pictures on the label of what's inside, since most people can't read English.

Colgate introduced a toothpaste in France called Cue, the name of a notorious porno magazine.

An American T-shirt maker in Miami printed shirts for the Spanish market which promoted the Pope's visit. Instead of "I saw the Pope" (el Papa), the shirts read "I saw the potato" (la papa).

In Italy, a campaign for Schweppes Tonic Water translated the name into "Schweppes Toilet Water."

Pepsi's "Come alive with the Pepsi Generation" translated into "Pepsi brings your ancestors back from the grave," in Chinese.

Frank Perdue's chicken slogan, "it takes a strong man to make a tender chicken" was translated into Spanish as "it takes an aroused man to make a chicken affectionate."

When Parker Pen marketed a ball-point pen in Mexico, its ads were supposed to have read, "it won't leak in your pocket and embarrass you." Instead, the company thought that the word "embarazar" (to impregnate) meant to embarrass, so the ad read: "It won't leak in your pocket and make you pregnant."

Although the subject of the electronic memo is "ad campaigns," the message can be applied to soap opera/telenovela exports. Language is the major means by which we structure our world—if the language is incorrect, our vision of the world may be similarly skewed.

However, language is not the sole determinant of cultural transmission (as any basic communication course would affirm). Other elements are also important—religion, art, music, transportation, legal systems, government hierarchy, educational standards, food, folktales, customs and nonverbal cues (to name a few). These are the basics of any society, and they are often communicated through the mass media, especially in dramatic shows.

Thus, soap operas and telenovelas have found their way into virtually every country, territory and protectorate in the world. Whether it be through local production, cable coaxials or satellite feed, somebody somewhere is likely to be viewing a serial drama each hour of every day. Each nation has its own perspective on the value of such program fare—some view it as instructional, whereas others see it as cultural imperialism. Still others find it to be a highly effective way of unifying their people with a strong sense of nationalism.

If one can believe such media determinists as Marshall McLuhan and Jacques Ellul, the media—and how it is used—plays an ever-growing part in the internalization of beliefs, attitudes and values. Thus, whoever controls the media can, in a sense, also control perceptions. As such, serial drama, as demonstrated throughout this book, is a convenient means to this end. Whether indigenous or imported, soap operas and telenovelas create a "cultural landscape" for their viewers. This process can have very positive results (such as population management, health education and comfort during times of political and economic crisis). Yet the opposite is often the case, however unintentional.

Often, a vital factor when considering whether serial drama effects are positive or negative is the program source. Many countries are still not able to produce their own soaps but have advanced technology with huge programming demands. Consequently, they are almost forced to import programming— whatever it may be. It is cheaper, better looking and more proven than a locally produced venture.

Conversely, some nations have found that program exports are an easy way to make money. After shows are produced, the above- and below-line costs are minimal; so even if syndication revenues from other markets are small, they are considered "found" money.

Thus, for the most part, program exporters may have no overt political agenda. Still, the effect is the same: power lies wherever media channels and show distribution are controlled.

In 1997, serial drama from the United States, United Kingdom, Japan, India, China, Hong Kong, Singapore, Thailand, Mexico, Brazil, Argentina and parts of Africa appeared throughout the world via several satellites, including RTP Internacional (Portugal), M-Net, Future TV (Lebanon), Orbit (Saudi Arabia), Zee TV (India), Star TV and Star Plus (Hong Kong).

But given the number of soap operas/telenovelas already on satellite channels, how many more can appear? More specifically, what does the future hold for the serial TV producers in the "global village"?

In 1995 reporter Wayne Walley wrote an article for *Electronic Media* entitled "Sellers Analyze Global Hot, Cold Spots." In it he summarized the results of a survey done on the future of global media distribution.[1] The participants cited in this survey included the following international television producers/syndicators: Christian Charret, chair and chief executive officer of Gaumont Television in Paris; Rola Zayed, president of Alliance International Television (Toronto and Paris); Cesar Diaz, vice president of Sales for Venevision (Miami); and Linda Frazier, vice president, and Joan Cavanaugh, director of international sales, Discovery Enterprises Worldwide (Bethesda, Maryland). Based on their responses, some interesting predictions can be made about the future of television and the global distribution business. Below is their assessment of the media growth potential in specific countries, as well as various regions of the world:

• In the United Kingdom, the debut of channel 5, along with expanded cable and satellite services, will increase program demand. But the Brits tend to be more domestically oriented in their programming—they are not as likely as some other nations to import programming.

• Despite declared program import quotas, the market in France is likely to open up to more outside influences.

• Germany continues to make strong relationships with other countries, whether in coproduction or program imports. However, Rola Zayed (Alliance International Television) cautioned that "[the country] has taken on a lot of responsibilities economically. It's managing its debt well, but it has a heavy debt load and can only withstand so many outlets."[2]

• Italy's market is still undergoing changes wrought by media mogul Silvio Berlusconi's move into politics. Although caution is important here, Italy may also be an emerging marketplace for joint media ventures.

• Spain has experienced some economic decline in recent years. Its previous reputation as a receptive market for outside ventures has paralleled this decline. Experts predict that the downward spiral will soon be over and that the market will recover (somewhat, if not entirely).

- Scandinavia and the Benelux countries (Belgium, Luxembourg and the Netherlands) are seen as "steady" markets for the future—conservative but strong.

- In central and eastern Europe, the countries that stand out for growth potential include Russia, Poland, Hungary and the Czech Republic. Economic stability (especially in Russia) looms as a large question mark for media investors.

- Because of an economic recession, Turkish media owners have not stood out as highly attractive clients for program imports. Once the recession ends, high growth is expected to take place.

- India's new PanAmSat's PAS-4 satellite has excited both viewers and station owners. The audience market has risen dramatically, and advertisers are now targeting an emerging middle class.

- Like India, China appears to be a "promised land" for programming distribution opportunities. The Discovery Channel has already made some interesting inroads there, according to company vice president Linda Frazier. And Canadian-based Alliance Television's Rola Zayed concurs with this rosy prediction: "There is a healthy appetite and a good track record…. They like that our programming has a more family-fare appeal where the violence and sex content is not as high."[3]

- Indonesia seems to have a growing appetite for Latin American telenovelas. Venevisión's Cesar Díaz says, "You may see as many as 20 titles broadcast on a weekly basis. What we hope is that the success in Indonesia for the telenovela travels across to other countries in Asia."[4]

- Mexico's economic slump has been felt strongly in the cable/satellite business. In spite of a small recovery, it seems unlikely that things will rebound quickly there.

- Brazil, on the other hand, continues to thrive—and will grow even stronger with Rupert Murdoch's investments there.

- Argentina, although also economically strong, seems less interested in program imports. Rather, it seems to be headed toward an emphasis on local productions for its cable viewers. Venevisión's Cesar Díaz notes: "It's become a very tough market…. The few foreign telenovelas that have aired there have not done well."[5]

- Despite a somewhat uncertain economic climate, Venezuelan TV producers continue to churn out large numbers of telenovelas for domestic and international distribution and seem likely to continue this trend well into the future.

- Ecuador, on the other hand, has been riddled with energy crises and political disputes with Peru. Within this uncertain climate, it's difficult to achieve a production momentum. The future for Ecuador to excel as a marketplace for media production seems doubtful at best at this point.[6]

From these observations, several generalizations can be made about the future of soap operas and telenovelas:

1. Latin America continues to set the standard for telenovelas worldwide. Despite the production drop in some countries like Argentina, Peru, Chile and Ecuador, this international success creates fertile ground for future projects, either in consultation or co-production with other countries. Warner Bros. has

already consolidated efforts with Venezuela's Marte TV to produce several telenovelas, and Rupert Murdoch and Mexico's Grupo Televisa recently invested $5 million each to produce 500 hours of bilingual programming.[7]

2. Asia—particularly China—is growing by leaps and bounds, and its audiences can't seem to get enough serial drama. Governments can also use this program genre to inform, educate and perhaps propagandize. The region is ripe for serious investment in soap opera/telenovela production, distribution and foreign importation.

3. Central and eastern Europe are enthusiastically opening their doors to joint production ventures as well as program imports. Once again, the interest in soap operas here is very high—in Russia many viewers have pay-TV to see their favorite telenovelas (on either NTV Plus or 2×2). Five hours of telenovela programming (provided by Madrid's Tepuy Films) air on 2×2 each week. Past favorites have included *La Viuda de Blanco/Blanco's Widow* and *Sueños y Espejos/Dreams and Mirrors.*[8] Although the economy is still shaky, the desire for serial drama is strong and likely to continue, if only through outside programming for the next few years.

4. The Pacific will continue to be a major force in serial drama, with the ongoing popularity of Australian and New Zealand soaps. In addition, one cannot ignore the global influence of Aussie Rupert Murdoch, who already offers a channel devoted completely to soaps as part of his multinational satellite empire (see Figure 10.2).

Figure 10.2

The Soap Channel Program Schedule
November 1997

6:00 A.M. *Guiding Light* (U.S.)	3:00 P.M. *Peyton Place* (U.S.)
7:00 A.M. *As the World Turns* (U.S.)	3:30 P.M. *Edge of Night* (U.S.)
8:00 A.M. *Search for Tomorrow* (U.S.)	4:00 P.M. *Days of Our Lives* (U.S.)
8:30 A.M. *Coronation Street* (U.K.)	5:00 P.M. *Another World* (U.S.)
9:00 A.M. *Peyton Place* (U.S.)	6:00 P.M. *Guiding Light* (U.S.)
9:30 A.M. *Edge of Night* (U.S.)	7:00 P.M. *As the World Turns* (U.S.)
10:00 A.M. *Days of Our Lives* (U.S.)	8:00 P.M. *Search for Tomorrow* (U.S.)
11:00 A.M. *Another World* (U.S.)	8:30 P.M. *Coronation Street* (U.K.)
12:00 P.M. *Guiding Light* (U.S.)	9:00 P.M. *Peyton Place* (U.S.)
1:00 P.M. *As the World Turns* (U.S.)	9:30 P.M. *Edge of Night* (U.S.)
2:00 P.M. *Search for Tomorrow* (U.S.)	10:00 P.M. *Days of Our Lives* (U.S.)
2:30 P.M. *Coronation Street* (U.K.)	11:00 P.M. *Another World* (U.S.)

Thus, soap opera/telenovela popularity continues to rise in most areas of the world today. In some countries the move has been toward more local production (either to preserve a homogeneous culture or because the costs are more complementary to current economic realities). Other nations have encouraged joint ventures and co-production, with plans for worldwide (or at least regional) distribution. Even African television, in its infancy (comparatively speaking), has found great purpose and popularity with its "life dramas." Serial drama continues to entertain, to culturally inform, to educate and to unify people across distant borders. Whereas some may fear cultural invasion, others welcome the integration of diverse populations, as demonstrated by the listener response to the BBC World Service's 1997 experiment with its first worldwide radio soap opera, *Westway*.[9]

Still, television (whether through satellite or cable) may not necessarily be the main showcase for serial drama in the future. Within the last few years a growing number of followers have nourished their soap opera hunger through another medium—the Internet. Trendy "cybersoaps" abound on the World Wide Web today—led (not surprisingly) by Aussies, Brits and Americans. The following examples (some of which need little more description than the title) are but a few among many:

The Spot—takes place in a Santa Monica beachhouse, with five main twentysomething characters and a Cyberian husky named Spotnik.[10]

Friday's Beach—focuses on the lives of five teenagers, rife with plots ranging from love, drugs and sex to steroid abuse.[11]

101 Hollywood Blvd.—features six film students "making love and making movies in Hollywood."[12]

Chuckleheads—best described as "'Married with Children' in Montana."[13]

California Beer Review and Soap Opera—a serial that takes place in pubs throughout California.[14]

Dogmandu—a fantasy about a dog who becomes a boy. It also features photographs of pets that need homes and provides web links to animal shelters.[15]

Zoloft—according to a Web site critic, "You can expect to find good mood music, wonderful shockwave effects and excellent photography. I've tuned in almost ten times and I still don't understand what the story is about. The viewer is supposed to be some kind of futuristic condominium tenant trying to evict a homeless squatter. You do this by eavesdropping."[16]

Cybersoaps range from promotional resumes, ad agency home pages and frustrated soap plots to political commentary to the "stuff" from which *Zoloft* is made. Each day new titles emerge with added visuals, sounds and imagination. For some this is the future home of serial drama; for others it will simply be remembered as a sidebar in soap opera history.

Notes

1. Wayne Walley, "Sellers Analyze Global Hot, Cold Spots," *Electronic Media* (October 23, 1995) [database on-line]; available from Lexis-Nexis.

2. *Ibid.*

3. *Ibid.*

4. *Ibid.*

5. *Ibid.*

6. The information for each of these countries/regions was collected from Walley's article (see above).

7. Meredith Amdur, "Cable Networks Head South: Latin America Ripe with Program Opportunities," *Broadcasting & Cable* (January 24, 1994), 118.

8. "The Scramble to Make Russia Pay," *Television Business International* (February 1997) [database on-line]; available from Lexis-Nexis.

9. "BBC to Broadcast Worldwide Radio Soap Opera," Reuters (October 2, 1997) [database on-line].

10. "Hitting the Spot," *The Economist* (August 26, 1995), 26.

11. "Cybersoap Opera," *New Straits Times Press (Malaysia) Berhad* (August 22, 1996), 36.

12. "Internet Soap Operas: Best Episodic Sites on the Web" <Merlin200@earthlink.net> (5/22/97) [database on-line].

13. *Ibid.*

14. *Ibid.*

15. *Ibid.*

16. *Ibid.*

Appendix A
Sample Soap Operas/Telenovelas

(Brief descriptions of some typical
soap operas/telenovelas seen worldwide)

NORTH AMERICA

United States

All My Children—Records the daily happenings in Pine Valley (a fictional community near New York City), a small town with many colorful characters whose families, by now, have almost all intermarried.

Another World—The first episode of this drama opened by introducing one of Bay City's most respectable families (the Matthewses) mourning the loss of brother William (who had been quite wealthy and even more arrogant). As the serial progressed, the less fortunate Matthewses had to endure William's widow and her children.

As the World Turns—This soap takes place in the fictitious town of Oakdale (allegedly near Chicago) and focuses on the personal and professional lives of several key characters and their families.

The Bold and the Beautiful—Originally titled *Rags*, it features the Forrester family, owners of an upscale design house, and the cutthroat competition of the fashion industry.

Capitol—Set in Washington, D.C., this drama featured two warring political families, the McCandlesses and Cleggs. In a plot twist straight out of *Romeo and Juliet*, one of the McCandless sons soon fell in love with a Clegg daughter. This provided enough grist for a five-year run at the soap mill.

Dark Shadows—An immediate cult hit, this serial featured a Gothic family (including a werewolf and a 200-year-old vampire) living on the dark shores of Maine.

191

Days of Our Lives—Features the trials and tribulations of the Horton family, as well as other, newer clans who have taken hold over the last three decades of the serial's broadcast history.

The Edge of Night—Named (in part) for its late-afternoon time slot, the serial featured crime/courtroom stories revolving around investigator Mike Karr, his colleagues and his friends.

General Hospital—Focuses on the intricate professional and personal lives of the medical staff of a Port Charles city hospital.

Guiding Light—Taking place in Springfield, the long-running serial looks at life from the vantage point of five families.

Loving (The City)—Focused on four major families living in the college town of Corinth.

One Life to Live—Set in Llanview, this story originally focused on the prominent Lord family, owners of the local newspaper. Victor (the widower father) tried to raise his two daughters (Victoria and Meredith) by himself while maintaining the legacy of the paper (through chosen daughter Victoria).

Port Charles—Premiering in a 1997 two-hour Sunday night made-for-television movie, this drama has tried to establish its own identity, while enjoying immediate viewer interest as a spin-off from *General Hospital*. The series began with the return of Scotty Baldwin (a character who had disappeared on *GH*), which caused immediate distress between Lucy Coe (his previous love) and her current boyfriend, Kevin Collins. From there, new characters have emerged.

Santa Barbara—Focusing on four families—the wealthy Capwells and Lockridges, the middle-class Perkinses and the lower-class Latino Andrades—this soap has achieved greater success in foreign export sales than in its domestic broadcasts.

Sunset Beach—The story takes place in a small Pacific coast town, where locals gather either at the local watering hole (The Deep) or the cyber coffeehouse (Java).

The Young and the Restless—Takes place in fictional Genoa City and features a culturally diverse blend of wealthy and middle-class families.

CENTRAL AMERICA

Jamaica

Lime Tree Lane—A look at life in a typical urban working-class environment.

Pullet Hall—Deals with the impact of urban migration on a rural farming family.

Mexico

Acapulco Cuerpo y Alma—Focuses on the main character, David Montalvo, whose successes are marred by jealousy and hatred in his family. This conflict becomes even worse, however, after David and his half-brother, Marcelo, both fall in love with the beautiful Lorena.

Agujetas de Color de Rosa—Reveals the pain endured by a widow (Elisa) after her mother-in-law tries to deprive her and her children (Paola, Daniel and Anita) of their rightful inheritance. They survive the ordeal as best they can, and Elisa also meets Gonzalo David, a single father, along the way.

Alondra—Features a young, idealistic woman who tries to escape her horrific family to find love and happiness with the man of her dreams.

Azul—Set in an amusement park, this story tells of love between an idealistic man and woman, both of whom care about humanitarian causes as much as they do for each other.

Con Todo el Alma—Recounts the rather dismal life of Daniel Linares, who has been cut out of his family's will, loses his actress girlfriend to her leading man, and barely survives a helicopter crash as he tries to win back his inheritance of his grandfather's ranch. Daniel's luck turns, however, when he meets a poor peasant girl and falls in love.

Corazón Salvaje—Recounts the hardships of Juan del Diablo, the illegitimate son of a wealthy landowner, Don Francisco (who is unaware Juan belongs to him). Shortly before his death, however, the landowner discovers the secret and acknowledges Juan's birthright. Unfortunately, Don Francisco's widow hides this letter, and for years afterward Juan must try to fend for himself in an unfriendly world. His suffering turns to bitterness, until he finally falls in love with Monica (the daughter of a poor aristocrat), who has been in a convent to hide from the humiliation of being left at the altar by Don Francisco's legitimate son.

La Culpa—Features two young lovers who must solve a murder mystery before they can find true happiness together.

María la del Barrio—Follows the travails of a 15-year-old waif, Maria, who tries to fight her way out of the ghetto by working for a wealthy landowner (Don Fernando). Along the way Maria is abused by Don Fernando's wife and niece but is hopeful all will turn out well when she falls in love with Don Fernando's son, Luis. Unfortunately, a great misunderstanding occurs after Maria and Luis are married, and unwittingly she gives away their newborn baby. Once the couple is reunited, however, Maria lives in the hopes of seeing her young son once more.

María Mercedes—Victimized by a poor, unloving family, Maria grows up to be a manipulative young woman on the streets. She will stop at nothing to keep her family fed and clothed. One day she meets a wealthy landowner named Santiago del Olmo, who falls in love with her (even though he is dying). However, del Olmo's evil sister-in-law will have none of this and tries to throw Maria out of the house before she is named as a major heiress in his will.

Marimar—The story of a young (apparently orphaned) girl who lives with her destitute, elderly grandparents on a beach, this serial tells how Marimar is forced to steal to feed her family. One day, as she tries to pinch some vegetables and eggs from a hacienda, she's caught by the foreman, who threatens to turn her in if she doesn't kiss him. As she screams for help, the wealthy, spoiled son of the house rushes to her rescue and later offers to marry her to humiliate his parents. Little does Marimar know, however, that her real father (a wealthy man in his own right) is not dead and is looking for her to make her his heiress.

Marisol—Centers on the life of Marisol, a young woman who has suffered through a life of poverty and facial disfigurement, all the while unaware that her true father is a wealthy man. Her mother dies without telling her this secret, and she mistakenly falls in love with a painter who shares the same grandfather.

Mirada de Mujer—Tells the story of a 50-year-old mother of three who starts an affair with a younger man after she discovers her husband has been cheating on her.

Nada Personal—Parallels the real-life drama of the assassination of a Mexican presidential candidate and a ruling party leader.

Los Parientes Pobres—Tells the story of Margarita Santos, a young woman who has lost her family fortune as well as the man she loves. Because of her bitterness she decides never to trust anyone again and to gather as much wealth as possible. While striving for her new goals, however, she meets Chucho, a poor but honest man, and the two fall in love. The love is then challenged by outsiders.

Pobre Niña Rica—Paralleling the story of Cinderella, little Consuelo is a slave to her mother and two selfish brothers. Her father, who loved her very much, dies, leaving her his fortune, but her family keeps this secret from her. Later, Consuelo meets Julio, who makes her feel beautiful both inside and out.

Los Ricos También Lloran—An impoverished young woman overcomes her lower social status by marrying into an aristocratic family. After giving birth to a beautiful son, she discovers to her dismay that her wealthy husband has been cheating on her. In desperation she gives her son to a poor street woman selling gum in the park. The husband finally reunites with his wife, but they must now spend the rest of their lives finding their lost child.

Triángulo—Centers on the very complicated life of Sara, a young, idealistic nurse, who unwittingly becomes pregnant by David (a spoiled son of the wealthy Villafranca family). David's brother Ivan then forces him to move to Brazil (without Sara). She then talks to Ivan about David's return, but when they call their contact in Brazil, they are told David is dead. In the meantime, Sara's father has committed suicide in his jail cell, having been falsely arrested for allegedly killing David's father. Ivan then feels sorry for Sara and the unborn child, falls in love with her, and asks her to marry him. Shortly afterward, David appears.

Ven Conmigo—(co-authored by Mexican novela icon Miguel Sabido and Celia Alcantara, an Argentine best known for *Simplemente María*) A dramatic portrayal of the lives of five major characters (including a servant, a farmer and a single mother). Within this drama is a strong message promoting adult literacy.

Puerto Rico

Al Son del Amor—Features Gabo, a poor stable boy, who falls in love with his boss's daughter, Vicky. At first Vicky is pampered and spoiled, but she adapts to a new lifestyle, and the couple ultimately finds happiness ... at least until Helen, a jealous schemer, interferes.

Natalia—Recounts the pain of a woman (Isabel) who seeks revenge after being raped. Unfortunately, she later finds out that the daughter conceived from the rape (Natalia) is in love with a man who is the grandson of her attacker.

SOUTH AMERICA

Argentina

Celeste—Follows the life of a young woman named Celeste as she tries to make a life for herself and her dying mother. In the midst of her sorrow, she meets a "mystery" man (Franco) with whom she immediately falls in love. Through a series of twists and turns (including some nasty business with Franco's mother, Teresa), Celeste comes to live with the family, only to discover later that Franco is the mystery man in her life. They fall in love ... and should live happily after, but they still live under a veil of secrecy that could destroy them.

Celeste, Siempre Celeste—The sequel to *Celeste*, the story picks up after Celeste and Franco prepare for their wedding and leave for their honeymoon. However, Franco's mother, Teresa, continues to wreak havoc by having Celeste kidnapped. Celeste escapes but is injured in the process and is hospitalized with pneumonia. In the meantime, Clara, Celeste's heretofore unknown twin sister, surfaces at the hospital. Confusion with each woman's identity occurs ... especially with Franco, who at first believes Clara is Celeste and later must continue this charade when he learns that Clara will put Celeste in greater peril if he tells the truth.

Chiquititas—Opens with a character named Martin Moran, who discovers during a business trip to Argentina that his sister is mentally ill. He gives up his job and moves back home to help her. After finding a new job in a factory, Martin meets and falls in love with Belen. In the meantime, Martin also develops a special friendship with Mili, an orphan who lives in his family-owned orphanage. From there, complications develop between these three and, of course, Martin's sister, Gabriela.

Nano—Features a young man named Nano (short for "Manuel") who decides, against his father's wishes, to open an oceanarium. By day he is the curator; by night, he plays a sort of "Robin Hood," taking risks to help people who have been victimized by upper-class corruption. Nano is not happily married but finds love with a deaf mute named Camila. His wife, however, will have none of it ... and proceeds to make his life even more difficult than before.

Brazil

Colégio Brasil—A novela aimed primarily at teens, this drama addresses the trials and tribulations of being a high school student.

Deus Nos Acuda—Portrays Brazil as an inferno that only God can save.

A Escrava Isaura—Focuses on a young white girl, born into slavery in nineteenth-century Brazil. From her childhood, Isaura yearns for freedom and will not be satisfied until she accomplishes her goal.

O Fim do Mundo—An experimental "short-form" novela, this drama prophesies what the world might look like in its final days. Viewers loved it; the Roman Catholic Church was less impressed.

Pantanal—A fantasy, featuring characters from Brazilian folklore, including a jaguar-woman and other river spirits. Often watched for its exquisitely photographed Amazon setting as well as its intermittent nude scenes, this soap became an instant hit for the Manchete network.

Tropicalmiente—Follows a heated romance between a rich, adventuresome girl and a poor (but handsome) fisherman amidst a sunbaked beach setting.

Colombia

Azúcar—A tale of wealth, power, and mistaken parentage, all taking place on a large sugarcane plantation.

Café con Aroma de Mujer—Centers on a powerful romance between the son of a wealthy ranch owner (Sebastian Vallejo) and one of the coffee-bean pickers on the property (Gaviota). After a single night of love-making, Sebastian travels to Europe to finish his studies. Gaviota soon realizes she's pregnant and sets out to find him. Along the way she falls onto hard times and is trapped in a prostitution ring. Sebastian hears that she is a prostitute and will not have anything to do with her ... until she takes on a new identity (Carolina) and he falls in love with her all over again.

Venezuela

Cristal—Starts with a woman's (Victoria Ascano) search for the daughter she abandoned years ago. At the same time, a young woman, Cristina, leaves her orphanage home to pursue a career in modeling and meets Victoria, the owner of a fashion house. As the story develops, Cristina falls in love with Victoria's stepson (Luis Alfredo), but Victoria separates them and forces Luis to marry his old girlfriend. In the meantime, Cristina discovers she's pregnant.

La Dama de Rosa—Gabriela, an ambitious, enterprising girl, works hard to help her family. She takes a job at a carwash, and has a romance with its owner (Tito), only to find out later that Tito has set her up to appear guilty of drug trafficking. Subsequently, she is taken to court and put into jail. As she awaits her freedom, Gabriela plots to change her appearance and get even with Tito.

Kassandra—Focuses on the determination of a young woman who must rise above the social class where she was born and search for professional success and personal love in her new life.

Por Estas Calles—A politically motivated novela in which the action centers around real-life Venezuela government scandals like diversion of public funds, drug trafficking and administrative corruption.

Quirpa de Tres Mujeres—A remake of a former hit, *Las Amazonas*, the story of a multgenerational family feud over love and an unfair land deal.

Señora—Eugenia, a young woman who is unfairly sent to prison, vows revenge on the man who put her there. She encounters several people along the way—some helpful, some harmful—but she cannot truly find love and contentment until she has gotten over her obsession.

EUROPE

France

Les Coeurs Brulées—Follows the path of a wealthy family who runs the lavish La Reserve Hotel on the Cote D'Azur.

Germany

Guten Zeiten, Schlechten Zeiten—Based on Australia's *Restless Years*, the soap focuses on the trials and tribulations of growing into adulthood.

Lindenstrasse (joint-produced with Austria)—Known as the German version of *Coronation Street*, this drama centers on the changing lives and relationships among the residents of Linden Street, a small suburban street in Cologne.

Marienhof—Takes place in a fictitious neighborhood in Cologne and focuses on the personal and professional lives of several key residents and their families. In recent years this serial has become more youth-oriented, addressing issues such as drug abuse, first love and teen pregnancy.

Open on Sunday—Set in a fictional Hamburg shopping mall (Neumarkt Center), the drama features mall manager Anna Schering, who serves as friend, "sounding board" and amateur psychologist to her tenants.

Schwarzwaldklinik—A German version of *General Hospital*, the serial focuses on the medical staff of The Black Forest Clinic.

Verbotene Liebe—Based on Australia's *Sons and Daughters*, this youth-oriented drama focuses on "growing pains" and the relationship changes that accompany them.

Poland

Clan—Focuses on an extended Polish family and how it deals with the new, capitalist way of life.

Russia

Dom Syem Podyezd 4—Set in a tough city housing project, this serial features the Mafia, drinking in epidemic proportions and a large dose of violence and bad language.

The Little Strawberry—Centers around six main characters who spend most of their time in a pub named Little Strawberry.

Spain/Catalonia

The Duty Chemist—Set in an old quarter of Madrid, this serial explores the lives and loves of the residents, who tell their troubles to Lourdes Cano, the owner of a neighborhood pharmacy.

Nissaga de Poder—Features the third generation of the wealthy Montsolis dynasty, who live in a small town in the heart of Catalonia's wine-producing region. Intrigue, suspicion

and cutthroat competition surround the lives of the members of the family and their relationships with others in the town. Beneath all this lies a secret that cannot be revealed.

Poblenou—Features a middle-aged couple with grown children. All lead fairly dull, predictable lives until a winning lottery ticket upsets their routine existence and sparks a
whirlwind of unexpected events.

Secretos de Familia—After a 25-year absence, Narcis unexpectedly returns to his
hometown and family. Why he returns—and why he left—nobody seems to know. But
as the web of mystery slowly unravels, buried feelings, secrets and deceit surface,
irrevocably changing the lives of all the characters in the series.

Sweden

High Seas—Filled with love, business, betrayal and intrigue, as a dedicated crew tries
to do its job (running a shipping service on the Baltic), despite constant intrusion from
the family that owns the business.

United Kingdom

The Archers—One of the most successful serials in Britain's soap opera history, this
program addresses the joys and troubles of a hard-working farming family. The Archers
face real problems like food shortages and possible crop failures in addition to idealistic love and romance. The drama later became a scripting model for serials in developing countries, as well as at home.

Brookside—Modeling the success of *Grange Hill*, this serial, set in a small housing
development outside of Liverpool, tries to address social issues (like date rape and
spousal abuse) through bold, dramatic story lines.

Coronation Street—Looks at life in a typical working-class neighborhoood in north-
ern England.

EastEnders—Set in the fictional community of Walford, in the east end of London, the
drama focuses on families and the problems they face in everyday life.

Emmerdale—Inspired by the success of *The Archers*, this serial takes place on a farm
in rural England and deals with the challenges faced by a family making a living in
agriculture.

Grange Hill—Begun in 1978, this soap focuses on daily dramatic action in a large secondary school located just outside of London. Its goals are both entertainment and education, focusing on the typical challenges of adolescence, as well as social issues of
abuse, alcoholism and drug addiction.

Hollyoaks—Set in the fictitional suburb of Chester, this story focuses on teenagers and
young adults from affluent families.

ASIA

China

Heroes Have No Regret—Features Situ Yuandong, director of the board of Hong Kong
Far East Company, who wants to invest in Nanbing, a small city in southern China. But

his nephew, Situ Wenbing, tries to foil Yuandong's investment. A battle of justice and sin begins.[1]

Sino-British Street—Focuses on the narrow and winding Zhongying Street, which has separated Hong Kong from the Chinese mainland since the late 1890s in the wake of Britain's signing an agreement with Qing Dynasty leaders renting Hong Kong until 1997. Disputes have occurred between the two sides about the street in the past 50 years. The serial depicts life and people on this street, featuring romance as well as social upheavals in Hong Kong.[2]

The Story of Lao Geng—Features a middle-aged peasant who has spent most of his adult life in the countryside. His wife had died several years earlier, leaving him to raise their two children—a son and a daughter. Now an adult, the son has chosen to marry and remain in the countryside with his father; the daughter has decided to move to the city. The serial follows Lao Geng as he tries to understand city life (while visiting his daughter) and to adjust to China after the Cultural Revolution.

Sun Wu, the Great Strategist—Tells the story of Sun Wu, a famous military strategy designer during the Autumn and Spring Period (770–476 B.C.). The story of Sun is interwoven with the fighting and diplomatic exchanges between the numerous kingdoms of that time. A glimpse of Sun's life is a review of the history of the period.[3]

India

Hum Log—Focuses on the problems caused by the centuries-old Indian tradition of sending young adolescent girls into early marriage, relegating them to second-class citizenship for the rest of their lives.

Humraahi—Centers on Angoori, a beautiful 14-year-old girl, eager for life and desperate to learn and better her life. But because of her poor family background, she enters into an arranged—and unhappy—marriage. Against her better judgment, Angoori then becomes pregnant, eventually dying in childbirth.

Mahabharat—Addressing religious issues, this serial is a comprehensive parable with themes of good vs. evil and justice vs. injustice.

Self-Esteem—Follows the fate of the wealthy and dishonest Malhotra family. The head of the clan dies, leaving behind a mistress named Svetlana, an alcoholic wife, a handsome son and an embittered younger brother to fight over the family business.[4]

Tara—Centers around "the lives of four women, their love affairs and scheming ambitions. The main character is the beautiful Tara, and the show spans three generations of her family's life."[5]

Japan

Fujisankei Drama—Recounts the story of Hideshi, a 35-year-old man in the midst of a midlife crisis. While enjoying his marriage with Akemi (also 35), Hideshi also carries on with one of the secretaries at his office. After his lover becomes pregnant (and decides to keep the baby), Hideshi tries to keep both relationships in balance, but Akemi begins to suspect him and has an affair herself with an old classmate from the Fine Arts University.[6]

The Good Wife—Features a 24-year-old female medical student who battles for recognition in a male world while also trying to maintain a stable marriage with her handsome businessman husband.

Hirari—Recounts the story of a young Tokyo woman who drops out of accounting school to enter the profession of sumo wrestling (a centuries-old "men only" sport).

The Last Friend—Tells of a 36-year-old magazine editor who becomes pregnant from an affair she initiated with her boss (who is also her best friend's husband).

Pearl Flower—Centers on a family who tries to run a pearl dealing house in Kobe after the father dies. The major character, Noriko, tries valiantly to keep everyone together; but after the business goes into bankruptcy, the brothers go very separate ways.[7]

Salon de Kinshiro Tokoyama—Follows the dilemmas of a man who must give up his barber shop and home to four feuding sisters.

Tokyo Love Story—Dramatizes the challenges of maintaining romantic relationships amid the pressures of urban life.

Kazakhstan

Crossroads—Based in the British working-class serial drama tradition, the serial follows a family as it tries to adjust to the nation's new free-market economy.

Thailand

Absent-Minded Cupid—The story of a little girl who is given the soul of a woman killed in an accident.

Darayan—Features a ghost who refuses reincarnation in order to wait for the rebirth of her lover and their enemies.

AFRICA

Kenya

Ndinga Nacio—Based on the famous British soap, *The Archers*, this drama focuses on the challenges faced by a family who makes a living on a farm. Because women do most of the farmwork in Kenya, the story lines particularly target them.

Tushauriane—Centers on the life of a beautiful young woman, a veterinarian, who [goes] out with a young man from another tribe.... The heroine's friends resent her for "abandoning" her tribe and, thus, [cause her] needless pain.[8]

Ushiwapo Shikimana—Addresses the joys and trials of family life, especially the problems of combining a professional career with having children.

Côte d'Ivoire

Sida dans la Cite—The first French language television serial addressing the AIDS epidemic in that country, this educational-entertainment drama deals with the social repercussions of contracting the HIV virus.

Niger

Shiga Ukku—Unbeknownst to her husband (or so she thinks), Abdu plans a rendezvous with Fati in a cabin. Her husband, aware of what is going on, surprises her first in the cabin. When he arrives, Abdu mistakenly believes it is Fati and gives him her baby for a while. Once the baby is in his hands, the husband runs away and Abdu runs after him. Fati then asks for the baby and total pandemonium occurs.

Dan Kagane—Dan Kagane explains a citizen's rights and duties. It also shows how to vote.

Hagoy da Waiboro—A wife wants to get rid of her husband she no longer loves. To do so, she decides to put poison in the porridge the husband is supposed to drink. When he is on the brink of drinking the poisonous porridge, a thief from under the bed gets out and orders him not to drink.

Uwar Miji—The tribulations of a mother-in-law. When she thinks the way her two daughters-in-law behave is not best, she plays her son's role and puts them out. She divorces them with her son.

Irkoy Beri—In this drama God punishes a woman. She has left her husband because he has no means to buy the sheep they must sacrifice on sacrifice day. Finally, the husband buys the sheep on credit. But when sacrifice day arrives, God refuses to accept the sacrificial animals that cannot be slaughtered (because the couple doesn't actually own them).

Kowa Ya Taka Doka—A policeman, accustomed to penalizing people who have no respect for the law, is judged himself. He has committed adultery and as law is law, he must go to prison.

El-hadji Ka Django—A story of El-hadji, an old rich man who falls in love with a very young girl. A dancing party is organized and El-hadji is invited to attend. His beloved accepts, too, but only when El-hadji changes his traditional clothes into western ones— to get dressed as Django (a cinema actor).

Bakauye Bakauye Ne—A country man comes to town with his donkey loaded with firewood to sell and is overtaken by thieves.

Ramen Mugunta—A dibia arrives in a village when another dibia welcomes him. But the guest, feeling that the host has more power than he, decides to eliminate him. He sends poisonous food to his host. As his host is away, the food is sent back and unfortunately, without knowing, he eats it and dies.

Laabu Si Tari—A story of a country man. He comes to town, thinking he can easily find a job and thereby get money. His hopes disappointed, he returns to his village and decides to till the land instead. He meets his challenge.

South Africa

Generations—Culled from such glamor serials as *Dynasty*, *Dallas* and *The Bold and the Beautiful*, *Generations* (comprised of a multiethnic cast) presents story lines ranging from business crises and courtroom hijinks to the strengths and weaknesses of cosmetic surgery.

Out of the Blue—A multicultural serial about six young friends who spend most of their time at a marine-life park. At the core of seemingly uncomplicated fun are intricate relationships and potential conflicts.

Soul City—An "edu-tainment" serial, this drama takes place in a health clinic, where friendship, love and romance occur, as well as valuable lessons in immunizations, preventive medicine and spousal abuse.

Suburban Bliss—Centers on the social complications of living in a multicultural neighborhood.

NEAR AND MIDDLE EAST

Israel

Mossad—Based on real events, this serial explores the lives of people who work in Israel's secret service. Unlike the James Bond archetypes, flawed character images and the general boredom of their daily existence dominate the story lines.

PACIFIC

Australia

Home and Away—Premiering in 1988, the story focuses on Tom and Pippa Fletcher and their five foster children, who decided to move to Summer Bay after Tom lost his job in the city. One or more of the children is constantly in love or in trouble, as they grow up in the beach community.[9]

Neighbours—Centered on the lives of the families on Ramsay Street, a working-class neighborhood in urban Australia.

Pacific Drive—Set in a vibrant city on Australia's Gold Coast, the serial features young professionals who divide their time between sandy beaches and hot boardrooms. Already shown in many areas of the world (including the U.S.), this soap is now being targeted for the Pacific Rim as well.

Paradise Beach—Produced in 1994, the soap features three teenagers who leave the drabness of the suburbs in search of sun, sand and surf and find it on Paradise Beach. Relationships blossom as the trio makes its journey.[10]

The Sullivans—Premiering in 1976, and running for more than 1,100 episodes, this drama focuses on a family during World War II, who share joys, tragedies, love and laughter.

New Zealand

Shortland Street—Set in a hospital emergency ward, this serial follows the lives and loves of doctors, nurses and patients.

Notes

1. "TV Highlights," *China Daily* (May 31, 1997), 6.
2. "TV Highlights," *China Daily* (May 17, 1997), 5.

3. *Ibid.*

4. Fred Hift, "Seeing the Issue in Black and White: Telenovels Created for Audiences from Rio to Bombay Are Prompting Big Changes," *WorldPaper* (January 1994), 10.

5. *The People* (November 5, 1995). Available on Lexis-Nexis.

6. International Channel Home Page (icinfo@i-channel.com). Available on Netscape.

7. NTV Web site (http://www.ntv.co.jp). Available on Netscape.

8. *Ibid.*

9. Information obtained from the "Home and Away" home page, featuring episode summaries (http://www.ozemail.com.au).

10. These descriptions were built from the contributions of Sarah Wiltshire, Programming Department, Nine Network Australia. Written correspondence (May 1996).

Appendix B
A Partial List of Current and Past Soap Operas/Telenovelas (with Country of Origin)

A

Abigail (Venezuela)
Absent-Minded Cupid (Thailand)
El Abuelo y Yo (Mexico)
Acapulco, Cuerpo Y Alma (Mexico)
Adriana (Venezuela)
Las Aguas Mansas (Colombia)
Agujetas de Color de Rosa (Mexico)
Alcanzar una Estrella, I (Mexico)
Alcanzar una Estrella, II (Mexico)
Alejandra (Venezuela)
Alejandra (Puerto Rico)
Alen do Horizonte (Argentina)
Alen Luz de Luna (Argentina)
Alguna Vez Tendremos Alas (Mexico)
All My Children (U.S.)
Alma Mia (Venezuela)
El Alma No Tiene Color (Mexico)
Almas de Piedra (Colombia)
Al Norte del Corazón (Mexico)
Alondra (Mexico)
Alondra (Venezuela)
Al Son del Amor (Puerto Rico)
Amalia Batista (Mexico)
Amanda Sabater (Venezuela)

Amor de Nadie (Mexico)
Amor de Papel (Venezuela)
Los Amores de Anita Peña (Venezuela)
Amores de Fin de Siglo (Venezuela)
Amor en Silencio (Mexico)
O Amor Esta No Ar (Brazil)
Anabel (Venezuela)
Andaz (India)
Ángeles sin Paraiso (Mexico)
Angélica, Mi Vida (Puerto Rico/U.S.)
Angélito (Venezuela)
El Ángel Rebelde (Venezuela)
Another World (U.S.)
Antonella (Argentina)
Antonio Alves, Taxista (Brazil)
La Antorcha Encendida (Mexico)
Apasionada (Argentina)
Aprendiendo a Amar (Mexico)
El Árbol Azul (Argentina)
The Archers (U.K.)
As the World Turns (U.S.)
Aspirations (China)
Atrapada (Mexico)
Aventurera (Puerto Rico)
Azúcar (Colombia)

Azucena (Venezuela)
Azul (Mexico)

B

Baila Conmigo (Mexico)
Bajo Un Mismo Rostro (Mexico)
Bakauye Bakauye Ne (Niger)
Balada por un Amor (Mexico)
Barrigo ... (Brazil)
Bellísima (Venezuela)
Bendita Mentira (Mexico)
Beto Rockefeller (Brazil)
Bianca Vidal (Mexico)
Bienvenida Esperanza (Venezuela)
Bodas de Odio (Mexico)
The Bold and the Beautiful (U.S.)
Brookside (U.K.)
Buscando el Paraiso (Mexico)

C

Cadenas de Amargura (Mexico)
Café con Aroma de Mujer (Colombia)
El Camino Secreto (Mexico)
Caminos Cruzados (Mexico)
O Campeão (Brazil)
Canaveral de Pasiones (Mexico)
Canción de Amor (Mexico)
Candela (Mexico)
Candida (Venezuela)
Capitol (U.S.)
Capricho (Mexico)
Cara Sucia (Venezuela)
Caribe (Venezuela)
Carmen Querida (Venezuela)
Carrusel (Mexico)
La Casa al Final de la Calle (Mexico)
La Casa de las Dos Palmas (Colombia)
Celeste (Argentina)
Celeste Siempre Celeste (Argentina)
Cenizas y Diamantes (Mexico)
Cheat Me Sweetly (Japan)
Chiquititas (Argentina)
Chispita (Mexico)
Cien Días de Ana (Argentina)
Ciao Cristina (Venezuela)
The City/Loving (U.S.)
Clan (Poland)
Clase Aparte (Colombia)
Colégio Brasil (Brazil)
Colorina (Mexico)

Como Pan Caliente (Argentina)
Copas Amargas (Colombia)
Como Tu, Ninguna (Venezuela)
Confidente de Secundaria (Mexico)
Con Todo el Alma (Mexico)
Coralito (Puerto Rico)
Corazón Salvaje (Mexico)
Coronation Street (U.K.)
Cosecharás Tu Siembra (Argentina)
A Country Practice (Australia)
Cristal (Venezuela)
Cristina Bazan (Puerto Rico)
Crossroads (Kazakhstan)
Crossroads (U.K.)
Cruz de Nadie (Venezuela)
Cuando Llega el Amor (Mexico)
La Culpa (Mexico)
Cuña de Lobos (Mexico)

D

La Dama de la Rosa (Venezuela)
Dan Kagane (Niger)
Dancin' Days (Brazil)
Darayan (Thailand)
Days of Our Lives (U.S.)
De Corpo e Alma (Brazil)
De Mujeres (Venezuela)
De Oro Puro (Venezuela)
De Pura Sangre (Mexico)
Deadly Fortune (Israel)
Dejate Querer (Spain/Argentina)
El Derecho de Nacer (Mexico)
El Desafío (Venezuela)
El Desprecio (Venezuela/Spain)
Detras de un Ángel (Colombia)
Días de Ilusión (Argentina)
Días sin Luna (Mexico)
Die Direktorin (Switzerland/Germany)
Divina Obsesión (Venezuela)
Dom Syem, Podyezd 4 (Russia)
Doña Anja (Brazil)
Doña Beija (Brazil)
Las Dos Dianas (Venezuela)
Dos Mujeres (Colombia)
Dos Mujeres, Un Camino (Mexico)
Dos Vidas (Mexico)
La Dueña (Mexico)
La Dueña (Venezuela)
Dulce Ave Negra (Colombia)
Dulce Desafío (Mexico)

Dulce Enemiga (Venezuela)
Dulce Ilusión (Venezuela)
Dulce María (Venezuela)

E
E-Street (Australia)
EastEnders (U.K.)
Echo Point (Australia)
The Editorial Office (China)
Eldorado (U.K.)
El-hadji Ka Django (Niger)
Elizabeth (Venezuela)
Emmerdale (U.K.)
Empire (U.S./Mexico)
Encadenados (Mexico)
En Carné Propia (Mexico)
En Cuerpo Ajeno (Colombia)
El Engaño (Venezuela)
Entre la Vida y la Muerte (Mexico)
Escalona (Colombia)
La Escrava Isaura (Brazil)
Esmeralda (Mexico)
Esos Que Dicen Amarse (Argentina)
El Esposo de Anaís (Venezuela)
Estrellita Mia (Argentina)
Eternamente Manuela (Colombia)
The Evolving of Three Countries (China)
El Extraño Retorno de Diana Salazar (Mexico)

F
Fabiola (Venezuela)
Fair City (Ireland)
Farewell to Moscow (China)
Fascht e Familie (Switzerland/Germany)
La Fiera (Mexico)
Al Filo de la Muerte (Mexico)
O Fim do Mundo (Brazil)
Flor de Oro (Colombia)
Florida Lady (Germany)
Fool's Gold (Israel)
Forsthaus Falkenau (Germany)
Fuego Verde (Colombia)
La Fuerza del Amor (Mexico)
Fujisankei Drama (Japan)

G
Gardenia (Venezuela)
La Gata Salvaje (Venezuela)
Géminis (Colombia)

General Hospital (U.S.)
Generations (South Africa)
Glenroe (Ireland)
La Goajirita (Venezuela)
Goede Tijden, Slechte Tijden (Netherlands)
The Good Wife (Japan)
Grange Hill (U.K.)
Guadalupe (U.S.)
Guajira (Colombia)
Guiding Light (U.S.)
Gute Zeiten, Schlechte Zeiten (Germany)

H
Habia una Vez un Circo (Argentina)
Hagoy da Waiboro (Niger)
Happy Family (China)
Healing Hearts (South Africa)
Heroes Have No Regret (China)
Het Oude Noorden (Netherlands)
High Seas (Sweden)
La Hija de Nadie (Venezuela)
Hijos de Nadie (Mexico)
Hirari (Japan)
Hollyoaks (U.K.)
Home and Away (Australia)
Hombres (Colombia)
Hong Kong in Troubled Times (China)
Hum Log (India)
Humraahi (India)
Huracán (Mexico)

I
I Prefer to Be Single (Japan)
Ich Heirate ein Familie (Germany)
Ilusiones (Venezuela)
Imperio de Cristal (Mexico)
La Indomable (Mexico)
A Indômada (Brazil)
Ines Duarte, Secretaría (Venezuela)
La Inolvidable (Venezuela)
La Intrusa (Venezuela)
Irkoy Beri (Niger)
Ivy (Italy)

J
La Jaula de Oro (Mexico)
Le Jeu Interdit (Japan)
The Journey West (China)
Juana Iris (Mexico)

Las Juanas (Colombia)
Jugando a Vivir (Venezuela)
Jugar a Morir (Argentina)
Just the Way You Are (Japan)

K

Kaina (Venezuela)
Kananga do Japão (Brazil)
Kapricho, S.A. (Venezuela)
Karina Montaner (Puerto Rico)
Kassandra (Venezuela)
Katochan Kenchan (Japan)
Kowa Ya Taka Doka (Niger)

L

Laabu Si Tari (Niger)
Labyrinth (Poland)
The Last Friend (Japan)
Lazos de Amor (Mexico)
Leonela (Venezuela)
Lime Tree Lane (Jamaica)
Lindenstrasse (Austria/Germany)
The Little Strawberry (Russia)
Llovizna (Venezuela)
Loba Herida (U.S.)
Loca Piel (Chile)
London's Burning (U.K.)
Long Vacation (Japan)
Loving/The City (U.S.)
Luisana Mia (Venezuela)
Luz Clarita (Mexico)
Luz y Sombra (Mexico)

M

Macarena (Venezuela)
Macht der Liedenschaft (Germany)
Madres Egoístas (Mexico)
Magica Juventud (Mexico)
El Magnate (US)
Mahabharat (India)
Maite (Venezuela)
Mala Mujer (Peru)
El Maléficio (Mexico)
Malhação (Brazil)
La Malvada (Venezuela)
Manuela (Argentina)
María (Colombia)
María Bonita (Colombia)
María Celeste (Venezuela)
María de los Angeles (Venezuela)

María de Nadie (Argentina)
María José (Mexico)
María la del Barrio (Mexico)
María María (Venezuela)
María Mercedes (Mexico)
Marielena (US)
Marielena (Venezuela)
Marienhof (Germany)
Marimar (Mexico)
Marisela (Venezuela)
Marisol (Mexico)
Marta y Javier (Venezuela)
Mas Allá del Horizonte (Argentina)
Mas Allá del Puente (Mexico)
Me, Lito Domestica (Cyprus)
Mediterranean Affairs (Israel)
Mi Adorable Mónica (Venezuela)
Mi Amada Beatriz (Venezuela)
Milagros (Argentina)
Micaela (Italy/Argentina)
Mi Nombre es Coraje (Argentina)
Mi Pequeña Soledad (Mexico)
Mi Querida Isabel (Mexico)
Mi Segunda Madre (Mexico)
Momposina (Colombia)
Monte Calvario (Mexico)
Morelia (U.S.)
Morena Clara (Venezuela)
Morir Dos Veces (Mexico)
Mossad (Israel)
Los Motivos de Lola (Colombia)
Muchachitas (Mexico)
Mulheres de Areia (Brazil)
Mundo de Fieras (Venezuela)

N

90-60-90 (Argentina)
Nada Personal (Mexico)
Nano (Argentina)
Natacha (Venezuela)
Ndinga Nacio (Kenya)
Neighbours (Australia)
Night Embrace (Japan)
Niña Bonita (Venezuela)
Nissaga de Poder (Spain/Catalonia)
No Tengo Madre (Mexico)

O

101st Proposal (Japan)
Onderweg Naar Morgen (Netherlands)

One Life to Live (U.S.)
Only My Beeper Knows (Japan)
Open on Sunday (Germany)
Oro Verde (Chile)
El Oro y el Barro (Argentina)
Os Ossos do Barao (Brazil)
Otra en Mi (Colombia)
Otra Mitad del Sol (Colombia)
Out of the Blue (South Africa)

P
Pacific Drive (Australia)
Pantanal de Amor (Brazil)
Papá Corazón (Argentina)
Para Toda la Vida (Mexico)
Paradise Beach (Australia)
Parampara (India)
Los Parientes Pobres (Mexico)
Pasión de Vivir (Puerto Rico/Spain)
Pasionaria (Venezuela)
Pasiones Secretas (Colombia)
Pearl Flower (Japan)
Pecado de Amor (Venezuela)
Pecado Santo (Colombia)
Peligrosa (Venezuela)
Perdidos de Amor (Brazil)
Perla Negra (Argentina)
Pero Sigo Siendo el Rey (Chile)
La Picara Sonadora (Mexico)
Piel (U.S.)
Poblenou (Spain/Catalonia)
Pobre Diabla (Venezuela)
Pobre Juventud (Mexico)
Pobre Niña Rica (Mexico)
Pole Position (Japan)
Poliladron (Argentina)
Por Amarte Tanto (Venezuela)
Por Estas Calles (Venezuela)
Porque Mataron a Betty? (Colombia)
Port Charles (U.S.)
La Potra Zaina (Colombia)
El Premio Mayor (Mexico)
Primeiro Amor (Brazil)
Primer Amor (Spain/Argentina)
Princesa (Argentina)
Prisionera de Amor (Mexico)
Prisoner of Cell Block H (Australia)
The Public Prosecutor (Japan)
Pueblo Chico, Infierno Grande (Mexico)
Puerta Grande (Colombia)

Pullet Hall (Jamaica)
Pura Sangre (Venezuela)

Q
Quem e Voce? (Brazil)
Que Paso con Jackeline? (Venezuela)
Quinceanera (Mexico)
Quirpa de Tres Mujeres (Venezuela)

R
Ramen Mugunta (Niger)
Razão de Viver (Brazil)
Rebeca (Venezuela)
Rebelde (Argentina)
Red Mansion Dream (China)
The Restless Years (Australia)
Retrato de Familia (Mexico)
La Revancha (Venezuela)
Los Ricos También Lloran (Mexico)
Riña (Mexico)
El Rincón de los Prodigios (Mexico)
Rojo y Miel (Chile)
The Romance of Three Kingdoms
  (China)
Roque Santeiro (Brazil)
Rosa Salvaje (Mexico)
Rosalinda (Venezuela)
Rostro de Mujer (Mexico)
Rubí (Venezuela)

S
Salon de Kinshiro Tokoyama (Japan)
Salsa y Merengue (Brazil)
Salvaje (Venezuela)
Santa Barbara (U.S.)
Schwarzwaldklinik (Germany)
Second Chance for Love (Japan)
Secrets (Italy)
Secrets de Familia (Spain/Catalonia)
Selva Maria (Venezuela)
Señora (Venezuela)
Señora Isabel (Colombia)
Señora Tentación (U.S.)
Señorita Perdomo (Venezuela)
Sentimientos Ajenos (Mexico)
Seven Men and Women: An Autumn
  Story (Japan)
Sheik (Argentina)
Shiga Ukku (Niger)
The Shining (Greece)

Shortland Street (New Zealand)
Si Dios Me Quita la Vida (Mexico)
Si Mañana Estoy Vivo (Colombia)
Sida dans la Cite (Côte d'Ivoire)
Simplemente María (Mexico)
Single-Parent Family (China)
Sinha Moca (Brazil)
Sino-British Street (China)
Sirena (Venezuela)
Sisters from Outside Make a Living in Beijing (China)
Soledad (Puerto Rico)
Solo una Mujer (Colombia)
La Sombra del Deseo (Colombia)
La Sombra de Otro (Mexico)
La Sonrisa del Diablo (Mexico)
Soul City (South Africa)
The Story of Lao Geng (China)
Suburban Bliss (South Africa)
Sueño de Amor (Mexico)
Sueños y Espejos (Colombia)
The Sullivans (Australia)
Sun Wu, the Great Strategist (China)
Sunset Beach (U.S.)
El Super (Spain)
Swabhimaan (India)

T
Take the High Road (Scotland)
Tal Como Somos (Mexico)
Tanairi (Puerto Rico)
Tara (India)
Te Dejare de Amar (Mexico)
Te Sigo Amando (Mexico)
Tenías Que Ser Tu (Mexico)
Theresa (Mexico)
Tobias (Switzerland/Germany)
Tocaia Grande (Brazil)
Tokyo Cinderella Story (Japan)
Tokyo Love Story (Japan)
Topacio (Venezuela)
La Traidora (Venezuela)
Das Traumschiff (Germany)
Tres Destinos (U.S.)
Triángulo (Mexico)
Tropicalmiente (Brazil)
Tu o Nadie (Mexico)
Tu y Yo (Mexico)
Tushauriana (Kenya)

U
Ugumba (Tanzania)
La Última Esperanza (Mexico)
El Último Verano (Argentina)
Under One Roof (Japan)
United Dreams (Germany)
Unter Uns (Germany)
Ushiwapo Shikimana (Kenya)
Uwar Miji (Niger)

V
Valentina (Mexico)
Valeria y Maximiliano (Mexico)
Vale Tudo (Brazil)
Vanessa (Mexico)
Verbotene Liebe (Germany)
A Viagem (Brazil)
Victoria (Mexico)
Vida de mi Vida (Colombia)
La Viuda de Blanco (Colombia)
Viviana (Mexico)
Vivir un Poco (Mexico)
Volver a Empezar (Mexico)
Volver a Vivir (Venezuela)
Vorágine (Colombia)
El Vuelo del Aguila (Mexico)

W
The Weekly (Denmark)
Die Wicherts van Nebenan (Germany)
Wolwedans in die Skemer (South Africa)
A Woman Does Her Best (Japan)

X
Xica de Silva (Brazil)

Y
Yesenia (Mexico)
Yo Compro Esa Mujer (Mexico)
Yolanda Lujan (Argentina)
Yo No Creo en los Hombres (Mexico)
The Young and the Restless (U.S.)

Z
Zaza (Brazil)
Zingara (Argentina)
O Zviratech a Lidech (Germany/Czech Republic)

Bibliography

Books

Allen, Robert C. *Speaking of Soap Operas*. Chapel Hill, NC: University of North Carolina Press, 1985.

_____, ed. *To Be Continued... Soap Operas Around the World*. London: Routledge, 1995.

Brunsdon, Charlotte. *Screen Tastes: Soap Opera to Satellite Dishes*. London: Routledge, 1997.

Cantor, Muriel, and Suzanne Pingree. *The Soap Opera*. Beverly Hills, CA: Sage, 1983.

Cole, Barry G., ed. *Television*. New York: Free Press, 1973.

Frentz, Suzanne, ed. *Staying Tuned: Contemporary Soap Opera Criticism*. Bowling Green, OH: Bowling Green University Popular Press, 1992.

Gitlin, Todd, ed. *Watching Television*. New York: Pantheon Press, 1986.

Groves, Seli. *The Ultimate Soap Opera Guide*. Detroit: Visible Ink Press, 1995.

Kisselhoff, Jeff. *The Box: An Oral History of Television*. New York: Viking, 1995.

LaGuardia, Robert. *Soap Opera World*. New York: Arbor House, 1983.

Lazarsfeld, Paul F., and Frank N. Stanton, eds. *Radio Research: 1942–1943*. New York: Essential, 1944.

MacDonald, J. Fred. *Don't Touch That Dial: Radio Programming in American Life from 1920 to 1960*. Chicago: Nelson-Hall, 1970.

McNeil, Alex. *Total Television: The Comprehensive Guide to Programming from 1948 to the Present*. New York: Penguin Books, 1996.

Martin, William. *Nerve Endings*. New York: Warner Books, 1994.

Matelski, Marilyn J. *The Soap Opera Evolution: America's Enduring Romance with Daytime Drama*. Jefferson, NC: McFarland, 1988.

Nariman, Heidi Noel. *Soap Operas for Social Change: Toward a Methodology for Entertainment-Education Television*. Westport, CT: Praeger, 1993.

Rouverol, Jean. *Writing for Daytime Drama*. Stoneham, MA: Focal Press, 1992.

Schemering, Christopher. *The Soap Opera Encyclopedia*. New York: Ballantine, 1985.

Sennitt, Andrew G., ed. *World Radio TV Handbook,* 1996 Edition. New York: Billboard Books, 1996.

_____. *World Radio TV Handbook,* 1997 Edition. New York: Billboard Books, 1997.

Television Monograph 13: Coronation Street. London: British Film Institute, 1981.

Waggett, Gerard J. *The Soap Opera Book of Lists*. New York: HarperCollins, 1996.

Wessels, Charlyn. *Soap Opera II—The Sequel*. Hertfordshire, UK: Phoenix ELT, 1996.

The World Almanac and Book of Facts 1998. Mahwah, NJ: K-III Reference Corporation, 1997.

Journals

Geraghty, Christine. "The Continuous Serial—A Definition." *Television Monograph 13: Coronation Street* (1981): 9–26.
Greenberg, Bradley S., and Rick W. Busselle. "Soap Operas and Sexual Activity: A Decade Later." *Journal of Communication* (Autumn 1996): 153–160.

Newspaper/Magazine Articles

Amdur, Meredith. "Cable Networks Head South: Latin America Ripe with Program Opportunities." *Broadcasting & Cable*, 24 January 1994, 118.
"And Now ... a Soap Channel!" *TV Magazine Africa*, August 1997.
Armstrong, Sue. "South African Soap Aids the Health of the Nation." *New Scientist*, 27 August 1994, 5.
Berlatsky-Kaplan, Rachel. "Surprise! Our Soaps Are Taking the World by Storm." *National Enquirer*, n.d.
"Brazil: Fiery Star Written Out of Globo Telenovela." *Television Business International*, March 1995, 12.
Coopman, Jeremy. "High Hopes for Soaps as Europe Lathers Up." *Variety*, 22 July 1991, 1.
"Cybersoap Opera." *New Straits Times Press (Malaysia) Berhad*, 22 August 1996, 36.
Da Cunha, Uma. "India's Cablers Join Forces." *Variety*, 2–8 December 1996, 50.
Dawtrey, Adam. "U.K.-bred Soaper Is Socko in Kazakh." *Variety*, 16–22 1996, 66.
Deshpande, Shekhar. "Religion, Art and Politics." *Ethnic News Watch*, 31 July 1994, 64.
Espiritu, Carol. "Philippines Eager to Buy Foreign Fare." *Variety*, 2–8 December 1996, 46.
"Forget Neighbours, the Poms Are Giving Us Cobber Nation Street." *Daily Mail*, 7 October 1994, 12.
Fuller, Chris. "Dutch Carve Soaps for Local Consumption." *Variety*, 26 October 1992, 48.
Guider, Elizabeth. "Foreign Sales in the 'Sunset.'" *Variety*, 2–8 December 1996, 82.
Harris, Mike. "Euros Awash in Sexy Soap Operas." *Variety*, 22 July 1991, 76.
Herskovitz, Jon. "Pumping Hot Drama, Variety Shows in the Asian Pipeline." *Variety*, 15–21 September 1997, 56.
"Hitting the Spot." *The Economist*, 26 August 1995, 26.
Hopewell, John. "Novelas Still a Staple but Waning." *Variety*, 25 September 1995, 90.
Mallet, Victor. "Thai Media Group Plans Flotation." *Financial Times*, 21 October 1994, 24.
Middlehurst, Lester. "Why the BBC Needs Eldorado." *Daily Mail*, 4 July 1992, 33.
Mitchell, Emily, Victoria Foote-Greenwell and Meenakshi Ganguly. "International Edition; Europe; Sightings." *Time*, 1 May 1995, 69.
Morrow, David J. "Ratings Climb as TV Soaps Show Savvy Career Women." *Detroit Free Press*, 12 May 1993, 7A.
_____. "Sumos and Soaps Provide Relief." *Detroit Free Press*, 29 March 1993, 3A.
Neff, Robert, and Larry Holyoke. "Show Biz: Don't Count Japan Out." *Business Week*, 24 April 1995, 126.
"No Independent Diplomatic Ties for HK." *China Daily*, 29 May 1997, 4.
Perlez, Jane. "Normal Soap Opera Formula in U.S. Is Groundbreaking in Poland." *Detroit Free Press*, 21 October 1997, 5A, 6A.
"Pull Plug on a Wasteful Program: TV Marti Accomplishes Nothing." *Sun Sentinel*, 18 October 1993, 6A.
Pursell, Chris. "Webs Lather Up with New Soaps." *Variety*, 29 August 1997, 44.
Quinones, Sam. "Suddenly, to the Fantasy Factory Known as the Mexican Telenovela Industry, Reality Matters." *Fort Worth Star-Telegram*, 23 April 1997, 3.

Schleier, Curt. "In a Lather: Ratings Drop, but Die-Hard Fans Keep Their Soaps Afloat," *Detroit News*, 24 May 1997, 1C, 6C.
Schmetzer, Uli. "Set of Russian TV Show Is a Soap Opera in Itself." *Chicago Tribune*, 26 December 1996, 24.
Soap Opera Magazine, 4 March 1997.
Stanley, Alessandra. "Russians Find Their Heroes in Mexican TV Soap Operas. *New York Times*, 20 March 1994, 12.
Werner, Laurie. "Working Class Heroes." *Northwest Portfolio*, July 1989, 24.
Williams, Michael. "Soccer Match Scores Big for Spanish Pubcaster." *Variety*, 7 June 1992, 41.
Woods, Mark. "Oz Outlets Exploding." *Variety*, 6–12 January 1997, N10.

Interviews/Letters

Correspondence with Eva Berquist, SVT I, Sweden, July 1996.
Correspondence with Josef Burry, SRG, August 1996.
Correspondence with Betsi Curdie@lass.gov.bc.ca, April 1997.
Correspondence with Valerio Fuenzalida, Televisión Nacional de Chile, September 1996.
Correspondence with Dr. Ronald Grabe, WDR, Germany, July 1996.
Correspondence with Dermot Horan, RTE, Ireland, July 1996.
Correspondence, Jamaica Broadcasting Corporation, September 1996.
Correspondence with Anestine Lafond, Marpin T.V. Company Limited, Dominica, August 1996.
Correspondence with Silvia Maric, ARD, Germany, July 1996.
Correspondence with Mauritius Broadcasting Corporation, July 1996.
Correspondence with Ken Mishima, Fuji Television Network, Japan, August 1996.
Correspondence with Tom Norman, KVZK-TV, American Samoa, October 1996.
Correspondence with O.R.T.N. (Direction de la Television Nationale—Niger), July 1996.
Correspondence with Ray Sorimachi, NTV, Japan, July 1996.
Correspondence with Connie Telfer-Smith, Norfolk Island Broadcasting Service, August 1996.
Correspondence with John Taylor, EMTV, Papua New Guinea, August 1996.
Correspondence with Sarah Wiltshire, Nine Network Australia, May 1996.
Interview with Tom Mwerka, PASA Assistant Coordinator, USIS, August 1997.
Interview with Franco Tramontano, Dar es Salaam, Tanzania, August 1997.

Electronic Documents

ABC Web site <http://www.abc.com>.
"BBC to Broadcast Worldwide Radio Soap Opera." Reuters, 2 October 1997.
Babakian, Genine. "'Neighbours' Hoping to Send 'Maria' Packing." *Moscow Times*, 11 February 1995. Available from Lexis-Nexis.
Barry, Ellen. "A New Dynasty Begins in Russia." *Moscow Times*, 11 August 1995. Available from Lexis-Nexis.
"Brazil: Bartering Novelas into 'Soap' Operas." *Television Business International*, July 1995, 12. Available from Lexis-Nexis.
Binyon, Michael. "BBC's Soap Opera Gets Russia in Free-Market Lather." *Times*, 4 August 1994. Available from Lexis-Nexis.

"Brazil: Fiery Star Written Out of Globo Telenovela." *Television Business International*, March 1995. Available from Lexis-Nexis.

"Brazil: Globo's Top Novelas in Ratings Stumble." *Television Business International*, May 1995, 6. Available from Lexis-Nexis.

"Brazilian Actor Accuses His Wife in Soap-Opera Murder Trial." CNN News, 23 January 1997.<http://www.cnn.news.com>.

"Brazilian Soaps—Popular, Racy and High-Budgeted." *Video Age International*, January 1992, 18. Available from Lexis-Nexis.

CBS Web site <http://www.cbs.com>.

CNN Web site archive <http://www.cnn.com>.

"Cable TV Comes to Thailand—Telcom Report International (1995).

Cabrera, Amy. "Poor Launch Wave of Bold Protests in Brazil." *Chattanooga Free Press*, 18 August 1996. Available from Lexis-Nexis.

Campbell, Colin. "Royal Soap Star." *Times*, 25 October 1994. Available from Lexis-Nexis.

Chamish, Barry. "Israel Awash in Soap Suds." *Hollywood Reporter*, 8 November 1994. Available from Lexis-Nexis.

Covington, Richard. "Latin America, Television Hotbed." *International Herald Tribune*, 8 May 1996. Available from Lexis-Nexis.

Culf, Andrew. "Soft Soap Gives Lead to Russia's Everyday Tale of Life with the Moscow Mafia." *Guardian*, 7 May 1994, 10. Available from Lexis-Nexis.

Dinapiera, di Donato. "Brazil: A Magnet for Talent." *UNESCO Courier*, October 1992, 41. Available from Lexis-Nexis.

Eagar, Charlotte. "African Archers Target Tribal Folk," *Observer*, 27 August 1995. Available from Lexis-Nexis.

Fell, Liz. "Ambassador Class." *Cable and Satellite Asia*, March 1996. Available from Lexis-Nexis.

Ferguson, Daniela. "Israeli Satellite Amos Begins Operations." R. R. Computers & Communication, Beer-Sheva, Israel <http://mandy.com/rrc001.html>.

Fletcher, Pascal. "Brazilian TV Soap Opera Is Cuba's Opium of the People." The Reuters Library Report, 12 February 1993. Available from Lexis-Nexis.

"From Venezuela with Love." *Television Business International*, January 1997, 16. Available from Lexis-Nexis.

Goering, Laurie. "Brutality Against Gay Men, Lesbians on Rise in Brazil." *Times Picayune*, 6 April 1997. Available from Lexis-Nexis.

Goldsmith, Belinda. "Australians Mold Soap Operas for Overseas Markets." Reuters North American Wire, 11 September 1995. Available from Lexis-Nexis.

"Hard-liners Blamed for Another Transmitter Outage." CNN News, 20 October 1997 <http://www.cnn.news.com>.

"Headline Russia: Ministry Attacks Move to Broadcast Parliament Programme at Time of US Soap Opera." BBC Summary of World Broadcasts, 17 August 1993. Available from Lexis-Nexis.

Hellen, Nicholas. "Sky Launches Bid to Wrest 'Coronation Street' from ITV" *Sunday Times*, 24 September 1995. Available from Lexis-Nexis.

Hift, Fred. "Seeing the Issue in Black and White; Telenovelas Created for Audiences from Rio to Bombay Are Prompting Big Changes." *Worldpaper*, January 1994, 10. Available from Lexis-Nexis.

Hispanic Institute of Radio & Television "Love Without Boundaries," Press Release, 6 November 1997.

"Hit TV Soap Producer Admits Child Sex Charges." Agence France Press, 18 December 1996. Available from Lexis-Nexis.

Hoffman, David. "A Communist Win? 'God Forbid!' in Russia." *Washington Post*, 30 April 1996, A08. Available from Lexis-Nexis.

"Home and Away" Web site <http://www.ozemail.com.au>.

Hopewell, John. "Novelas Still a Staple but Waning." *Variety*, 25 September 1995. Available from Lexis-Nexis.

International Channel Web site <icinfo@i-channel.com>.

"Internet Soap Operas: Best Episodic Sites on the Web" <Merlin200@earthlink.net>.

Israel Broadcasting Authority Law, Israel Broadcasting Authority, Jerusalem, Israel.

Jones, Gareth. "Education Is What Counts, UK's Blair Tells Russians." Reuters, 7 October 1997.

"Kenya to Show 'Culturally Devastating' Films Late." Reuters North American Wire, 29 August 1995. Available from Lexis-Nexis.

Kingsley, Hilary. "Strange but True; If Boris Yeltsin Wins the Russian Presidential Election, Will History Credit His Victory to the Rescheduling of a Television Soap Opera?" *Guardian*, 4 July 1996, T12. Available from Lexis-Nexis.

Landler, Mark, Joyce Barnathan, Geri Smith and Gail Edmundson. "Think Globally, Program Locally." *Business Week*, 18 November 1994. Available from Lexis-Nexis.

"Lesbian Kiss on Colombian Soap Stirs Up Controversy." *Stuart News/Port St. Lucie News*, 15 June 1997, 15. Available from Lexis-Nexis.

Levaux, Janet Purdy. "Univision Communications, Inc.: The New America." *Investor's Business Daily*, 26 November 1996, A6. Available from Lexis-Nexis.

Martin, Lydia. "Queen of the Novelas: Thalia Has Conquered the Soap Opera World and Now Sets Sights on Hollywood." *Fort Worth Star-Telegram*, 19 March 1997, 9. Available from Lexis-Nexis.

Miller, Jonathan. "Behind the Screen." *Sunday Times*, 9 August 1992. Available from Lexis-Nexis.

Molinski, Michael. "Sky Entertainment Starts Brazil Satellite TV." *Bloomberg Business News*, 30 October 1996.

Mycio, Mary. "The Great Soap Wars of 1995; Television: Ethnic Russians in Ukraine Protest When Characters on Their Beloved 'Santa Barbara' Begin Speaking Ukrainian." *Los Angeles Times*, 9 October 1995. Available from Lexis-Nexis.

Mylrea, Paul. "UK's Blair to Star in Russian Radio Soap." Reuters, 7 October 1997.

NBC Web site <http://www.nbc.com>.

NTV Web site <http://www.ntv.co.jp>.

Neal, Pat. "Bosnian Relief from an Unlikely Source." CNN News, 11 November 1997 <http://www.cnn.news.com>.

"Newsbytes Pacifica Headlines." Newsbytes Pacifica Web site <http://www.nb-pacifica.com>.

"Oh Ahrr, Tovarich." Press Association Limited, 4 December 1994. Available from Lexis-Nexis.

Palchikoff, Kim. "Town in a Lather Over Latin Soaps." *Moscow Times*, 4 December 1996. Available from Lexis-Nexis.

Paxman, Andrew. "Instruments of Change." *Variety*, 7–13 October 1996, 63. Available from Lexis-Nexis.

PSI: Communications to Motivate Healthy Behavior. Population Services International, Inc., 1996 <webmaster@psiwash.org>.

Rede Globo Web site <http://redeglobo.com.br>.

Robinson, Edward. "Sex, Drugs and Dinero." *Fortune*, 10 November 1997.

Robinson, Eugene. "Over the Brazilian Rainbow: In This Multi-Hued Society, the Color Line Is a State of Mind." *Washington Post*, 10 December 1995. Available from Lexis-Nexis.

Sampson, Catherine. "Television Tear-Jerker Enraptures China." *Times*, 30 January 1991. Available from Lexis-Nexis.

Sanz, Marie. "Private Restaurants Booming." Agence France Presse, 23 March 1996. Available from Lexis-Nexis.

"SBT Chases Telenovela Top Spot." *Television Business International*, April 1996. Available from Lexis-Nexis.
"The Scramble to Make Russia Pay." *Television Business International*, February 1997. Available from Lexis-Nexis.
"Series/Novelas at Mipcom '95." *Television Business International*, October 1995. Available from Lexis-Nexis.
Schomberg, William. "Brazil Television Giant Wages Soap Opera Wars." Reuters, 6 May 1996. Available from Lexis-Nexis.
Simpson, Ian. "Heads Roll as Brazil's Globo TV Faces Competition," Reuters European Business Report, 25 July 1995. Available from Lexis-Nexis.
"Skullduggery Behind the Soap." *Financial Times, London Edition*, 10 January 1997, 11. Available from Lexis-Nexis.
South African Broadcasting Corporation <http://www.sabc.co.za.
"Special Report." *Variety*, 7–13 October 1996, 64. Available from Lexis-Nexis.
Stanley, Alessandra. "A 20th Century Prophet Joins Media Revolution; Exile Hero Finds New Role Back Home: Solzhenitsyn Shines as Talk Show Host." *International Herald Tribune*, 15 April 1995. Available from Lexis-Nexis.
Swartzberg, Terry. "Players' Perilous Paradise in Central and Eastern Europe." *Video Age*, 13 March 1996, 46. Available from Lexis-Nexis.
"Swedes Taste the Street." *Daily Mail*, 4 January 1996. Available from Lexis-Nexis.
"TV Highlights," *China Daily*, 17 and 31 May 1997.
"Telenovela Archives" <yoletten@x.site.net>.
"Telenovela Fever Goes Globo." *Television Business International*, February 1995, 64. Available from Lexis-Nexis.
"Thailand: Thai Soap Opera on the Net." *Bangkok Post*, 27 March 1996. As reported on the Reuter Textline. Available from Lexis-Nexis.
Trofimov, Yaroslav. "Israeli Soap Reveals Mossad's Dark Side." *Asia Times*, 6 November 1996, 7. Available from Lexis-Nexis.
"Tuning in the Global Village: What They'll be Watching This Week." *Los Angeles Times*, 22 October 1992. Available from Lexis-Nexis.
"Urgent Hit TV Soap Producer Admits Child Sex Charges." Agence France Press, 18 December 1996. Available from Lexis-Nexis.
Valdespino, Anne. "A Novela Approach: Spanish-Language Soap Operas, the Highest-Rated Programming in Latin America, Are Gaining Fans in the United States." *Orange County Register*, 29 September 1996, F12. Available from Lexis-Nexis.
Walker, S. Lynne. "Mexico's 'Telenovelas' Breaking Their Traditional Themes." Copley News Service, 20 February 1997. Available from Lexis-Nexis.
Walley, Wayne. "Sellers Analyze Global Hot, Cold Spots." *Electronic Media*, 23 October 1995. Available from Lexis-Nexis.
"Warner Bros. International Television Distribution Signs Its Largest Deal Ever in Poland with Telewizja Polska S.A." Warner Bros. press release.
Williams, Philip. "Kenya Uses a Soap Opera to Preach Population Control," UPI, 23 May 1987. Available from Lexis-Nexis.
WOWOW Japan Satellite Broadcasting, Inc. Web site <http://www.wowow.co.jp>.
Wudunn, Sheryl. "Beijing Journal; Why So Many Chinese Are Teary: The Soap Opera Epoch Has Dawned." *New York Times*, 1 February 1991. Available from Lexis-Nexis.
Zona Latina Web site <http://www.zonalatina.com>.

Other

"The Koppel Report: Technology in a Box." Aired on ABC-TV, September 1989.

Index